S0-BTE-094

943.07
M36r

93786

WITHDRAWN
L. R. COLLEGE LIBRARY

DATE DUE			
Mar31 '76			

KARL MARX

FREDERICK ENGELS

THE REVOLUTION
OF 1848-49

Articles from the
Neue Rheinische Zeitung

by KARL MARX and FREDERICK ENGELS

INTERNATIONAL PUBLISHERS

New York

CARL A. RUDISILL LIBRARY
LENOIR RHYNE COLLEGE

Translated from the German by *S. Ryazanskaya*

Edited by *Bernard Isaacs*

Published simultaneously by Progress Publishers, Moscow, and International Publishers, New York

PUBLISHERS' NOTE

The translation has been made from Marx/Engels, *Werke*, Band 5 and Band 6, Dietz Verlag, Berlin. The aim has been to make the translation as close as possible to the original. When for the sake of clarity it has been found necessary to insert a few words, these are inclosed in square brackets. Italicised passages and words indicate emphasis by Marx; but following the English custom, titles of publications and foreign words are also italicised.

This volume is a selected cross-section of articles and editorials; the complete *Neue Rheinische Zeitung* writings by Marx and Engels will be published in the English Edition of the *Collected Works*, now in preparation.

943.09

M36r

93786

July 1975

ALL RIGHTS RESERVED

First printing, 1972

Library of Congress Catalog Card Number: 77-188755

ISBN 0-7178-0339-2 (cloth); 0-7178-0340-6 (paperback)

Printed in the Union of Soviet Socialist Republics

CONTENTS

---

* Headings given by the Institute of Marxism-Leninism are indicated by an asterisk.

1*

ILLUSTRATIONS

FOREWORD

The articles included in this volume were written by Karl Marx and Frederick Engels during the stormy period of 1848-49, the period of European revolutions.

In 1848 the revolutionary movement was building up, with more or less greater momentum, in most of the European countries. The masses came out onto the streets demanding political liberty, the overthrow of the hated monarchist regimes, the convocation of national assemblies and remedies to improve the unendurable conditions of life of the urban poor, the workers and artisans. Demonstrations and meetings grew into barricade battles, armed uprisings. The revolutionary people won a number of brilliant—but, alas! temporary—victories over the regular troops, which were armed to the teeth. In the wake of the townspeople the peasantry joined the struggle demanding land and the abolition of feudal dependency on the landed aristocracy. The peoples under the heel of foreign oppressors rose in rebellion one after the other—Italians, Poles, Hungarians and Czechs—fighting for national freedom and independence.

On February 22-24, 1848, the workers and artisans of Paris toppled the monarchy of Louis Philippe; the King abdicated and fled to England. On March 13 demonstrations started in Vienna and developed into an armed struggle between the people and the troops. The people won, but the constitution, which the Austrian government drafted soon afterwards, deprived the majority of the working people of the franchise and raised a storm of popular anger. On May 26-27 barricades were thrown up once more in the streets of Vienna and fighting broke out. March saw the beginning of armed risings in other German states—Prussia, Baden, Saxony, Württemberg and Bavaria. On March 18 the streets of Berlin were blocked with barricades and fighting went on all night between the people and the troops. On the morning of March 19 Frederick William IV, King of Prussia, frightened by the revolution, promised to have the troops withdrawn from the capital, asked the people to take down the barricades, and formed a new government headed by Camphausen, the leader of the Rhine bourgeois liberals. In Italy the revolutionary movement started in the South. The uprising which had broken out in Palermo (Sicily) on January 12 overthrew the Bourbon dynasty. Soon afterwards Naples rose in revolt, followed by Piedmont, Tuscany, Lombardy, Milan and Venice. In September 1848 a popular uprising took place in Rome; Pope Pius IX fled, the Pope's temporal power was abrogated and the Roman republic proclaimed.

The revolution of 1848 found Marx and Engels in Brussels. After a stay of several weeks in Paris they arrived in Germany, which was in the grip of revolution, in April 1848. In Cologne, capital of the Rhine Province of Prussia, Marx and Engels founded the *Neue Rheinische Zeitung*, a revolutionary daily, which defended the interests of the popular masses, first and foremost those of the working class, and expressed the political ideas and aspirations of the most consistent and resolute wing of the revolutionary movement in Germany. Karl Marx was Editor-in-Chief of the paper, around which were grouped proletarian revolutionaries and revolutionary democrats. The newspaper highlighted all the major issues of the European revolution. It supported the revolutionary movement in all countries, demonstrated the social nature of the sharpening political struggle, analysed the alignment of class forces, defined the chief aims of the Left, revolutionary wing of the democratic movements, criticised the inconsistent half-way policy of the petty bourgeoisie and exposed the treacherous policy of the big bourgeoisie.

In June 1848 an uprising of the workers broke out in Paris. Duped by the bourgeoisie, who took advantage of the fruits of the workers' victory in February to further their own selfish interests and did nothing to improve the unendurable conditions of life of the working class, and having learned from experience that all the talk of the liberals about unity and brotherhood among all classes of society was merely a screen to hide their concern for the interests of a single class—that of the bourgeoisie, the workers threw up barricades in the streets of Paris and in the course of four days courageously fought the armed forces of bourgeois society who outnumbered them several times over. The troops of General Cavaignac, the bourgeois republican, gunned the workers. The uprising was crushed. The bourgeoisie took ferocious reprisals against the insurgents.

As soon as the Paris uprising started, Marx and Engels declared their solidarity with the insurgents in the columns of their paper. In response to the savage attacks and the slander which the bourgeois press in all countries hurled upon the workers of the French capital Marx and Engels, in a number of brilliant articles, came out in defence of the June uprising, and revealed its character and historical significance. It was "the first great battle fought between the two classes that split modern society. It was a fight for the preservation or annihilation of the *bourgeois* order", wrote Marx.

A number of articles in the *Neue Rheinische Zeitung* were devoted to the struggle of the Italian people for their country's freedom and independence.

Difficult problems confronted the revolution in Italy. The country represented a conglomeration of states, large and small. A considerable part of it was under Austrian domination. Liberation from foreign rule was an essential condition for the country's political unification. At the same time Italy's progressive development was impossible unless the feudal-monarchist system was destroyed. But the liberal bourgeoisie, which had seized control of the movement, betrayed the interests of the masses. It sought to unite the country "from above", within the framework of a constitutional monarchy. Marx and Engels called upon the Italian people not to trust the liberals and to take the cause of national liberation into their own hands. Independence could

only be won if the monarchist regimes of the various Italian
states were overthrown. Only an uprising of the masses and
a revolutionary people's war could put an end to the Austrian yoke, said Engels.

The national liberation movement of the oppressed peoples
was an integral part of the European revolution of 1848-49.
The *Neue Rheinische Zeitung* warmly supported the Poles,
Hungarians and Czechs as well as the Italians in their fight
against the Hohenzollerns, the Hapsburgs and the Russian
Tsar, who had seized their lands. In standing up for national
freedom and independence, Marx and Engels stressed the
fact that the fight for democracy was closely identified with
the struggle against national oppression. Engels wrote:
"Germany will liberate herself to the extent to which she
sets free neighbouring nations."

In the spring of 1848 the Polish population of Poznan,
which formed part of Prussia, rose up in arms against their
oppressors. The revolt was brutally suppressed by the Prussian military. Marx and Engels were strongly in sympathy
with the struggle of the Polish people for an independent
Polish state. They wrote with anger and indignation about
the colonialist policy of the Prussian government in Poznan
and considered the decision of the Frankfurt Assembly to
incorporate the greater part of Poznan in the German Confederation a disgrace.

In 1848-49 the liberation struggle spread among the
Hungarian people, who were under the heel of the Austrian
empire of the Hapsburgs. A Hungarian revolutionary government was formed, headed by Kossuth, which carried out
a number of measures aimed at abolishing feudal relations.
In April 1849 Kossuth's government proclaimed Hungary's
secession from Austria. The Hungarian revolutionary army
fought successfully against the Austrian regular troops.
Marx and Engels commented on the genuinely popular
character of the war in Hungary. They came out in support
of the Hungarian revolution, for they believed that its victory could lead to the fall of the Hapsburg monarchy and
affect the course of the revolution in Germany.

Naturally, the attention of the *Neue Rheinische Zeitung*
was focussed on Germany.

Germany at that time was divided into several dozen small and tiny states, of which only Prussia and Austria stood apart as large states possessing considerable armed forces. Every German kingdom and duchy, however small, had its own laws, its own absolute monarch, its own feudal services, soldiers, custom-houses, taxes and duties. Germany as a whole was an extremely backward country economically and politically, with a feudal system of exploitation of the peasantry surviving since the Middle Ages, with a people robbed of political suffrage, and its kings and dukes enjoying unlimited power. The country's disunity and the existence of customs and other barriers between the states greatly hampered the growth of German industry and commerce, and the country's economy as a whole.

How did events develop in Germany after the March revolution of 1848?

In May 1848 the all-German National Assembly gathered in Frankfurt am Main. The majority in this national parliament were bourgeois liberals. The Right flank was made up of a relatively small group of supporters of the absolute monarchy. The petty-bourgeois democrats formed its Left wing.

From the very outset the Frankfurt Assembly evaded the basic issues of the revolution and engaged in petty affairs of little importance. The liberal bourgeoisie, which had the greatest say in the Assembly, had no intention of tackling any of the major problems that confronted Germany, namely, the problems of uniting the country, overthrowing the monarchy, and doing away with the feudal dependency of the peasants. The leaders of the Frankfurt Assembly feared nothing so much as the further development of the revolution and they would have been quite content with such a deal with the monarchy as would have put an end to the popular movement and given the representatives of the bourgeoisie access to power.

In contrast to the pusillanimous, evasive and double-faced policy of the liberals, the *Neue Rheinische Zeitung* put forward a bold and consistent revolutionary programme. This was:

Reunification of Germany on a democratic basis through

the overthrow of the Hohenzollerns and Hapsburgs in
Prussia and Austria; formation of a united democratic
German republic; the carrying through of democratic
reforms in the interests of the popular masses.

This programme differed radically from the plans of the
bourgeois liberals, who wanted to see Germany united "from
above" in the form of a constitutional monarchy; it differed
also from the views of the petty-bourgeois republicans, who
dreamt of turning the country into a federative republic
along the lines of neighbouring Switzerland.

Abolition of feudal relations, that hoary relic of the
Middle Ages, was another problem of paramount importance
which the German revolution had to deal with. In the course
of the revolution the peasants rose to the struggle for their
emancipation from the oppression of the landowners. The
flames of the peasant war raged throughout Germany, the
walls of feudal castles fell to the ground, and ancient
charters containing an endless list of peasant dues and services were reduced to ashes. But instead of supporting the
peasants, who were their closest allies in the struggle against
the feudalists, the bourgeoisie, on coming to power, made a
deal with the landowning clique and refused to enact the
abolition of feudal services. In the columns of the *Neue
Rheinische Zeitung* Marx branded the treachery of the
bourgeoisie, who had joined the camp of the people's
enemies. Marx and his associates wholeheartedly supported
the peasant movement. They called upon the peasants to
fight for the immediate, complete and final abolition of all
feudal services. Without a revolutionary solution of the
agrarian question it would be impossible to carry out the
unification and democratisation of Germany.

Marx and Engels regarded the German revolution as a
popular revolution in its motive forces and aims. They
repeatedly stressed in their articles that the only force that
could and should go through with the revolution and secure
political and social reforms was the people, that is, the
proletariat, the peasantry and the petty bourgeoisie of the
towns. The people were to wield supreme state power. The
representative institutions—the Prussian National Assembly
in Berlin and especially the all-German National Assembly

at Frankfurt convened as a result of the March revolution—
were to uphold the interests of the people against the counter-revolutionary governments of Germany. Criticising the
inactivity and impotence of the Frankfurt Assembly, the
Neue Rheinische Zeitung wrote: "It [the National Assembly]
only had to oppose authoritatively all reactionary encroachments by obsolete governments in order to win such strength
of public opinion as would make all bayonets and rifle butts
ineffective against it."

The bourgeois revolution in Germany, Marx and Engels
stressed, should have as its outcome the overthrow of the
existing governments and the establishment of a new
rule. "We must achieve a really popular government, and
the old edifice must be razed to the ground," wrote the
newspaper.

Marx envisaged this new rule as a revolutionary dictatorship of the people—the workers, peasants and petty bourgeois—who, by means of decisive action, would paralyse the
attacks of the counter-revolution and carry out a broad
programme of revolutionary democratic reforms.

One of the most important events of the German revolution was the uprising in Vienna in October 1848. The populace of the Austrian capital—the workers, students and
democratic intellectuals—heroically fought against the
superior forces of the feudal-monarchist reaction. The
uprising in Vienna stirred up the whole of Germany. The
sympathies of all revolutionary democrats were with the
insurgents. The forces, however, were unequal, and this
decided the outcome of the uprising. The government troops
under General Windischgrätz took revolutionary Vienna by
storm. Analysing the reasons for the uprising's defeat, Marx
pointed out the disgraceful behaviour of the Austrian bourgeoisie, who betrayed the fighting people and surrendered
to the forces of counter-revolution.

In November 1848 an acute political crisis was coming
to a head in Prussia. The counter-revolutionary government
was preparing a coup d'état. The appeals of the Rhenish
District Committee of Democrats, of which Marx was a
member, called for the organisation of a Civil Guard to
fight the enemy and for the setting-up of revolutionary

organs of power—committees of public safety. As opposed
to the passive resistance proclaimed by the democratic leaders in the National Assembly, Marx and his associates
called upon the people to respond with violence to the acts
of violence on the part of the Prussian government, which
intended to dissolve the National Assembly. Defending the
people's right to revolution and active interference in the
course of the political struggle, Marx stated in his address
to the jury during his trial in February 1849: "If the
Crown makes a counter-revolution, the people has the right
to reply with a revolution."

However, the capitulation of the bourgeois majority of
the Assembly and the indecisive, wavering stand of the
petty-bourgeois democrats paralysed the people's resistance.
The royal power, backed by the civil servants and the military, carried out a coup in Prussia in December 1848 and
dismissed the National Assembly. A decisive factor contrib-
uting to the victory of the reactionary clique was the
attitude adopted by the Prussian bourgeoisie. The big commercial and industrial bourgeoisie threw themselves into
"the arms of the counter-revolution for fear of the revolution", Marx wrote. Despite the fact that the Prussian
bourgeoisie had a vested interest in the unification of
Germany and in the introduction of a number of political
reforms, they yielded control of the country to the
monarchist camarilla and the feudalists out of fear that the
continuation of the revolution would threaten bourgeois as
well as feudalist property.

The consolidation of the reactionary forces in Prussia
led to a sharpening of class antagonisms within the country.
The bourgeoisie launched an attack upon the vital interests
of the proletariat. While wringing profits out of the workers,
the bourgeois robbed them of the means of subsistence. The
Neue Rheinische Zeitung denounced the oppressive policy
of the German bourgeoisie. It wrote with wrath and indignation that the capitalists refused to grant elementary human
rights to the workers of whom they demanded absolute
submission to conditions of slavery under the threat of police
reprisals. Marx presented to the bourgeoisie the shameful

list of their crimes and accused them of "shameless maltreatment of the working class".

The spring of 1849 brought signs of a new upswing in the German revolution. In May an uprising broke out in South-Western Germany in defence of the imperial constitution. Framed by the Frankfurt parliament in March 1849, this constitution was a compromise. It preserved the existence of the 36 German states and at the same time provided for the establishment of a central all-German government headed by a hereditary emperor. The constitution proclaimed a number of bourgeois-democratic freedoms and was a step towards the unification of Germany. "The Imperial Constitution," Engels wrote, "not only was distinguished by its apparently exclusive popular origin, but at the same time, full of contradiction as it was, it yet was the most liberal Constitution of all Germany." The refusal of the counter-revolutionary governments of Austria, Prussia, Bavaria, Hannover and Saxony to recognise the imperial constitution threw up a new wave of protest among the masses. The workers, artisans and peasants took up arms in defence of the constitution. The uprising spread with great force to both banks of the Rhine, overrunning Rhenish Prussia, Pfalz and Baden. Engels fought in one of the units of the revolutionary army.

The Prussian government sent a 60,000-strong army against the insurgents and by the end of July 1849 the uprising was suppressed.

In 1848-49 the working class of the European countries entered the arena of political struggle. It was an active force of the general democratic front. Hegemony in the democratic movement, however, belonged to the petty bourgeoisie and its leaders. The labour movement was taking its first steps at the time. One of its advanced detachments was the English Chartists—the organised party of the proletariat, which directed the class struggle of the workers in Europe's most industrialised country. The *Neue Rheinische Zeitung* defended the Chartists against the attacks of the reactionary press and considered the fight of the Chartists an example to be emulated by the German workers. The revolutionary struggle in France, Germany and other countries tended to widen the political horizon of the European workers and awaken in them a sense of international solidarity. Engels noted with satisfaction the successes achieved by the labour movement even in such a small country as Switzerland, where the growing class-consciousness of the workers gradually drew them into the socialist movement, and made them follow with sympathy the struggle of their brothers in other countries.

The activities of the *Neue Rheinische Zeitung* were imbued with a spirit of proletarian internationalism. As opposed to the coalition between international reaction and the counter-revolutionary big bourgeoisie, Marx and Engels worked for the unity of the European proletarian forces, whose militant symbol was the red flag flying on the barricades of many European cities.

The *Neue Rheinische Zeitung* succeeded in winning the sympathy and love of the broad popular masses. The Prussian government, quick to see in it a dangerous opponent, did everything it could to hamper and prevent its activities. From the very first months of the paper's existence the legal authorities and the police started to persecute its editors. Two trials against the paper's editors were held in February 1849. Marx used the courtroom as a rostrum from which to arraign the counter-revolutionary policy of the Prussian government and publicise his revolutionary views. At both trials the accused were acquitted.

In May 1849 the counter-revolution went into the offensive all over Germany, and the Prussian government resorted to further police repressions against Marx and the other editors of the *Neue Rheinische Zeitung*. The newspaper closed down. Its last issue, which came out on May 19, 1849, was printed in red ink. Taking leave of the workers, to whom the paper's revolutionary propaganda was chiefly addressed, its editors issued the battle-cry of "Emancipation of the Working Class". Reviewing the honourable path the paper had traversed, Marx wrote: "We have saved the revolutionary honour of our homeland."

The revolution of 1848-49 ended with the defeat of the people. The struggle of the working masses—the proletariat, peasantry and lower strata of the towns—met with growing resistance not only on the part of the forces of obsolete feudal society, the monarchist parties, nobility, clergy, the military and reactionary officialdom, but also on the part of the big bourgeoisie. Seeing in the victory of the revolutionary people a threat to their propertied interests and class privileges, the bourgeoisie made a deal with the feudal-monarchist reaction, betrayed the interests of their original allies—the popular masses—and took a direct part in crushing the revolution.

In their works written immediately after the defeat of the revolution, Marx and Engels subjected the development and results of the revolution of 1848-49 to a scientific analysis from the standpoint of historical materialism. The theory of Marxism withstood the historical test of revolutionary practice in the course of the revolution. This test revealed the vital force of Marxism as the only correct revolutionary doctrine. Only Marxism was capable of demonstrating the inner objective laws of development of the revolution in the different countries, correctly assessing the attitudes of the fighting classes and parties, and pointing out to the masses the prospects of the further struggle for democracy and socialism against feudal oppression and disfranchisement.

S. Z. Leviova

KARL MARX
AND
FREDERICK ENGELS

THE REVOLUTION OF 1848-49

Articles from
the *Neue Rheinische Zeitung*

[STATEMENT OF THE EDITORIAL BOARD OF THE *NEUE RHEINISCHE ZEITUNG*[1]]

Originally the date of publication of the *Neue Rheinische Zeitung* was to be the first of July, and arrangements with correspondents, etc., were made with that date in view.

But since the brazen attitude reassumed by the reactionaries foreshadows the enactment of German September Laws[2] in the near future, we have decided to make use of every available day and to publish the paper as from June the first. Our readers will therefore have to bear with us if during the first days we cannot offer so wide a variety of news and reports as our widespread connections should enable us to do. In a few days we shall be able to satisfy all requirements in this respect too.

Editorial Board:
Karl Marx, Editor-in-Chief
Heinrich Bürgers,
Ernst Dronke,
Friedrich Engels, } editors
Georg Weerth,
Ferdinand Wolff,
Wilhelm Wolff

Written on May 31, 1848
Neue Rheinische Zeitung No. 1,
June 1, 1848

THE ASSEMBLY AT FRANKFURT

Cologne, May 31. For a fortnight Germany has had a constituent National Assembly elected by the German people as a whole.

The German people won its sovereign status by fighting in the streets of almost all towns in the country, large and small, and especially on the barricades of Vienna and Berlin. It exercised this sovereignty in the elections to the National Assembly.

The bold and public proclamation of the sovereignty of the German people should have been the first act of the National Assembly.

Its second act should have been the drafting of a German constitution based on the sovereignty of the people and the elimination from the conditions actually existing in Germany of everything that conflicts with this principle.

During the whole of its session the Assembly ought to have taken all necessary measures to frustrate any reactionary sallies, to maintain the revolutionary basis on which it depends and to safeguard the sovereignty of the people, won by the revolution, against all attacks.

Though the German National Assembly has met about a dozen times already, it has done none of these things.

But it has ensured the salvation of Germany by the following great deeds.

The National Assembly realised that it must have rules, for it knew that when two or three Germans get together they must have a set of rules, otherwise chair legs will be used to decide matters. And now some school-master had foreseen this contingency and drawn up special regulations for this high Assembly. A motion was submitted to adopt this scheme provisionally; though most deputies had not read it, the Assembly adopted it without more ado, for what would become of Germany's representatives without regulations? *Fiat reglementum partout et toujours!*

Herr Raveaux of Cologne tables a quite simple motion dealing with conflicts between the assemblies at Frankfurt and at Berlin.[3] But the Assembly debates the final regulations, and although Raveaux's motion is urgent, the regulations are still more urgent. *Pereat mundus, fiat reglementum!* However, the elected philistines in their wisdom cannot refrain from making a few remarks concerning Raveaux's motion, and while they are debating whether the regulations or the motion should take precedence, they have already produced up to two dozen amendments to this motion. They ventilate the thing, talk, get stuck, raise a din, waste time and postpone voting from the 19th to the 22nd of May. The matter is brought up again on the 22nd, there is a deluge of new amendments and new digressions, and after long-winded speeches and endless confusion they decide that the question, which was already placed on the agenda, is to be referred back to the sections. Thus the time has happily slipped by and the deputies leave to take their meal.

On May 23 they first wrangle about the minutes, then have innumerable motions read out again, and just when they are about to return to the agenda, that is, to the beloved regulations, Zitz of Mainz mentions the brutalities of the Prussian army and the despotic abuses of the Prussian commandant at Mainz.[4] This was an indubitable and successful sally on the part of the reaction, an event with which the Assembly was especially competent to deal. It ought to have called to account the presumptuous soldier who dared threaten to shell Mainz almost within sight of the National Assembly, it ought to have protected the unarmed citizens of Mainz in their own houses from the atrocities of a coarse soldiery which had been forced upon them and incited against them. But Herr Bassermann, the waterman of

Baden,* declares that these are trifles. Mainz must be left to its fate, the whole is more important, the Assembly meets here to consider a set of regulations in the interests of Germany as a whole—indeed, what is the shelling of Mainz compared with this! *Pereat Moguntia, fiat reglementum!* But the Assembly is soft-hearted, it elects a commission that is to go to Mainz to investigate matters and—it is again just time to adjourn and dine.

And then, on May 24, we lose the parliamentary thread altogether. The regulations would seem to have been completed or to have got lost, at any rate we hear nothing more about them. Instead we are inundated by a veritable flood of well-intentioned motions in which numerous representatives of the sovereign people obstinately demonstrate the limited understanding of a loyal subject.[5] Then follow applications, petitions, protests, etc., and in the end the national slops find an outlet in innumerable speeches skipping from one subject to another. The fact, however, that four committees have been set up cannot be passed over in silence.

Finally Herr Schlöffel asked for the floor. Three German citizens, Esselen, Pelz and Löwenstein, had been ordered to leave Frankfurt that very day, before 4 p.m. The wise and all-knowing police asserted that these gentlemen had incurred the wrath of the townspeople by their speeches in the Workers' Association and must therefore clear out. And the police dare to do this after German right of citizenship was proclaimed by the Preparliament[6] and even after it was endorsed in the draft constitution of the 17 "trusted men" (*hommes de confiance de la diète*).[7] The matter is urgent. Herr Schlöffel asks to be allowed to speak on this point. He is refused permission. He asks for the floor to speak on the urgency of the subject, which he is entitled to do according to the regulations, but on this occasion it was a case of *fiat politia, pereat reglementum!* Naturally, for it was time to go home and eat.

On the 25th, the flood of tabled motions caused the pensive heads of the deputies to droop like ripe ears of corn

---

* A pun on the words "Bassermann" and "Wassermann" (waterman). —*Ed.*

Neue Rheinische Zeitung.

Organ der Demokratie.

№ 1.   Köln, Donnerstag, 1. Juni   1848.

Die „Neue Rheinische Zeitung" erscheint vom 1. Juni an täglich.

Der Abonnementspreis beträgt: Für das Vierteljahr in Köln 1 Thlr. 15 Sgr.; für alle übrigen Orte Preußens jene 2 Thlr. 3 Sgr. 9 Pf. Außerhalb Preußens mit Zuschlag des fremden Zeitungsporto's.

Das Abonnement für den Monat Juni kann nur unter gleichzeitiger Bestellung des nächsten Quartals (Juli, August, September) geschehen. Der Preis dieses viermonatlichen Abonnements beträgt: für Köln 2 Thlr., auswärts 2 Thlr. 25 Sgr.

Man abonnirt bei allen Postanstalter und Buchhandlungen des In- und Auslandes; — für Köln in der Expedition der Zeitung bei Hrn. W. Clouth, St. Agatha 12, Köln.

Fernere Abonnements werden entgegen genommen in der Expedition der Zeitung. Inserate werden gebeten, sich ebenfalls dorthin franco zu wenden.

Insertionsgebühren.

Für die vierspaltige Petitzeile oder deren Raum . . . . 1 Sgr. 6 Pf.

Die Expedition der „Neuen Rheinischen Zeitung."

Das Erscheinen der Neuen Rheinischen Zeitung war ursprünglich auf den ersten Juli festgesetzt. Die Arrangements mit den Correspondenten &c. waren auf diesen Termin getroffen.

Da jedoch bei dem erneuten frechen Auftreten der Reaktion deutsche Septembergesetze in naher Aussicht stehen, so haben wir jeden freien Tag benutzen wollen, und erscheinen schon mit dem ersten Juni. Unsre Leser werden es uns also nachsehen müssen, wenn wir in den ersten Tagen an Nachrichten und mannigfaltigen Correspondenzen noch nicht das reichhaltige Material liefern, wozu unsere ausgedehnten Verbindungen uns befähigen. In wenig Tagen werden wir auch hierin allen Anforderungen genügen können.

Redactions-Comité.

Karl Marx, Redakteur en Chef.

Heinrich Bürgers,
Ernst Dronke,
Friedrich Engels,
Georg Weerth,
Ferdinand Wolff,
Wilhelm Wolff,
    Redakteure.

Uebersicht.

Deutschland. Köln (die Frankfurter Versammlung). — Herausgeberische Skizze aus dem deutschen Handelsleben.

Deutschland.

** Köln, 31. Mai. Seit vierzehn Tagen besitzt Deutschland eine konstituirende Nationalversammlung, hervorgegangen aus der Wahl der gesammten deutschen Volkes.

Amtliche Nachrichten.

Der bisherige Privat-Docent, Dr. jur. Breyer hierselbst, ist zum außerordentlichen Professor in der juristischen Fakultät der hiesigen Universität ernannt worden.

Humoristische Skizze aus dem deutschen Handelsleben.

Von Georg Weerth.

Der Herr Preiß in Köthen.

The first issue of the *Neue Rheinische Zeitung*

in a downpour. Two deputies then attempted once more to raise the question of the expulsion, but they too did not get a chance to speak, even about the urgency of the matter. Some of the documents received, especially one sent by Poles, were much more interesting than all the motions of the deputies. Finally the commission that was sent to Mainz was given the floor. It announced that it could not report until the following day; moreover it had, of course, arrived too late: 8,000 Prussian bayonets had restored order by disarming 1,200 men of the Civil Guard. Meantime, there was nothing for it but to pass on to the agenda. This was done promptly, the item on the agenda being Raveaux's motion. Since in Frankfurt this had not yet been settled, whereas in Berlin it had already lost all significance because of Auerswald's decree, the National Assembly decided to defer the question till the next day and to go and dine.

On the 26th innumerable new motions were introduced and after that the Mainz commission delivered its final and very indecisive report. Herr Hergenhahn, ex-people's representative and pro tempore minister, presented the report. He moved an extremely moderate resolution, but after a lengthy debate the Assembly concluded that even this docile proposition was too strong and resolved to leave the citizens of Mainz to the tender mercies of the Prussians commanded by a Herr Hüser, and "in the hope that the government will do its duty" the Assembly passed on to the agenda, that is, the gentlemen left to have a meal.

Finally, on May 27, after lengthy preliminaries over the minutes, Raveaux's motion was discussed. There was some desultory talk until half past two and then the deputies went to dine, but this time they assembled again for an evening session and at last brought the matter to a close. Because of the extreme tardiness of the National Assembly, Herr Auerswald had already disposed of Raveaux's motion, therefore Herr Raveaux decided to support an amendment proposed by Herr Werner, which settled the question of the people's sovereignty neither in the affirmative nor in the negative.

Our information concerning the National Assembly ends here, but there is every reason to assume that after having taken this decision the meeting was adjourned and the deputies went to dine. That they were able to do this so early, they have to thank Robert Blum, who said:

"Gentlemen, if you decide to pass on to the agenda today, then the whole agenda of this Assembly may be cut short in a very curious manner."

Written by Engels

Neue Rheinische Zeitung No. 1,
June 1, 1848

THE DEMOCRATIC PARTY

Cologne, June 1. Every new organ of public opinion is generally expected to show enthusism for the party whose principles it supports, unqualified confidence in the strength of this party, and constant readiness either to use the real power to back the principles, or to use the glamour of the principles to cover up real weaknesses. We shall not live up to these expectations. We shall not seek to gild defeats with deceptive illusions.

The democratic party has suffered defeat; the principles which it proclaimed at the moment of victory are called in question; the ground it has actually won is being contested inch by inch; much has been lost already and soon the question will arise—what is left?

What is important for us is that the democratic party should understand its position. People may ask why we are concerned with a party, why we do not concentrate on the aims of the democratic movement, the welfare of the people, the happiness of all without distinction.

For such is the law and usage of struggle, and only from the *struggle* of parties can the future welfare arise—not from pseudo-judicious compromises or from a hypocritical alliance brought about despite conflicting views, interests and aims.

We demand of the democratic party that it grasp the significance of its position. This demand springs from the experience of the past months. The democratic party has allowed the elation of its first victory to go to its head. Intoxicated with the joy of being able at last to proclaim its principles openly for all to hear, it imagined that one had merely to proclaim these principles for them to be immediately realised. It did not go beyond this proclamation after its first victory and the concessions which directly followed it. But while the party was lavish with its ideas and treated as a brother everyone who did not immediately dare to challenge it, the others—those who retained or obtained power—were active. And their activity is not to be made light of. Keeping their principles to themselves and divulging only those parts that were directed against old conditions already overthrown by the revolution, they carefully held the movement in check, ostensibly in the interests of the evolving legal system or the establishment of formal order. They made would-be concessions to the advocates of the old order to secure their support for their own plans; then they gradually built up the basic elements of their own political system and thus succeeded in occupying an intermediate position between the democratic party and the defenders of absolutism, on the one hand advancing and on the other retarding the movement, being at once progressive—as regards the absolutists—and reactionary—as regards the democrats.

In its first intoxication the people's party allowed itself to be taken in by the party of the prudent, moderate bourgeoisie, till finally it began to see things in their true light after having been contemptuously spurned, after all sorts of reprehensible intentions had been imputed to it, and its members denounced as demagogues. Then it perceived that it had actually achieved nothing but what the gentlemen of the bourgeoisie regarded as compatible with their own well-understood interests. Set in conflict with itself by an undemocratic electoral law and defeated in the elections, the party now has against it two elected bodies; the only doubtful thing about them is, which of them will more strongly oppose its demands. Consequently, the enthusiasm of the party has of course melted away and has been replaced by the sober recognition of the fact that a powerful reaction has gained control, and this, strangely enough, happened before any revolutionary action took place.

Although all this is undoubtedly true, it would be dangerous if the bitter feeling engendered by the first and partly self-induced defeat would impel the democratic party now to revert to that wretched idealism, which is unfortunately characteristic of the German temperament, and according to which a principle that cannot be put into practice immediately is relegated to the distant future while for the present its innocuous elaboration is left to the "thinkers".

We must clearly warn against those hypocritical friends who, while declaring that they agree with the principles, doubt whether they are practicable, because, they allege, the world is not yet ready for them, and who have no intention of making it ready, but on the contrary prefer to share the common lot of the wicked in this wicked earthly life. If these are the crypto-republicans whom the privy councillor Gervinus fears so much, then we wholeheartedly agree with him: "Such men are dangerous."

Neue Rheinische Zeitung No. 2,
June 2, 1848

THE PROGRAMMES
OF THE RADICAL-DEMOCRATIC PARTY
AND OF THE LEFT AT FRANKFURT

Cologne, June 6. Yesterday we acquainted our readers with the "reasoned manifesto of the Radical-Democratic Party[8] in the constituent National Assembly at Frankfurt am Main". Today they will find the manifesto of the Left under the heading Frankfurt. At first sight the two manifestos appear to be almost identical except in form, as the Radical-Democratic Party has a clumsy editor and the Left a skilful one. On closer scrutiny, however, several substantially different points stand out. The manifesto of the Radicals demands a National Assembly to be set up *"by direct voting without any electoral qualifications"*, that of the Left wants it to be convened by *"free universal elections"*. *Free universal elections* exclude *electoral qualifications*, but do not exclude *indirect* methods. In any case why use this vague and ambiguous term?

We encounter once more this greater latitude and flexibility in the demands of the Left compared with the demands of the Radical Party. The Left wants "an executive central authority elected *by* the National Assembly for a definite period and responsible to it". It does not say whether this central authority has to be elected *from the ranks of the National Assembly*, as the manifesto of the Radicals expressly states.

Finally the manifesto of the Left calls for the immediate definition, proclamation and maintenance of the basic rights of the German people against all encroachments by individual governments. The manifesto of the Radicals is not content with this. It declares that

"all political power of the federal state is now concentrated in the Assembly which must *immediately* bring into operation the various forces and political institutions falling within its jurisdiction, and direct the home and foreign policies of the federal state".

Both manifestos agree that the "drafting of the German constitution should be left solely to the National Assembly" and the governments debarred from taking part in it. Both agree that "without prejudice to the people's rights to be proclaimed by the National Assembly" it should be left to the individual states to choose the form of government, whether that of a constitutional monarchy or a republic. Both finally agree that Germany should be transformed into a confederation or a federative state.

The manifesto of the Radicals at least expresses the *revolutionary* nature of the National Assembly. It demands appropriate revolutionary action. Does not the mere existence of a *constituent* National Assembly prove that *there is no* longer any constitution? But if there is no constitution, then there is no government either. And if there is no government the National Assembly must govern. Its first move should have been a decree of seven words: *"The Federal Diet*[9] *is dissolved for ever."*

A constituent National Assembly must above all be an *active*, revolutionarily active assembly. The Assembly at Frankfurt is engaged in parliamentary school exercises and leaves it to the governments to act. Assuming that this learned gathering succeeds, after mature consideration, in framing the best of agendas and the best of constitutions, of what use is the best agenda and the best constitution if the governments meanwhile have placed bayonets on the agenda?

Apart from the fact that it was the outcome of *indirect* elections, the German National Assembly suffers from a specifically German malady. It sits at Frankfurt am Main, and Frankfurt am Main is merely an ideal centre, which corresponded to the hitherto ideal, that is, merely imaginary, German unity. Frankfurt moreover is not a big city with a numerous revolutionary population that can back the National Assembly, partly defending it, partly spurring it on. It is the first time in human history that the constituent assembly of a big nation holds its sessions in a small town. This is the result of Germany's previous history. While the

French and English national assemblies met on volcanic ground—Paris and London—the German National Assembly considered itself lucky to find *neutral* ground, where in the most comfortable peace of mind it could ponder over the best constitution and the best agenda. Yet the present state of affairs in Germany offered the assembly an opportunity to overcome the drawbacks of its unfortunate physical situation. It only had to oppose authoritatively all reactionary encroachments by obsolete governments in order to win such strength of public opinion as would make all bayonets and rifle butts ineffective against it. Instead Mainz, almost within sight of the Assembly, is abandoned to the arbitrary actions of the army, and German citizens from other parts of the country are exposed to the chicanery of the philistines in Frankfurt.* The Assembly bores the German people instead of inspiring it or being inspired by it. Although there is a *public* which for the time being still looks with good-natured humour upon the antics performed by the spectre of the resurrected Diet of the Holy Roman Empire, there is no *people* that can find its own life reflected in the life of the Assembly. Far from being the central organ of the revolutionary movement, the Assembly, up till now, was not even its echo.

If the National Assembly forms a central authority from its own midst, little satisfaction can be expected from such a provisional government, in view of the Assembly's present composition and the fact that it let the favourable moment slip by. If it forms no central authority, it puts its seal to its own abdication and will be scattered to the winds at the first stir of a revolutionary current.

It is to the credit of both the programme of the Left and that of the Radical group that they have grasped this necessity. Both exclaim with Heine:

> After very careful consideration
> I see that we need no emperor at all.[10]

Because it is so difficult to decide "*who* shall be emperor", and because there are as many good reasons for an elected

---

* See this volume, pp. 23-25.—*Ed.*

emperor as there are for a hereditary emperor, even the conservative majority of the Assembly will be compelled to cut the Gordian knot by electing *no emperor at all.*

It is quite incomprehensible how the so-called Radical-Democratic Party can advocate, as the ultimate political structure of Germany, a *federation* of constitutional monarchies, small principalities and tiny republics, i.e., a federal union of such heterogeneous elements, headed by a republican government—for this is what the central body agreed to by the Left really amounts to.

First of all the German central government elected by the National Assembly must undoubtedly be set up *alongside* the governments which still actually exist. But its struggle against the separate governments begins as soon as it comes into existence, and in the course of this struggle either the federal government and the unity of Germany are wrecked, or the separate governments with their constitutional princes or petty republics are destroyed.

We do not make the utopian demand that at the outset a *united indivisible German republic* should be proclaimed, but we ask the so-called Radical-Democratic Party not to confuse the starting-point of the struggle and of the revolutionary movement with the goal. Both German unity and the German constitution can result only from a movement in which the internal conflicts and the war with the East will play an equally decisive role. The final act of constitution cannot be *decreed*, it coincides with the movement we have to go through. It is therefore not a question of putting into practice this or that view, this or that political idea, but of understanding the course of development. The National Assembly has to take only such steps as are practicable in the first instance.

Nothing can be more confused than the notion advanced by the editor of the democratic manifesto—for all his assurances that "everybody is glad to get rid of his confusion" —that the *federal state of North America* should serve as a model for the German constitution.

Leaving alone the fact that all its constituent parts have a similar structure, the United States of America covers an area equal to that of civilised Europe. Only a *European* federation would be analogous to it. But in order to federate with other states Germany must first of all become *one* state. The conflict between centralisation and federalism in Germany is a conflict between modern culture and feudalism. Germany fell into a kind of bourgeoisified feudalism at the very moment the great monarchies arose in the West; she was moreover excluded from the world market just when this market was opened up to the countries of Western Europe. Germany became impoverished while the Western countries grew rich; she became countrified while they became urbanised. Even if Russia did not knock at the gates of Germany, the economic conditions alone would compel the latter to introduce rigorous centralisation. Even from a purely bourgeois point of view, the solid unity of Germany is a primary condition for her deliverance from her present wretchedness and for the building up of her national wealth. And how could modern social problems be solved in a territory that is split into 39 small states?

Incidentally, the editor of the democratic programme does not bother about such a minor question as material economic conditions. He relies on the concept of federation in his reasoning. *Federation* is *an alliance of free* and *equal partners. Hence* Germany must be a *federal state.* But cannot the Germans unite in *one* great state without offence to the concept of an alliance of free and equal partners?

Neue Rheinische Zeitung No. 7,
June 7, 1848

THE BERLIN DEBATE ON THE REVOLUTION

Cologne, June 13. At last the Assembly of conciliation has made its position clear. It has rejected the idea of revolution and accepted the theory of agreement.[11]

The matter the Assembly had to decide was this.

On March 18 the King promised a constitution, introduced freedom of the press together with caution money, and made a series of proposals in which he declared that Germany's unity must be achieved by the merging of Germany in Prussia.

These sum up the crux of the concessions made on March 18. The fact that the people of Berlin were satisfied with this and that they marched to the palace to thank the King is the clearest proof of the necessity of the March 18 revolution. Not only the state, its *citizens* too had to be revolutionised. Their submissiveness could only be shed in a sanguinary liberation struggle.

A well-known "misunderstanding" led to the revolution. There was indeed a misunderstanding. The attack by the soldiers, the 16-hour fight, and the fact that the troops had to be forced by the people to withdraw are sufficient proof that the people completely *misunderstood* the concessions of March 18.

The results of the revolution were, on the one hand, the arming of the people, the right of association and the sovereignty of the people, won de facto; on the other hand, the retention of the monarchy and the Camphausen-Hansemann ministry, that is, a government representing the big bourgeoisie.

Thus the revolution produced two sets of results, which were bound to fall apart. The people was victorious; it had won liberties of a pronounced democratic nature, but direct control passed into the hands of the big bourgeoisie and not into those of the people.

2*

In short, the revolution was not carried through to the end. The people left the formation of a cabinet to the big bourgeoisie, and the big bourgeoisie promptly revealed its intentions by inviting the old Prussian nobility and the bureaucracy to enter into an alliance with it. Arnim, Kanitz and Schwerin became members of the government.

The upper middle class was all along anti-revolutionary; through fear of the people, i.e., of the workers and the democratic lower middle class, it concluded a defensive and offensive alliance with the reaction.

The united reactionary parties began their fight against the democratic movement by *calling the revolution in question*. The victory of the people was denied, the famous list of the "seventeen dead soldiers" was fabricated, and those who had fought on the barricades were slandered in every possible way. But this was not all. The United Provincial Diet[12] convoked before the revolution was now actually convened by the government, in order rather belatedly to fabricate a legal transition from absolutism to the constitution. Thus the government openly repudiated the revolution. It moreover invented the theory of agreement, once more repudiating the revolution and with it the sovereignty of the people.

The revolution was accordingly really called in question, and this could be done because it was only a partial revolution, only the beginning of a long revolutionary movement.

We cannot here go into the question as to why and to what extent the present rule of the big bourgeoisie in Prussia is a necessary transitional stage towards democracy, and why, directly after its ascension, the big bourgeoisie joined the reactionary camp. For the present we merely report the fact.

The Assembly of conciliation was now to declare whether it recognised the revolution or not.

But to recognise the revolution under these circumstances meant recognising the democratic aspects of the revolution, which the big bourgeoisie wanted to appropriate to itself.

Recognising the revolution at this moment meant recognising the *half-and-half* nature of the revolution, and consequently recognising the democratic movement, which was directed against some of the results of the revolution. It meant recognising that Germany was in the grip of a revolutionary movement, and that the Camphausen ministry, the theory of agreement, indirect elections, the rule of the big capitalists and the decisions of the Assembly itself could indeed be regarded as unavoidable transitional steps, but by no means as final results.

The debate on the recognition of the revolution was carried on by both sides with great prolixity and great interest, but with remarkably little intelligence. One seldom reads anything so unedifying as these long-winded deliberations, constantly interrupted by noisy scenes or fine-spun arguments about standing orders. Instead of the great passion of party strife, we have a cold, placid temper which threatens at any moment to lapse into amiable colloquy; instead of the biting edge of argument we have interminable and confused talk rambling from one subject to another; instead of neat retorts we have tedious sermons on the essence and nature of morality.

Neither has the Left exactly distinguished itself in these debates. Most of its speakers repeat one another; none of them dare tackle the matter head-on and speak their mind in frank revolutionary terms. They are always afraid to give offence, to hurt or to frighten people away. Germany would have been in a sorry plight if the people who fought on March 18 had not shown more energy and passion in battle than the gentlemen of the Left showed in the debate.

Written by Engels

Neue Rheinische Zeitung No. 14,
June 14, 1848

THE PRAGUE UPRISING

Cologne, June 17. Another massacre similar to that of Poznan[13] is being prepared in *Bohemia*. The possibility of a peaceful association of Bohemia and Germany has been drowned in the blood of the Czech people shed by the Austrian army.

Prince Windischgrätz had cannons mounted on the Wyshehrad and Hradschin[14] and trained on Prague. Troops were massed and a sudden attack on the Slavic Congress[15] and the Czechs was being prepared.

The people discovered these preparations; they went in a body to the residence of the prince and demanded arms. The demand was rejected. Feeling began to run high and the crowds of people with and without arms were growing. Then a shot was fired from an inn opposite the commandant's palace and Princess Windischgrätz dropped, mortally wounded. The order to attack followed immediately; the Grenadiers advanced, the people were driven back. But barricades were thrown up everywhere, checking the advance of the military. Cannons were brought into position and the barricades raked with grape-shot. Torrents of blood were shed. The fighting went on throughout the night of the 12th and continued on the 13th. Eventually the troops succeeded in occupying the wide streets and pressing the people back into the narrower quarters of the city where artillery could not be used.

That is as far as our latest news goes. But in addition it is stated that many members of the Slavic Congress were sent out of the city under a strong escort. It would appear that the military won at least a partial victory.

However the uprising may end, a war of attrition between

the Germans and Czechs is now the only possible outcome.

In their revolution the Germans have to suffer for the sins of their whole past. They suffered for them in Italy. In Poznan they have brought down upon themselves once more the curse of the whole of Poland, and to that is now added Bohemia.

The French were able to win the recognition and sympathy even of the countries to which they came as enemies. The Germans win recognition nowhere and find sympathy nowhere. Even where they adopt the role of magnanimous apostles of liberty, they are spurned with bitter scorn.

And so they deserve to be. A nation which throughout its history allowed itself to be used as a tool of oppression against all other nations must first of all prove that it has been really revolutionised. It must prove this not merely by a few indecisive revolutions, as a result of which the old irresolution, impotence and discord are allowed to continue in a modified form; revolutions which allow a Radetzky to remain in Milan, a Colomb and Steinäcker in Poznan, a Windischgrätz in Prague, a Hüser in Mainz, as if nothing had changed.

A revolutionised Germany ought to have renounced her entire past, especially as far as the neighbouring nations are concerned. Together with her own freedom, she should have proclaimed the freedom of the nations hitherto suppressed by her.

And what *has* revolutionised Germany done? She has fully endorsed the old oppression of Italy, Poland, and now of Bohemia too, by German troops. Kaunitz and Metternich have been completely vindicated.

And the Germans, after this, demand that the Czechs should trust them?

Are the Czechs to be blamed for not wanting to join a nation that oppresses and maltreats other nations, while liberating itself?

Are they to be blamed for not wanting to send their representatives to the despondent and faint-hearted National Assembly at Frankfurt, which is afraid of its own sovereignty?

Are they to be blamed for dissociating themselves from the impotent Austrian government, which is in such a perplexed and helpless state that it seems to exist only in order to register the disintegration of Austria, which it is unable to prevent, or at least to give it an orderly course? A government which is even too weak to save Prague from the guns and soldiers of a Windischgrätz?

But it is the gallant Czechs themselves who are most of all to be pitied. Whether they win or are defeated, their doom is sealed. They have been driven into the arms of the Russians by 400 years of German oppression, which is being continued now in the street-fighting waged in Prague. In the great struggle between Western and Eastern Europe, which may begin very soon, perhaps in a few weeks, the Czechs are placed by an unhappy fate on the side of the Russians, the side of despotism opposed to the revolution. The revolution will triumph and the Czechs will be the first to be crushed by it.

The Germans once again bear the responsibility for the ruin of the Czech people, for the Germans have betrayed them to the Russians.

Written by Engels

Neue Rheinische Zeitung No. 18,
June 18, 1848

Barricades on the Brückenplatz in Prague, June 12, 1848
(*Lithograph*)

A DEMOCRATIC UPRISING

Prague. Every day brings further confirmation of our view of the Prague uprising (No. 18 of this paper*), and shows that the insinuations of the German papers which alleged that the Czech party served reaction, the aristocracy, the Russians, etc., were downright lies.

They only saw Count Leo Thun and his aristocrats, and failed to notice the mass of the people of Bohemia—the numerous industrial workers and peasants. The fact that at one moment the aristocracy tried to use the Czech movement in its own interests and those of the camarilla at Innsbruck, was regarded by them as evidence that the revolutionary proletariat of Prague, who, already in 1844, held full control of Prague for three days,[16] represented the interests of the nobility and reaction in general.

All these calumnies, however, were exploded by the first decisive act of the Czech party. The uprising was so decidedly democratic that the counts *Thun*, instead of heading it, immediately withdrew from it, and were detained by the people as Austrian hostages. It was so definitely democratic that all Czechs belonging to the aristocratic party shunned it. It was aimed as much against the Czech feudal lords as against the Austrian troops.

The Austrians attacked the people not because they were Czechs, but because they were *revolutionaries*. The military

---

* See this volume, pp. 38-40.—*Ed.*

regarded the storming of Prague simply as a prelude to the storming and burning down of Vienna.

Thus the *Berliner Zeitungs-Halle*[17] writes:

"*Vienna*, June 20. The deputation which the Viennese Citizens' Committee[18] had sent to Prague has returned today. Its sole errand was to arrange for some sort of supervision of telegraphic communications, so that we should not have to wait for information 24 hours, as was often the case during the last few days. The deputation reported back to the Committee. They related dreadful things about the military rule in Prague. Words failed them to describe the horrors of a conquered, shelled and besieged city. At the peril of their lives they drove into the city from the last station before Prague by cart, and at the peril of their lives they passed through the lines of soldiers to the castle of Prague.

"Everywhere the soldiers met them with exclamations of: 'So you're here, too, you Viennese dogs! Now we've got you!' Many wanted to set upon them, even the officers were shockingly rude. Finally the deputies reached the castle. Count Wallmoden took the credentials the Committee had given them, looked at the signature and said: '*Pillersdorf*? He has nothing to say here.' Windischgrätz treated the plebeian rabble more arrogantly than ever, saying: '*The revolution has been victorious everywhere; here we are the victors and we recognise no civilian authority*. While I was in Vienna things were quiet there. But the moment I left everything was upset.' The members of the deputation were disarmed and confined in one of the rooms of the castle. They were not allowed to leave until two days later, and their arms were not returned to them.

"This is what our deputies reported, this is how they were treated by the Tilly of Prague and the soldiers, yet people here still act as though they believe that this is merely a fight against the Czechs. Did our deputies perhaps speak Czech? Did they not wear the uniform of the Viennese National Guard? Did they not have a warrant from the ministry and the Citizens' Committee which the ministry had recognised as a legal authority?

"But the revolution has gone too far. Windischgrätz thinks he is the man who can stem it. The Bohemians are shot down like dogs, and when the time for the venture comes the advance against Vienna will begin. Why did Windischgrätz set Leo Thun free, the same Leo Thun who headed the Provisional Government in Prague and who advocated the separation of Bohemia? Why, we ask, was he freed from Czech hands if his entire activity were not a game prearranged with the aristocracy in order to bring about the explosion?

"A train left Prague the day before yesterday. On it travelled German students, Viennese National Guards, and families who were leaving Prague, for, despite the fact that tranquility had been restored, they no longer felt at home there. At the first station the military guard posted there demanded that all the passengers without exception hand over their weapons, and when they refused the soldiers fired into the carriages at the defenceless men, women and children. Six bodies were removed from the carriages and the passengers wiped the blood of the murdered people from their faces. This was how Germans were treated by the very military whom people here would like to regard as the guardian angels of German liberty."

Written by Engels on June 24, 1848

Neue Rheinische Zeitung No. 25, June 25, 1848

NEWS FROM PARIS

Cologne, June 26. The news just received from Paris takes up so much space that we are obliged to omit all articles of critical comment.

Therefore only a few words to our readers. Our latest news from Paris gives this:—the *resignation of Ledru-Rollin* and *Lamartine* and their ministers; the transfer of *Cavaignac's military dictatorship* from Algiers to Paris; *Marrast the dictator in plain clothes; Paris bathed in blood;* the *insurrection* growing into the *greatest revolution that has ever taken place*, into a *revolution of the proletariat against the bourgeoisie.* Three days which sufficed for the *July revolution* and the *February revolution* are insufficient for the colossal contours of this *June revolution,* but the *victory of the people is more certain than ever. The French bourgeoisie has dared to do what the French kings never dared—it has itself cast the die.* This *second act of the French revolution* is only the beginning of the *European tragedy.*

Neue Rheinische Zeitung No. 27,
June 27, 1848

THE JUNE REVOLUTION

The workers of Paris were *overwhelmed* by superior strength, but they were not *subdued*. They have been *defeated* but their enemies are *vanquished*. The momentary triumph of brute force has been purchased with the destruction of all the delusions and illusions of the February revolution, the dissolution of the entire moderate republican party and the division of the French nation into two nations, the nation of owners and the nation of workers. The tricolour republic now displays only *one colour*, the colour of the defeated, the *colour of blood*. It has become a *red republic*.

None of the big republican figures, whether of the *National*[19] or of the *Réforme*,[20] sided with the people. In the absence of leaders and means other than those thrown up by the rebellion itself, the people stood up to the united forces of the bourgeoisie and army longer than any French dynasty with the entire military apparatus at its disposal was ever able to stand up to any group of the bourgeoisie allied with the people. To have the people lose its last illusions and break completely with the past, it was necessary that the customary poetic trimmings of French uprisings—the enthusiastic bourgeois youth, the students of the école polytechnique, the tricornes—should join the side of the suppressors. The medical students had to deny the wounded plebeians the succour of their science. Science does not exist for the plebeian who has committed the heinous, unutterable crime of fighting this time for his own existence instead of for Louis Philippe or Monsieur Marrast.

The Executive Committee,[21] that last official vestige of the February revolution, vanished like a ghost in the face

of these grave events. Lamartine's fireworks have turned
into the incendiary shells of Cavaignac.

Fraternité, the brotherhood of antagonistic classes, one of
which exploits the other, this fraternité which in February
was proclaimed and inscribed in large letters on the façades
of Paris, on every prison and every barracks—this fraternity
found its true, unadulterated and prosaic expression in *civil
war*, civil war in its most terrible aspect, the war of labour
against capital. This brotherhood blazed in front of the
windows of Paris on the evening of June 25, when the Paris
of the bourgeoisie held illuminations while the Paris of the
proletariat was burning, bleeding, groaning in the throes of
death.

This brotherhood lasted only as long as there was a con-
sanguinity of interests between the bourgeoisie and the proletariat. Pedants sticking to the old revolutionary tradition
of 1793; socialist doctrinaires who begged alms for the
people from the bourgeoisie and who were allowed to deliver lengthy sermons and compromise themselves so long as
the proletarian lion had to be lulled to sleep; republicans
who wanted to keep the old bourgeois order in toto, but
without the crowned head; members of the Dynastic Opposition[22] on whom chance imposed the task of bringing about
the downfall of a dynasty instead of a change of government;
legitimists,[23] who did not want to cast off their livery but
merely to change its style—these were the allies with whom
the people had fought their February revolution. What the
people instinctively hated in Louis Philippe was not Louis
Philippe himself, but the crowned rule of a class, the capital
on the throne. But magnanimous as always, the people
thought they had destroyed their enemy when they had overthrown the enemy of their enemies, their *common* enemy.

The *February revolution* was the *nice* revolution, the
revolution of universal sympathies, because the contradictions
which erupted in it against the monarchy were still *unde-
veloped* and peacefully dormant, because the social struggle
which formed their background had only achieved an ephem-
eral existence, an existence in phrases, in words. The *June
revolution* is the *ugly* revolution, the nasty revolution, because the phrases have given place to the real thing, be-

cause the republic has bared the head of the monster by knocking off the crown which shielded and concealed it.

Order! was Guizot's war-cry. *Order!* shouted Sébastiani, the Guizotist, when Warsaw became Russian. *Order!* shouts Cavaignac, the brutal echo of the French National Assembly and of the republican bourgeoisie.

Order! thundered his grape-shot as it tore into the body of the proletariat.

None of the numerous revolutions of the French bourgeoisie since 1789 assailed the existing *order*, for they retained the class rule, the slavery of the workers, the *bourgeois system*, even though the political form of this rule and this slavery changed frequently. The June uprising did assail this *system*. Woe to the June uprising!

Under the *Provisional Government* it was considered good form and, moreover, a *necessity* to preach to the magnanimous workers—who, as a thousand official posters proclaimed, *"placed three months of misery at the disposal of the Republic"*—it was both good politics and a sign of enthusiasm to preach to the workers that the February revolution had been carried out *in their own interests* and that the principal issue of the February revolution was the *interests of the workers*. With the *opening* of the National Assembly the speeches have become more prosaic. Now it was only a matter of *leading labour back to its old conditions*, as Minister Trélat said. Thus the workers fought in February in order to be engulfed in an industrial crisis.

It is the business of the National Assembly to undo the work of February, at least as far as the workers are concerned, and to throw them back to their old conditions. But even this was not done, because it is not within the power of any assembly any more than of a king to will a universal industrial crisis—*advance up to this point and no further*. In its crude eagerness to put an end to the tiresome February phraseology, the National Assembly did not even take the measures that were possible on the basis of the old conditions. Parisian workers aged 17 to 25 were either pressed into the army or thrown onto the street; those from other parts were ordered out of Paris to the Sologne without even receiving the money that went with such an order; adult Parisians could for the time being secure a pittance in workshops organised on military lines on condition that they did not attend any public meetings, in other words on condition that they ceased to be republicans. Neither the sentimental rhetoric which followed the February events nor the brutal legislation after May 15[24] achieved their purpose. A real, practical decision had to be taken. For whom did you make the February revolution, you rascals—for *yourselves* or for *us*? The bourgeoisie put this question in such a way that it had to be answered in June with grape-shot and barricades.

The entire National Assembly is nevertheless struck with paralysis, as one deputy* put it on June 25. Its members are stunned when question and answer make the streets of Paris flow with blood; some are stunned because their illusions are lost in the smoke of gunpowder, others because they cannot understand how the people dare stand up *on their own* for their *own vital* interests. *Russian money, British money, the Bonapartist eagle, the lily*, amulets of all kinds—this is where they sought an explanation of this strange event. Both parts of the Assembly feel however that a vast gulf separates them from the people. None of them dare stand up for the people.

As soon as the stupor has passed frenzy breaks out. The majority quite rightly greets with catcalls those hapless utopians and hypocrites guilty of the anachronism of still using the term fraternité, brotherhood. The question at issue was precisely that of doing away with this term and with the illusions arising from its ambiguity. When the legitimist *Larochejaquelein*, the chivalrous dreamer, protested against the infamy of those who cried *"Uae victis! Woe to the vanquished!"* the majority of the deputies broke into a St. Vitus's dance as if stung by a tarantula. They shouted *woe!* to the workers in order to hide the fact that they themselves are the *"vanquished"*. Either the Assembly must perish now, or the republic. And that is why it frantically yells—long live the republic!

Is the deep chasm which has opened at our feet to mislead us, democrats, or cause us to believe that the struggle for a form of polity is meaningless, illusory and futile?

* Ducoux.—*Ed.*

Street-fighting in the Faubourg St. Antoine (Paris),
June 1848 (*Lithograph*)

Only weak, cowardly minds can pose such a question. Collisions proceeding from the very conditions of bourgeois society must be overcome by fighting, they cannot be reasoned out of existence. The best form of polity is that in which the social contradictions are not blurred, not arbitrarily—that is, merely artificially, and therefore only seemingly—kept down. The best form of polity is that in which these contradictions reach a stage of open struggle in the course of which they are resolved.

We may be asked, do we not find a tear, a sigh, a word for the victims of the people's wrath, for the National Guard, the mobile guard,[25] the republican guard and the line?

The state will care for their widows and orphans, decrees extolling them will be issued, their remains will be carried to the grave in solemn procession, the official press will declare them immortal, the European reaction in the East and the West will pay homage to them.

But the plebeians are tormented by hunger, abused by the press, forsaken by the physicians, called thieves, incendiaries and galley-slaves by the respectabilities; their wives and children are plunged into still greater misery and the best of those who have survived are sent overseas. It is the *right* and the *privilege of the democratic press* to place laurels on their gloomy threatening brow.

Written by Marx on June 28, 1848

Neue Rheinische Zeitung No. 29, June 29, 1848

THE JUNE REVOLUTION
[The Course of the Paris Uprising]

[I]

Gradually we gain a more comprehensive view of the June Revolution; fuller reports arrive, it becomes possible to distinguish facts from either hearsay or lies, and the nature of the uprising stands out with increasing clarity. The more one succeeds in grasping the interconnection of the events of the four days in June, the more is one astonished by the vast magnitude of the uprising, the heroic courage, the rapidly improvised organisation and the unanimity of the insurgents.

The workers' plan of action, which Kersausie, a friend of Raspail and a former officer, is said to have drawn up, was as follows:

The insurgents, moving in four columns, advance concentrically towards the town hall.

The first column, whose base were the suburbs of Montmartre, La Chapelle and La Villette, advance southwards from the gates of Poissonnière, Rochechouart, St. Denis and La Villette, occupy the Boulevards and approach the town hall through the streets Montorgueil, St. Denis and St. Martin.

The second column, whose base were the faubourgs du Temple and St. Antoine, which are inhabited almost entirely by workers and protected by the St. Martin canal, advance towards the same centre through the streets du Temple and St. Antoine and along the quais of the northern bank of the Seine as well as through all other streets running in the same direction in this part of the city.

The third column based on the Faubourg St. Marceau move towards the Île de la Cité through the Rue St. Victor and the quais of the southern bank of the Seine.

The fourth column, based on the Faubourg St. Jacques and the vicinity of the Medical School, move down the Rue Saint Jacques also to the Cité. There the two columns join, cross to the right bank of the Seine and envelop the town hall from the rear and flank.

Thus the plan, quite correctly, was based on the districts in which only workers lived. These districts form a semicircular belt, which surrounds the entire eastern half of Paris, widening out towards the east. First of all the eastern part of Paris was to be cleared of enemies, and then it was intended to move along both banks of the Seine towards the west and its centres, the Tuileries and the National Assembly.

These columns were to be supported by numerous flying squads which, operating independently alongside and between the columns, were to build barricades, occupy the smaller streets and be responsible for maintaining communication.

The operational bases were strongly fortified and skilfully transformed into formidable fortresses, e.g., the Clos St. Lazare, the Faubourg and Quartier St. Antoine and the Faubourg St. Jacques, in case it should become necessary to retreat.

If there was any flaw in this plan it was that in the beginning of the operations the western part of Paris was completely overlooked. There are several districts eminently suitable for armed action on both sides of the Rue St. Honoré near the market halls and the Palais National, which have very narrow, winding streets tenanted mainly by workers. It was important to set up a fifth centre of the insurrection there, thus cutting off the town hall and at the same time holding up a considerable number of troops at this projecting strongpoint. The success of the uprising depended on the insurgents reaching the centre of Paris as quickly as possible and seizing the town hall. We cannot know what prevented Kersausie from organising insurgent action in this part. But it is a fact that no uprising was ever successful which did not at the outset succeed in seizing the centre of Paris adjoining the Tuileries. Suffice to mention the uprising* which took

---

* The uprising took place in Paris on June 5-6, 1832.—*Ed.*

place during General Lamarque's funeral when the insurgents got as far as the Rue Montorgueil and were then driven back.

The insurgents advanced in accordance with their plan. They immediately began to separate their territory, the Paris of the workers, from the Paris of the bourgeoisie, by two main fortifications—the barricades at the Porte Saint Denis and those of the Cité. They were dislodged from the former, but were able to hold the latter. June 23, the first day, was merely a prelude. The plan of the insurgents already began to emerge clearly (and the *Neue Rheinische Zeitung* grasped it correctly at the outset, see No. 26, special supplement*), especially after the first skirmishes between the advanced guards which took place in the morning. The Boulevard St. Martin, which crosses the line of operation of the first column, became the scene of fierce fighting, which, partly due to the nature of the terrain, ended with a victory for the forces of "order".

The approaches to the Cité were blocked on the right by a flying squad, which entrenched itself in the Rue de la Planche-Mibray; on the left by the third and fourth columns, which occupied and fortified the three southern bridges of the Cité. Here too a very fierce battle raged. The forces of "order" succeeded in taking the St. Michel bridge and advancing to the Rue St. Jacques. They felt sure that by the evening the revolt would be suppressed.

The plan of the forces of "order" stood out even more clearly than that of the insurgents. To begin with, their plan was merely to crush the insurrection with all available means. They announced their design to the insurgents with cannon-ball and grape-shot.

But the government believed it was dealing with an uncouth gang of common rioters acting without any plan. After clearing the main streets by the evening, the government declared that the revolt was quelled, and the stationing of troops in the conquered districts was arranged in an exceedingly negligent manner.

---

* See "Details über den 23. Juni" by Engels in : Marx/Engels, *Werke*, Bd. 5, Berlin, 1969, S. 112-15.—*Ed.*

The insurgents made excellent use of this negligence by launching the great battle which followed the skirmishes of June 23. It is simply amazing how quickly the workers mastered the plan of campaign, how well-concerted their actions were and how skilfully they used the difficult terrain. This would be quite inexplicable if in the national workshops the workers had not already been to a certain extent organised on military lines and divided into companies, so that they only needed to apply their industrial organisation to their military enterprise in order to create a fully organised army.

On the morning of the 24th they had not only completely regained the ground they had lost, but even added new strips to it. True, the line of Boulevards up to the Boulevard du Temple remained in the hands of the troops, thus cutting off the first column from the centre, but on the other hand the second column pushed forward from the Quartier St. Antoine until it almost surrounded the town hall. It established its headquarters in the church of St. Gervais, within 300 paces of the town hall. It captured the St. Merri monastery and the adjoining streets and advanced far beyond the town hall so that together with the columns in the Cité it almost completely encircled the town hall. Only one way of approach, the quais of the right bank, remained open. In the south the Faubourg St. Jacques was completely reoccupied, communication with the Cité was restored, reinforcements were sent there, and preparations were made for crossing to the right bank.

There was no time to be lost. The town hall, the revolutionary centre of Paris, was threatened and was bound to fall unless resolute measures were taken immediately.

[II]

Cavaignac was appointed dictator by a frightened National Assembly. Accustomed as he was in Algeria to "energetic" action, he did not have to be told what to do.

Ten battalions promptly moved towards the town hall along the wide Quai de l'École. They cut off the insurgents in the Cité from the right bank, secured the safety of the town hall and made it even possible to attack the barricades surrounding it.

The Rue de la Planche-Mibray and its continuation, Rue Saint Martin, were cleared and kept permanently clear by cavalry. The Notre-Dame bridge, which lies opposite and leads to the Cité, was swept by heavy guns, and then Cavaignac advanced directly on the Cité in order to take "energetic" measures there. The "Belle Jardinière", the strongpoint of the insurgents, was first destroyed by cannon and then set on fire by rockets. The Rue de la Cité was also seized with the aid of gun-fire; three bridges leading to the left bank were stormed and the insurgents on the left bank were pressed back. Meanwhile, the 14 battalions deployed on the Place de Grève and the quais freed the besieged town hall, and reduced the church of Saint Gervais from a headquarters to a lost outpost of the insurgents.

The Rue St. Jacques was bombarded not only from the Cité but also in the flank from the left bank. General Damesme broke through along the Luxembourg to the Sorbonne, seized the Quartier Latin and sent his columns against the Panthéon. The Panthéon square had been transformed into a formidable stronghold. The forces of "order" still faced this unassailable bulwark long after they had taken the Rue St. Jacques. Gun-fire and bayonet attacks were of no avail until finally exhaustion, lack of ammunition and the threat of the bourgeois to set the place on fire compelled the 1,500 workers, who were completely hemmed in, to surrender. At about the same time, the Place Maubert fell into the hands of the forces of "order" after a long and courageous resistance, and the insurgents, deprived of their strongest positions, were forced to abandon the entire left bank of the Seine.

Meanwhile the troops and National Guards stationed on the Boulevards of the right bank of the Seine were likewise put into action in two directions. Lamoricière, who commanded them, had the streets of the faubourgs St. Denis and St. Martin, the Boulevard du Temple and part of the Rue du Temple cleared by heavy artillery and swift infantry attacks. By the evening he could boast of brilliant successes. He had cut off and partly surrounded the first column in the Clos St. Lazare; he had pushed back the second column, and by advancing along the Boulevards had thrust a wedge into it.

How did Cavaignac win these advantages?

First, by the vastly superior force he was able to use against the insurgents. On the 24th he had at his disposal not only the 20,000-strong Paris garrison, the 20,000 to 25,000 men of the Garde mobile and the 60,000 to 80,000 available men of the Garde national, but also the Garde national from the whole vicinity of Paris and from many of the more distant towns (20,000 to 30,000 men) and in addition 20,000 to 30,000 soldiers who were called in with the utmost dispatch from the neighbouring garrisons. Even on the morning of the 24th he had well over 100,000 men at his disposal, and by the evening their numbers had increased by half. The insurgents, on the other hand, numbered 40,000 to 50,000 men at most!

Secondly, by the brutal means he used. Until then guns had been fired in the streets of Paris *only once*, i.e., in Vendémiaire 1795, when Napoleon dispersed the insurgents in the Rue Saint Honoré with grape-shot. But no artillery, let alone grenades and incendiary rockets, was ever used against barricades and against houses. The people were unprepared for this, they were defenceless, for the only counteraction they could take was to set fire to houses, but this was repugnant to their noble sentiments. Up till then the people had no idea that this brand of Algerian warfare could be used right in the centre of Paris. They therefore retreated, and their first retreat spelt their defeat.

On the 25th Cavaignac attacked with even larger forces. The insurgents were confined to a single district, the faubourgs Saint Antoine and du Temple; in addition they still held two outposts, the Clos St. Lazare and a part of the St. Antoine district up to the Damiette bridge.

Cavaignac, who had received further reinforcements of 20,000 to 30,000 men as well as a substantial park of artillery, first attacked the isolated outposts of the insurgents, especially the Clos St. Lazare. The insurgents were entrenched here as in a fortress. After a 12-hour bombardment with shells and grenades, Lamoricière finally succeeded in dislodging the insurgents and occupying the Clos St. Lazare, but not until he had mounted a flank attack from the Rue Rochechouart and the Rue Poissonnière, and had demolished the barricades by bombarding them with 40 guns on the first day and with an even greater number on the next.

Another part of his column penetrated through the Faubourg Saint Martin into the Faubourg du Temple, but was not very successful. A third section moved along the Boulevards towards the Bastille, but it did not get very far either, because a number of the most formidable barricades there resisted for a long time and only succumbed after a fierce cannonade. The houses here suffered appalling destruction.

Duvivier's column advancing from the town hall pressed the insurgents back still further with the aid of incessant artillery fire. The church of St. Gervais was captured, a long stretch of the Rue St. Antoine well beyond the town hall was cleared, and several columns moving along the quai and streets running parallel to it seized the Damiette bridge, which connected the insurgents of the St. Antoine district with those of the St. Louis and Cité islands. The St. Antoine district was outflanked and the insurgents had no choice but to fall back into the faubourg, which they did in fierce combat with a column advancing along the quais to the mouth of the St. Martin canal and thence along the Boulevard Bourdon skirting the canal. Several insurgents who were cut off were massacred, hardly any were taken prisoner.

The St. Antoine district and the Place de la Bastille were seized in this operation. Lamoricière's column managed to occupy the whole Boulevard Beaumarchais by the evening and join up with Duvivier's troops on the Place de la Bastille.

The capture of the Damiette bridge enabled Duvivier to dislodge the insurgents from the St. Louis island and the former Louvier island. He did this with a commendable display of Algerian barbarity. Hardly anywhere in the city was heavy artillery used with such devastating effect as in the island of St. Louis. But what did that matter? The insurgents were either driven out or massacred and among the blood-stained ruins "order" triumphed.

One more post remained to be seized on the left bank of the Seine. The Austerlitz bridge, which east of the St. Martin canal links the Faubourg St. Antoine with the left bank of the Seine, was heavily barricaded and had a strong bridgehead on the left bank where it adjoins the Place Valhubert in front of the Botanical Gardens. This bridgehead, which after the fall of the Panthéon and the Place Maubert was the last stronghold of the insurgents on the left bank, was taken after stubborn resistance.

Only their last bulwark, the Faubourg St. Antoine and a part of the Faubourg du Temple, was thus left to the insurgents on the following day, the 26th. Neither of these is quite suitable for street-fighting; the streets there are fairly wide and almost perfectly straight, offering full play for the artillery. Their western side is well protected by the St. Martin canal, but the northern side is completely exposed. Five or six perfectly straight, wide streets run from the north right into the centre of the Faubourg St. Antoine.

The principal fortifications were at the Place de la Bastille and in the Rue du Faubourg St. Antoine, the main street of the whole district. Remarkably strong barricades were set up there, built partly of big flagstones and partly of wooden beams. They were constructed in the form of an angle pointing inward in order partly to weaken the effect of the gun-fire, partly to offer a larger defence front making cross-fire possible. Openings had been made in the fireproof walls of the houses so that the rows of houses were connected with each other, thus enabling the insurgents to open rifle fire on the troops or withdraw behind the barricades as circumstances demanded. The bridges and quais along the canal as well as the streets running parallel to it were also strongly fortified. In short, the two faubourgs the insurgents still held resembled a veritable fortress, in which the troops had to wage a bloody battle for every inch of ground.

On the morning of the 26th the fighting was to be resumed, but Cavaignac was not keen on sending his troops into this maze of barricades. He threatened to shell them; mortars and howitzers were brought up. A parley was held. Cavaignac meanwhile ordered the nearest houses to be undermined, but this could only be done to a very limited extent, because the time was too short and because the canal covered one of the lines of attack; he also ordered internal communication to be established between the occupied houses and the adjoining houses through gaps in the fire-proof walls.

The negotiations broke down and fighting was resumed. Cavaignac ordered General Perrot to attack from the Faubourg du Temple and General Lamoricière from the Place de la Bastille. The barricades were heavily shelled from both directions. Perrot pushed forward fairly rapidly, occupied the remaining section of the Faubourg du Temple and even penetrated into the Faubourg St. Antoine at several points. Lamoricière's advance was slower. The first barricades withstood his guns, although his grenades set the first houses of the faubourg on fire. He began once more to negotiate. Watch in hand he awaited the moment when he would have the pleasure of shelling and razing to the ground the most thickly populated district of Paris. Some of the insurgents at last capitulated, while others, attacked in the flank, withdrew from the city after a short battle.

That saw the end of the June barricade fighting. Skirmishes still continued outside the city, but they were of no significance. The insurgents who fled were scattered in the neighbourhood and were one by one captured by cavalry.

We have given this purely military description of the struggle to show our readers with what heroic courage, unity, discipline and military skill the Paris workers fought. For four days 40,000 of them opposed forces four times their strength, and were within a hairbreadth of victory. They almost succeeded in gaining a footing in the centre of Paris, taking the town hall, forming a provisional government and doubling their number not only by people from the captured parts of the city joining them but also from the ranks of the Garde mobile, who at that time needed but a slight impetus to make them go over to their side.

German newspapers assert that this was the decisive battle between the red and the tricolour republics, between workers and bourgeois. We are convinced that this battle will decide nothing but the disintegration of the victors. Moreover, the whole course of events proves that, even from a purely military standpoint, the workers are bound to triumph within a fairly short space of time. If 40,000 Paris workers could achieve such tremendous things against forces four times their number, what will the whole mass of Paris workers accomplish by concerted and co-ordinated action.

Kersausie was captured and by now has probably been shot. The bourgeois can kill him, but cannot take from him the fame of having been the *first to organise street-fighting.* They can kill him, but no power on earth can prevent his techniques from being used in all future street-fighting. They can kill him, but they cannot prevent his name from going down in history as the *first commander-in-chief of barricade fighting.*

Written by Engels
on June 30 and July 1, 1848

Neue Rheinische Zeitung Nos. 31
and 32, July 1 and 2, 1848

GERMANY'S FOREIGN POLICY

Cologne, July 2. All hitherto existing rulers and their diplomats have employed their skill and efforts to set one nation against another and use one nation to suppress another, and in this manner to perpetuate absolute rule. Germany has distinguished herself in this respect. During the last 70 years alone, she had furnished the British, in exchange for English gold, with mercenaries to be used against the North Americans fighting for their independence; when the first French revolution broke out it was the Germans again who, like a rabid pack, allowed themselves to be set upon the French; in a vicious manifesto issued by the Duke of Brunswick they threatened to raze the whole of Paris to the ground; they conspired with the émigré aristocrats against the new order in France and were paid for this in the form of subsidies received from England. When the Dutch, for the first time in two hundred years, finally hit upon the sensible idea of putting an end to the mad rule of the House of Orange and establishing a republic,[26] it was the Germans again who acted as the hangmen of freedom. The Swiss, too, could tell a tale about their German neighbours, and it will be some time before the Hungarians recover from the harm which Austria, i.e., the German imperial court, inflicted upon them. German mercenary troops were even sent to Greece to prop up the little throne of dear Otto,[27] and German policemen were sent even to Portugal. Then there were the congresses after 1815, Austria's expeditions to Naples, Turin and the Romagna, the imprisonment of Ypsilanti, the German-imposed war of suppression which France waged against Spain,[28] Dom Miguel[29] and Don Carlos[30] who were supported by Germany; the reaction in Britain had Hannoverian troops at its disposal; German influence led to the dismemberment of Belgium and the establishment of a Thermidorian rule there; in the very heart of Russia Germans are the mainstay of the *one* autocrat and of the smaller ones, all Europe is flooded with sprigs of the House of Coburg.

Poland was plundered and dismembered and Cracow throttled with the help of German soldiers.[31] German money and blood helped to enslave and impoverish Lombardy and Venice, and directly or indirectly to stifle any movement of liberation throughout Italy by means of bayonets, gallows, prisons and galleys. The list of sins is much longer, let us close it.

The blame for the infamies committed with the aid of Germany in other countries falls not only on the governments but to a large extent also on the German people. But for the delusions of the Germans, their slavish spirit, their flair for acting as mercenaries and "benign" jailers and tools of the masters "by divine right", the German name abroad would not be so detested, cursed and despised, and the nations oppressed by Germany would have long since been able to develop freely. Now that the Germans are throwing off their own yoke, their whole foreign policy must change too. Otherwise the fetters with which we have chained other nations will shackle our own new, barely prescient, freedom. Germany will liberate herself to the extent to which she sets free neighbouring nations.

Things are indeed beginning to look up. The lies and misrepresentations which the old government organs have been so busy spreading about Poland and Italy, the attempts to artificially create enmity, the turgid phrases proclaiming that German honour or German power is at stake—all these magic formulas are no longer effective. The official patriotism is effective only when these patriotic postures conceal material interests, i.e., only among a section of the big bourgeoisie whose business depends on this official patriotism. The reactionary party knows this and makes use of it. But the great mass of the German middle class and the working class understand or feel that the freedom of the neighbouring nations is the guarantee of their own freedom. Is Austria's

war against Italy's independence or Prussia's war against
the restoration of Poland popular, or do these "patriotic"
crusades on the contrary destroy the last illusions? However, neither this understanding nor this feeling is sufficient.
If Germany's blood and money is no longer to be squan-
dered, to her own detriment, in suppressing other nations, then
we must achieve a really popular government, and the old
edifice must be razed to the ground. Only then can an international policy of democracy take the place of the sanguinary, cowardly policy of the old, revived system. How can
a democratic foreign policy be carried through while democracy at home is stifled? Meanwhile, everything possible
must be done to prepare the way for the democratic system
on this side and the other side of the Alps. The *Italians* have
issued a number of declarations which make their friendly
attitude towards Germany perfectly clear. We would mention the Manifesto of the Provisional Government at Milan
addressed to the German people[32] and the numerous articles
written in the same vein, which are published in the Italian
press. We have now received further evidence of this attitude—a private letter from the administrative committee of
the newspaper *L'Alba*,[33] published in Florence, to the editors of the *Neue Rheinische Zeitung*. It is dated June 20,
and says among other things:

"We thank you sincerely for the esteem in which you hold our poor
Italy. Meanwhile we wholeheartedly assure you that all Italians know
who really violates and attacks their liberty; they know that their most
deadly enemy is not the strong and magnanimous German people, but
rather their unjust, despotic, and cruel government; we assure you
that every true Italian longs for the moment when he will be free to
shake hands with his German brother, who, once his inalienable rights
are established, will be able to defend them, to respect them himself
and to secure the respect of all his brothers for them. Placing our
trust in the principles to whose careful elaboration you have dedicated
yourselves, we remain

your faithful friends and brothers
(signed) *L. Alinari"*

The *Alba* is one of the few papers in Italy which advocate
thoroughly democratic principles.

Written by Engels
Neue Rheinische Zeitung No. 33,
July 3, 1848

THE DEBATE ON JACOBY'S MOTION

Cologne, July 17. Again a "great debate", to use an expression of Herr Camphausen, has taken place, a debate which lasted two full days.

The substance of the debate is well known—the reservations the government advanced regarding the immediate validity of the decisions passed by the National Assembly and Jacoby's motion asserting the Assembly's right to pass legally binding decisions requiring no one's consent, and at the same time objecting to the resolution on the central authority.[34]

That a debate on this subject was possible at all may seem incomprehensible to other nations. But we live in a land of oaks and lime-trees where nothing should surprise us.

The people send their representatives to Frankfurt with the mandate that the Assembly assume sovereign power over the whole of Germany and all her governments, and, by virtue of the sovereignty the people have vested in the Assembly, adopt a constitution for Germany.

Instead of immediately proclaiming its sovereignty in respect to the separate states and the Federal Diet, the Assembly timidly avoids any question relating to this subject and maintains an irresolute and vacillating attitude.

Finally it is confronted with a decisive issue—the appointment of a provisional central authority. Seemingly independent, but in fact guided by the governments with the help of Gagern, the Assembly elects as Vice Regent of the Empire a man whom these governments had in advance designated for this post.

The Federal Diet recognises the election, pretending, as it were, that only its confirmation makes the election valid.

Reservations are nevertheless made by Hannover and even by Prussia, and it is the Prussian reservation that has caused the debate of the 11th and 12th.

This time, therefore, it is not so much the fault of the Chamber in Berlin that the debates are vague and hazy. The irresolute, weak-kneed, ineffectual Frankfurt National Assembly itself is to blame for the fact that its decisions can only be described as so much twaddle.

Jacoby introduces his motion with a brief speech made with his usual precision. He makes things very difficult for the speakers of the Left, because he says everything that can be said about the motion if one is to avoid enlarging upon the origin of the central authority, whose history is rather discreditable to the National Assembly.

In fact, the deputies of the Left who follow him advance hardly any new arguments, while those of the Right fare much worse—they lapse either into sheer twaddle or juridical hair-splitting. Both sides endlessly repeat themselves.

The honour of first presenting the case for the Right devolves on Deputy *Schneider*.

He begins with the grand argument that the motion is self-contradictory. On the one hand, the motion recognises the sovereignty of the National Assembly, on the other hand, it calls upon the Chamber of conciliation to censure the National Assembly, thus placing itself above it. Any individual could express his disapproval but not the Chamber.

This subtle argument, of which the Right seems to be very proud seeing that it recurs in all the speeches of its deputies, advances an entirely new theory. According to this theory, the Chamber has fewer rights with regard to the National Assembly than an individual.

This first grand argument is followed by a republican one. Germany consists for the most part of constitutional monarchies, and must therefore be headed by a constitutional, irresponsible authority and not by a republican, responsible one. This argument was rebutted on the second day by Herr *Stein*, who said that Germany, under her federal constitution, had always been a republic, indeed a very edifying republic.

"We have been given a mandate," says Herr Schneider, "to agree on a constitutional monarchy, and those in Frankfurt have been given a similar mandate, i.e., to agree with the German governments on a constitution for Germany."

The reaction indulges in wishful thinking. When, by order of the so-called Preparliament—an assembly having no valid mandate—the trembling Federal Diet convened the German National Assembly, there was no question at the time of any agreement; the National Assembly was then considered to be a sovereign power. But things now have changed. The June events in Paris have revived the hopes of both the big bourgeoisie and the supporters of the over-thrown system. Every country bumpkin of a squire hopes to see the old rule of the knout re-established, and a clamour for "an agreed German constitution" is already arising from the imperial court at Innsbruck to the ancestral castle of Henry LXXII. The Frankfurt Assembly has no one but itself to blame for this.

"In electing a constitutional head the National Assembly has there-fore acted according to its mandate. But it has also acted in accordance with the will of the people; the great majority want a constitutional monarchy. Indeed, had the National Assembly come to a different decision, I would have regarded it as a misfortune. *Not* because I am *against the republic*; in *principle* I admit that the republic—and I have quite definitely made up my mind about it—*is the most perfect and lofty form of polity*, but in reality we are still very far from it. We cannot have the form unless we have the spirit. We cannot have a republic while we lack *republicans*, that is to say, noble minds capable, at all times, with a clear conscience and noble selflessness, and not only in a fit of enthusiasm, of sinking their own interests in the com-mon interest."

Can anyone ask for better proof of the virtues represent-ed in the Berlin Chamber than these noble and modest words of Deputy Schneider? Surely, if any doubt still exist-ed about the fitness of the Germans to set up a republic, it must have completely vanished in face of these examples of true civic virtue, of the noble and most modest self-sacrifice of our Cincinnatus-Schneider. Let Cincinnatus pluck up courage and have faith in himself and the numerous noble citizens of Germany who likewise regard the republic as the most noble political form but consider themselves bad re-publicans—they are ripe for the republic, they would endure

the republic with the same equanimity with which they have
endured the absolute monarchy. The republic of worthies
would be the happiest republic that ever existed—
a republic without Brutus and Catiline, without Marat and
upheavals like those of June, it would be a republic of well-
fed virtue and solvent morality.[35]

How mistaken is Cincinnatus-Schneider when he exclaims:

"A republican mentality cannot be formed under absolutism; it is
not possible to create a republican spirit *offhand,* we must first educate
our children and grandchildren in this way. At present I would regard
a republic as the greatest calamity, for it would be anarchy under the
desecrated name of republic, despotism under the cloak of liberty."

On the contrary, as Herr *Vogt (from Giessen)* said in the
National Assembly, the Germans are republicans *by nature,*
and to educate his children in the republican spirit Cincinnatus-Schneider could do no better than bring them up in the
old German discipline, tradition of modesty and God-fear-
ing piety, the way he himself grew up. Not anarchy and
despotism, but those cozy beer-swilling proceedings, in which
Cincinnatus-Schneider excels, would be brought to the highest perfection in the republic of worthies. Far removed
from all the atrocities and crimes which defiled the first
French republic, unstained by blood, and detesting the red
flag, the republic of worthies would make possible something
hitherto unattainable: it would enable every respectable
burgher to lead a quiet, peaceful life marked by godliness
and propriety. The republic of worthies might even revive
the guilds together with all the amusing trials of non-guild
artisans. This republic of worthies is by no means a fanci-
ful dream; it is a reality existing in Bremen, Hamburg,
Lübeck and Frankfurt, and even in some parts of Switzerland. But its existence is everywhere threatened by the contemporary storms, which bid fair to engulf it everywhere.

Therefore rise up, Cincinnatus-Schneider, leave your
plough and turnip field, your beer and conciliation, mount
your steed and save the threatened republic, *your* republic,
the *republic of worthies*!

Written by Engels
Neue Rheinische Zeitung No. 48.
July 18, 1848

THE ARMISTICE WITH DENMARK

Cologne, July 21. As our readers know, we have always regarded the Danish war[36] with great equanimity. We have joined neither in the blatant bluster of the nationalists, nor in the well-worn tune of the sea-girt Schleswig-Holstein fraternity with their sham enthusiasm. We knew our country too well, we knew what it means to rely on Germany.

Events have fully borne out our views. The unimpeded capture of Schleswig by the Danes, the recapture of the country and the march to Jutland, the retreat to the Schlei, the repeated capture of the duchy up to Königsau—this utterly incomprehensible conduct of the war from first to last has shown the Schleswigers what sort of protection they can expect from the revolutionary, great, strong, united, etc., Germany, from the supposedly sovereign nation of forty-five million. However, in order that they lose all desire to become German, and that "the Danish yoke" appear infinitely more desirable to them than "German liberty", the Prussians, in the name of the German Confederation, negotiated the armistice of which we print today a word-for-word translation.

Hitherto it has been the custom, when signing an armistice, for the two armies to maintain their positions, or as a last resort, a narrow neutral strip was interposed between them. Under this armistice, the first result of "the prowess of Prussian arms", the victorious Prussians withdraw over 20 miles, from Kolding to this side of Lauenburg, whereas the defeated Danes maintain their positions at Kolding and relinquish only Alsen. Furthermore, in the event of the armistice being called off, the Danes are to advance to the positions they held on June 24, in other words they are to

occupy a six to seven miles wide stretch of North Schleswig
without firing a shot—a stretch from which they were *twice*
driven out—whereas the Germans are allowed to advance
only to Apenrade and its environs. Thus "the honour of the
German arms is preserved" and North Schleswig, already
exhausted because it was deluged with troops four times, is
promised a possible fifth and sixth invasion.

But that is not all. A part of Schleswig is to be occupied
by Danish troops even during the armistice. Under Clause
8, Schleswig is to be occupied by regiments recruited in the
duchy, i.e., partly by soldiers from Schleswig who took part
in the movement, and partly by soldiers who at that time
were stationed in Denmark and fought in the ranks of the
Danish army against the Provisional Government. They are
commanded by Danish officers and are in every respect
Danish troops. That is how the Danish papers, too, size up
the situation.

The *Fädrelandet*[37] of July 13 writes:

"The presence in the duchy of *loyal* troops from Schleswig will
undoubtedly substantially harden popular feeling which, now that the
country has experienced the misfortunes of war, will forcefully turn
against those who are the cause of these misfortunes."

On top of that we have the movement in Schleswig-Holstein. The Danes call it a *riot*, and the Prussians *treat it as
a riot*. The Provisional Government, which has been recognised by Prussia and the German Confederation, is mercilessly sacrificed; all laws, decrees, etc., issued after Schleswig became independent are abrogated; on the other hand,
the repealed Danish laws have again come into force. In
short, the reply concerning *Wildenbruch*'s famous Note,[38]
a reply which Herr Auerswald refused to give, can be found
here in Clause 7 of the proposed armistice. Everything that
was revolutionary in the movement is ruthlessly destroyed,
and the government created by the revolution is to be replaced by a legitimate administration nominated by three
legitimate monarchs. The troops of Holstein and Schleswig
are again to be *commanded by Danes and thrashed by
Danes*; the ships of Holstein and Schleswig are to remain
"Danish property" as before, despite the latest order of the
Provisional Government.

The new government which they intend to set up puts the finishing touch to all this. The *Fädrelandet* declares:

"Though in the limited electoral district from which the Danish-elected members of the new government are to be chosen we shall probably not find the combination of energy, talent, intelligence, and experience which Prussia will dispose of when making her selection", this is not decisive. "The members of the government must of course be elected from among the population of the duchies, but nothing is to prevent us giving them secretaries and assistants *residing* and *born in other parts of the country*. In selecting these secretaries and administrative advisers one can be guided by considerations of fitness and talent without regard to local considerations, and it is likely that these men will exert a great influence on the spirit and trend of the entire administration. Indeed, it is to be hoped that even *high-ranking Danish officials* will accept such a post, though its official status may be inferior. Every true Dane will consider such a post an honour under the present circumstances."

This semi-official paper thus promises the duchies that they will be swamped not only with Danish troops but also with Danish civil servants. A partly-Danish government will take up its residence in Rendsburg on the officially recognised territory of the German Confederation.

These are the advantages which the armistice brings Schleswig. The advantages for Germany are just as great. The admission of Schleswig to the German Confederation is not mentioned at all. On the contrary, the decision of the Confederation is *flatly repudiated* by the composition of the new government. The German Confederation chooses the members for Holstein, and the King of Denmark chooses those *for Schleswig*. Schleswig is therefore under Danish, and not German, jurisdiction.

Germany would have rendered a real service in this Danish war if she had compelled Denmark to abolish the Sound tax, a form of old feudal robbery.[39] The German seaports, hard hit by the blockade and the seizure of their ships, would have willingly borne the burden even longer if it led to the abolition of the Sound tax. The governments also made it known everywhere that the abolition of this tax must at any rate be brought about. And what came of all this boasting? Britain and Russia want the tax kept, and of course Germany obediently acquiesces.

It goes without saying that in exchange for the return of the ships, the supplies requisitioned in Jutland have to be refunded, on the principle that Germany is rich enough to pay for her glory.

These are the advantages which the Hansemann ministry offers in this draft armistice to the German nation. These are the fruits of a war waged for three months against a small nation of a million and a half. That is the result of all the boasting by our national papers, our formidable Dane-haters!

It is said that the armistice will not be concluded. General Wrangel, encouraged by Beseler, has definitely refused to sing it, despite repeated requests by Count Pourtalès, who brought him Auerswald's order to sign it, and despite numerous reminders that it was his duty as a Prussian general to do so. Wrangel stated that he is above all subordinated to the German central authority, and the latter will not approve of the armistice unless the armies maintain their present positions and the Provisional Government remains in office until the peace is concluded.

Thus the Prussian project will probably not be carried out, but it is nevertheless interesting as a demonstration of how Prussia, when she takes over the reins, is capable of defending Germany's honour and interests.

Written by **Engels**

Neue Rheinische Zeitung No. 52,
July 22, 1848

THE BILL PROPOSING THE ABOLITION
OF FEUDAL OBLIGATIONS

Cologne, July 29. If any Rhinelander should have forgotten what he owes to the "foreign rule", to "the yoke of the Corsican tyrant", he ought to read the Bill providing for the abolition without compensation of various services and dues. The Bill has been submitted by Herr Hansemann in this year of grace 1848 for the "consideration" of his conciliators. Liegedom, allodification rent, death dues, heriot, protection money, legal dues and fines, signet money, tithes on live-stock, bees, etc.—what a strange, what a barbaric ring these absurd terms have for our ears, which have been civilised by the French Revolution's destruction of feudalism and by the Code Napoléon. How incomprehensible to us is this farrago of medieval duties and taxes, this collection of musty junk from an antediluvian age.

Nevertheless, put off thy shoes from off thy feet, German patriot, for the place whereon thou standest is holy ground. These barbarities are the last remnants of Christian-German glory, the last links of the historical chain which connects you with your illustrious ancestors all the way back to the forest of the Cherusci. The musty air, the feudal mire which we find here in their classic unadulterated form are the very own products of our fatherland, and every true German should exclaim with the poet:

> 'Tis my own native air, and the glow
> > on my cheek
> Could bear no other construction;
> The very dirt in the highway itself
> Is my fatherland's production![40]

Reading the Bill, it seems to you at first glance that our Minister of Agriculture Herr *Gierke*, on the orders of Herr

Hansemann, has brought off a terrifically "bold stroke", has done away with the Middle Ages by a stroke of the pen, and of course quite gratuitously.

But when one looks at the Bill's *motivation*, one discovers that it sets out straight away to prove that *no* feudal obligations *whatever* ought to be abolished without compensation, that is to say, it starts with a bold assertion which directly contradicts the "bold stroke".

The minister's practical timidity now manoeuvres warily and prudently between these two bold postures. On the left "the general welfare" and "the demands of the spirit of our time"; on the right the "established rights of the lords of the manor"; in the middle the "praiseworthy idea of a freer development of rural relations" represented by Herr Gierke's shamefaced embarrassment—what a picture!

In short, Herr Gierke fully recognises that feudal obligations in general ought to be abolished only against compensation. Thus the most onerous, the most widespread, the principal obligations are to *continue* or, seeing that the peasants have in fact already done away with them, they are to be *reimposed*.

But, Herr Gierke observes,

"if, nevertheless, particular relations, whose intrinsic justification is insufficient or whose continued existence is incompatible with the demands of the spirit of our time and the general welfare, are abolished *without compensation,* then the persons affected by this should appreciate that they are making a few sacrifices not only for the good of all but also in their own well-understood interests, in order that relations between those who have claims and those who have duties shall be peaceful and friendly, thereby helping landed property generally to maintain the political status which befits it for the good of the whole".

The revolution in the countryside consisted in the actual elimination of all feudal obligations. The government of action, which recognises the revolution, recognises it in the countryside by destroying it underhandedly. It is quite impossible to restore the old status quo completely; the peasants would promptly kill their feudal lords—even Herr Gierke realises that. An impressive list of insignificant feudal obligations existing only in a few places is therefore abolished, but the principal feudal obligation epitomised in the simple term *corvée* is revived.

As a result of all the rights that are to be abolished, the aristocracy will sacrifice less than 50,000 thaler a year, but will thereby save several million. Indeed the minister hopes that they will thus placate the peasants and even gain their votes at future parliamentary elections. This would really be a very good deal, provided Herr Gierke does not miscalculate.

In this way the objections of the peasants would be eliminated, and so would those of the aristocrats, in so far as they correctly understand their position. There remains the Chamber, the scruples of the inflexible legalists and radicals. The distinction between obligations that are to be abolished and those that are to be retained—which is simply the distinction between practically worthless obligations and very valuable obligations—must be based as regards the Chamber on some semblance of legal and economic justification. Herr Gierke must prove that the obligations to be abolished 1. have an insufficient inner justification, 2. are incompatible with the general welfare, 3. are incompatible with the demands of the spirit of our time, and 4. that their abolition is fundamentally no infringement of property rights, i.e., no expropriation without compensation.

In order to prove the insufficient justification of these dues and services Herr Gierke delves into the darkest recesses of feudal law. He invokes the entire, "originally very slow development of the Germanic states over a period of a thousand years". But what good will it do? The deeper he digs, the more he rakes up the stagnant mire of feudal law, the more does that feudal law prove that the obligations in question have, not an insufficient justification, but from the feudal point of view, a very solid justification. The hapless minister merely causes general amusement when he tries his hardest to induce feudal law to make cryptic pronouncements in the style of modern civil law, or to let the feudal lord of the twelfth century think and judge like a bourgeois of the nineteenth century.

Herr Gierke fortunately has inherited Herr von Patow's principle that everything emanating from feudal sovereignty and serfdom is to be abolished without payment, but everything else is to be abolished only against payment of compensation. But does Herr Gierke really think that special perspicacity is required in order to show taht all and every obligation subject to repeal emanates from feudal sovereignty?

It is hardly necessary to add that for the sake of consistency Herr Gierke constantly insinuates modern legal concepts into feudal legal regulations, and in an extremity he always invokes them. But if Herr Gierke evaluates some of these obligations in terms of the modern ideas of law, then it is incomprehensible why the same should not be done with all obligations. In that case, however, the corvée, faced with the freedom of the individual and of property, would certainly come off badly.

Herr Gierke fares even worse when he advances the argument of public welfare and the demands of the spirit of our time in support of his differentiations. Surely it is self-evident that if these insignificant obligations impede the public, welfare and are incompatible with the demands of the spirit of our time, then this applies in still greater measure to such obligations as labour service, the corvée, laudemium, etc. Or does Herr Gierke consider that the right to pluck the peasants' *geese* (§ 1, No. 14) is out of date, but the right to pluck the *peasants* is not?

Then follows the demonstration that the abolition of those particular obligations does not infringe any property rights. Of course, only spurious arguments can be adduced to prove such a glaring falsehood; it can indeed only be done by reckoning up these rights to show the squires how worthless they are for them, though this, obviously, can be proved only approximately. And so Herr Gierke sedulously reckons up all the 18 sections of Clause 1, and does not notice that, to the extent in which he succeeds in proving the given *obligations* to be worthless, he also succeeds in proving the *proposed legislation to be worthless*. Virtuous Herr Gierke! How it pains us to have to destroy his fond delusions and obliterate his Archimedean-feudalist diagrams.

But there is another difficulty. Both in previous commutations of the obligations now to be abolished and in all other commutations, the peasants were flagrantly cheated in favour of the aristocracy by corrupt commissions. The peasants now demand the revision of all commutation agreements concluded under the previous government, and they are quite justified in doing so.

But Herr Gierke will have nothing to do with this, since "formal right and law are opposed" to it; such an attitude is altogether opposed to any progress, since every new law nullifies some old formal right and law.

"The consequences of this, it can confidently be predicted, will be that, in order to secure advantages to those under obligations by means that run counter to the eternal legal principles" (revolutions, too, run counter to the eternal legal principles), "*incalculable damage* must be done to a very large section of landed property in the state, and hence" (!) "to the state itself."

Herr Gierke now proves with staggering thoroughness that such a procedure

"would call in question and undermine the entire legal framework of landed property and this together with numerous lawsuits and the great expenditure involved would cause great damage to landed property, which is the principal foundation of the national welfare"; that it "would be an encroachment on the legal principles underlying the validity of contracts, an attack on the most indubitable contractual relations, the consequences of which would shake all confidence in the stability of civil law, thereby constituting a grave menace to the whole of commercial intercourse"!!

Herr Gierke thus sees in this an infringement of the rights of property, which would undermine all legal principles. Why is the abolition of the obligations under discussion without compensation not an infringement? These are not merely indubitable contractual relations, but claims that were invariably met and not contested since time immemorial, whereas the demand for revision concerns contracts that are by no means uncontested, since the bribery and swindling are notorious, and can be proved in many cases.

It cannot be denied that, though the abolished obligations are quite insignificant, Herr Gierke, by abolishing them, secures "advantages to those under obligations by means that run counter to the eternal legal principles" and this is "directly opposed to formal right and law"; he "undermines the entire legal framework of landed property" and attacks the very foundation of the "most indubitable" rights.

Really, Herr Gierke, was it worth while to go to all this trouble and commit such a grievous sin in order to achieve such paltry results?

Herr Gierke does indeed *attack property*—that is quite indisputable—but it is feudal property he attacks, not modern, bourgeois property. By destroying feudal property he *strengthens* bourgeois property which arises on the ruins of feudal property. The only reason he does not want the commutation agreements revised is because by means of these contracts feudal ownership relations were converted into *bourgeois* ones, and consequently he cannot revise them without at the same time formally infringing bourgeois property. Bourgeois property is, of course, as sacred and inviolable as feudal property is vulnerable and—depending on the requirements and courage of the ministers—violable.

What in brief is the significance of this lengthy law?

It is the most striking proof that the German revolution of 1848 is merely a *parody of the French revolution of 1789.*

On August 4, 1789, three weeks after the storming of the Bastille, the French people, in a *single* day, got the better of the feudal obligations.

On July 11, 1848, four months after the March barricades, the feudal obligations got the better of the German people. *Teste Gierke cum Hansemanno.*

The French bourgeoisie of 1789 never left its allies, the peasants, in the lurch. It knew that the abolition of feudalism in the countryside and the creation of a free, landowning peasant class was the basis of its rule.

The German bourgeoisie of 1848 unhesitatingly betrays the peasants, who are its *natural allies*, flesh of its own flesh, and without whom it cannot stand up to the aristocracy.

The perpetuation of feudal rights and their endorsement in the form of the (illusory) commutations—such is the result of the German revolution of 1848. There was much ado about nothing.

Written by Marx
Neue Rheinische Zeitung No. 60.
July 30, 1848

THE *KÖLNISCHE ZEITUNG* ON THE
STATE OF AFFAIRS IN ENGLAND

Cologne, July 31.

"Where is it possible in England to discover *any trace of hatred* against the class which *in France is called the bourgeoisie?* This hatred was *at one time* directed against the aristocracy, which by means of its corn monopoly imposed a heavy and unjust tax on industry. The bourgeois *in England enjoys no privileges*, he depends on his own diligence; in France under Louis Philippe he depended on monopolies, on privileges."

This great, this scholarly, this veracious proposition can be found in Herr Wolfers' leading article in the always well-informed *Kölnische Zeitung*.[41]

It is indeed strange. England has the most numerous, the most concentrated, the most classic proletariat, a proletariat which every five or six years is decimated by the crushing misery of a commercial crisis, by hunger and typhus; a proletariat which for half its life is redundant to industry and unemployed. One man in every ten in England is a pauper, and one pauper in every three is an inmate in one of the Poor Law Bastilles.[42] The annual cost of poor-relief in England almost equals the entire expenditure of the Prussian state. Poverty and pauperism have been openly declared in England to be necessary elements of the present industrial system and the national wealth. Yet, despite this, where is it possible in England to discover any trace of hatred against the bourgeoisie?

There is no other country in the world where, simultaneously with the enormous growth of the proletariat, the contradiction between proletariat and bourgeoisie has reached such a high level as in England; no other country presents such glaring contrasts between extreme poverty and

immense wealth—yet where can one find even a trace of
hatred against the bourgeoisie?

Obviously, the associations of workers, set up secretly
before 1825 and openly after 1825, associations not for just
a day against *any* single manufacturer, but permanent associations directed against entire groups of manufacturers,
workers' associations of entire industries, entire towns,
finally associations uniting large numbers of workers throughout England, all these associations and their numerous fights
against the manufacturers, the strikes, which led to acts of
violence, revengeful destructions, arson, armed attacks and
assassinations—all these actions just prove the love of the
proletariat for the bourgeoisie.

The entire struggle of the workers against the manufacturers over the last 80 years, a struggle which, beginning
with machine wrecking, has developed through associations,
through isolated attacks on the person and property of the
manufacturers and on the few workers who were loyal to
them, through bigger and smaller rebellions, through the
insurrections of 1839 and 1842, has become the most advanced class struggle the world has seen. The class war of the
Chartists,[43] the organised party of the proletariat, against
the organised political power of the bourgeoisie, has not yet
led to those terrible bloody clashes which took place during
the June uprising in Paris, but it is waged by a far larger
number of people with much greater tenacity and on a much
larger territory—this social civil war is of course regarded
by the *Kölnische Zeitung* and its Wolfers as nothing but a
long demonstration of the love of the English proletariat for
its bourgeois employers.

Not so long ago it was fashionable to present England as
the classic land of social contradictions and struggles, and to
declare that France, compared with England's so-called
"unnatural situation", was a happy land with her Citizen
King, her bourgeois parliamentary adversaries and her upright workers, who always fought so bravely for the bourgeoisie. It was not so long ago that the *Kölnische Zeitung*
kept harping on this well-worn tune and saw in the English
class struggles a reason for warning Germany against pro-
tectionism and the "unnatural" hot-house industry to which

it gives rise. But the June days have changed everything. The horrors of the June battles have shaken the *Kölnische Zeitung*, and the millions of Chartists in London, Manchester and Glasgow vanish into thin air in face of the forty thousand Paris insurgents.

France has become the classic country as regards hatred of the bourgeoisie and, according to the present assertions of the *Kölnische Zeitung*, this has been the case since 1830. How strange. For the last ten years English agitators, received with acclamation by the entire proletariat, have untiringly preached fervent hatred of the bourgeoisie at meetings and in pamphlets and journals, whereas the French working-class and socialist literature has always advocated reconciliation with the bourgeoisie on the grounds that the class antagonisms in France were far less developed than in England. The men at whose very name the *Kölnische Zeitung* makes the triple sign of the cross, men like Louis Blanc, Cabet, Caussidière and Ledru-Rollin, have, for many years before and after the February revolution, preached peace with the bourgeoisie, and they generally did it in good faith. Let the *Kölnische Zeitung* look through any of the writings of these people, or through the *Réforme*,[44] the *Populaire*,[45] or even the working-class journals published during the last few years like the *Union*,[46] the *Ruche populaire*[47] and the *Fraternité*[48]—though it should be sufficient to mention two works which everybody knows, Louis Blanc's entire *Histoire de dix ans*, especially the last part, and his *Histoire de la révolution française* in two volumes.

But the *Kölnische Zeitung* is not content with merely *asserting* that no hatred exists in England against "the class which in France is called the *bourgeoisie*" (in England too, our well-informed colleague, cf. *The Northern Star*[49] for the last two years)—it also explains *why* this must be so.

Peel saved the English bourgeoisie from this hatred by repealing the monopolies and establishing Free Trade.

"The bourgeois in England enjoys no privileges, no monopolies; in France he depended on monopolies.... It was Peel's measures that saved England from the most appalling upheavals."

By doing away with the monopoly of the *aristocracy*, Peel saved the *bourgeoisie* from the threatening hatred of the proletariat, according to the amazing logic of the *Kölnische Zeitung*.

"The English people, we say: the *English people* realises more and more that only from *Free Trade* can it expect a solution of the vital problems bearing on all its present afflictions and apprehensions, a solution which was recently attempted amid streams of blood.... We must not forget that the first notions of Free Trade came from the *English people*."

The English people! But the "English *people*" have been fighting the Free Traders since 1839 at all their meetings and in the press, and compelled them, when the Anti-Corn Law League was at the height of its fame, to hold their meetings in *secret* and to admit only persons who had a ticket. The people with bitter irony compared the practice of the Free Traders with their fine words, and fully identified the bourgeois with the Free Trader. Sometimes the English people were even forced temporarily to seek the support of the aristocracy, the monopolists, against the bourgeoisie, e.g., in their fight for the ten-hour day.[50] And we are asked to believe that the people who were so well able to drive the Free Traders off the rostrum at *public* meetings, that it was these "English *people*" who originally conceived the ideas of Free Trade! The *Kölnische Zeitung*, in its artless simplicity, not only repeats mechanically the illusions of the big capitalists of Manchester and Leeds, but lends a gullible ear to their deliberate lies.

"The bourgeois in England enjoys no privileges, no monopolies." But in France things are different:

"The worker for a long time regarded the bourgeois as the monopolist who imposed a tax of 60 per cent on the poor farmer for the iron of his plough, who made extortionate profits on his coal, who exposed the vine-growers throughout France to death from starvation, who added 20, 40, 50 per cent to the price of everything he sold them...."

The only monopoly which the worthy *Kölnische Zeitung* knows is the *customs* monopoly, i.e., the monopoly which only *appears* to affect the workers, but actually falls on the bourgeoisie, on all industrialists, who do not profit from the tariff-protection. The *Kölnische Zeitung* knows only the local, legally imposed monopoly, the monopoly which was attacked by the Free Traders from Adam Smith to Cobden.

But the *monopoly of capital*, which comes into being without the aid of legislation and often exists despite it, this monopoly is not recognised by the gentlemen of the *Kölnische Zeitung*. Yet it is this monopoly which directly and ruthlessly weighs upon the workers and causes the struggle between the proletariat and the bourgeoisie. Precisely this monopoly is the *specifically modern* monopoly, which produces the modern class contradictions, and the solution of just these contradictions is the specific task of the nineteenth century.

But this *monopoly of capital* becomes more powerful, more comprehensive, and more threatening *in proportion as the other small and localised monopolies disappear.*

The freer competition becomes as a result of the abolition of all "monopolies", the more rapidly is capital concentrated in the hands of the industrial barons, the more rapidly does the petty bourgeoisie become ruined and the faster does the industry of England, the country of capital's monopoly, subjugate the neighbouring countries. If the "monopolies" of the French, German and Italian bourgeoisie were abolished, Germany, France and Italy would be reduced to proletarians compared with the all-absorbing English bourgeoisie. The pressure which the individual English bourgeois exerts on the individual English proletarian would then be matched by the pressure exerted by the English bourgeoisie as a whole on Germany, France and Italy, and it is particularly the petty bourgeoisie of these countries which would suffer most.

These are such commonplace ideas that today can no longer be explained without causing offence—to anybody but the learned gentlemen of the *Kölnische Zeitung*.

These profound thinkers see in Free Trade the only means by which France can be saved from a devastating war between the workers and the bourgeois.

To reduce the bourgeoisie of a country to the level of the proletariat is indeed a means of solving class contradictions, which is worthy of the *Kölnische Zeitung*.

Written by Engels

Neue Rheinische Zeitung No. 62,
August 1, 1848

THE FRANKFURT ASSEMBLY DEBATES
THE POLISH QUESTION

[I]

Cologne, August 7. The Frankfurt Assembly, whose debates even during the most exciting moments were conducted in a truly German spirit of geniality, at last pulled itself together when the Poznan question came up. On this question, the ground for which had been prepared by Prussian shrapnel and the docile resolutions of the Federal Diet, the Assembly had to pass a clear-cut resolution. No mediation was possible: it had either to save Germany's honour or to blot it once again. The Assembly acted as we had expected; it sanctioned the seven partitions of Poland, and shifted the disgrace of 1772, 1794 and 1815 from the shoulders of the German princes to its own shoulders.

The Frankfurt Assembly, moreover, declared that the seven partitions of Poland were benefactions wasted on the Poles. Had not the forcible intrusion of the Jewish-German race lifted Poland to a level of culture and a stage of science which that country could never have dreamed of! Deluded, ungrateful Poles! If your country had not been partitioned you would have had to ask this favour yourselves of the Frankfurt Assembly.

Pastor Bonavita Blank of the Paradise monastery near Schaffhausen trained magpies and starlings to fly in and out. He had cut away the lower part of their bill so that they were unable to get their own food and could only receive it from his hands. The philistines who from a distance saw the birds alight on the Reverend's shoulders and seem to be friendly with him, admired his great culture and learning. His biographer says that the birds *loved their benefactor*.

Yet the fettered, maimed, branded Poles refuse to love their Prussian benefactors.

We could not give a better description of the benefactions which Prussia bestowed on the Poles than that provided by the report which the learned historiographer Herr *Stenzel* submitted on behalf of the Committee for International Law, a report which forms the basis of the debate.

The report, entirely in the style of the conventional diplomatic documents, first recounts how the Grand Duchy of Poznan was set up in 1815 by "incorporation" and "merging". Then follow the promises which at the same time Frederick William III made to the inhabitants of Poznan, i.e., the safeguarding of their nationality, language and religion, the appointment of a native governor, and participation in the famous Prussian constitution.[51]

The extent to which these promises were kept is well known. The freedom of communication between the three sections of Poland, to which the Congress of Vienna could the more easily agree the less feasible it was, was of course never put into effect.

The make-up of the population is then examined. Herr Stenzel calculates that 790,000 Poles, 420,000 Germans and about 80,000 Jews lived in the Grand Duchy in 1843, making a total of 1,300,000.

Herr Stenzel's statement is challenged by the Poles, notably by Archbishop Przyluski, according to whom there are considerably more than 800,000 Poles, and, if one deducts the Jews, officials and soldiers, hardly 250,000 Germans, living in Poznan.

Let us, however, accept Herr Stenzel's figures. For our purposes it is quite sufficient. To avoid all further discussion, let us concede that there are 420,000 Germans living in Poznan. Who are these Germans, who by the inclusion of the Jews have been brought up to half a million?

The Slavs are a predominantly agricultural people with little aptitude for urban trades in the form in which they were hitherto carried on in the Slav countries. The first crude stage of commerce, when it was still mere hawking, was left to *Jewish* pedlars. With the growth of culture and population the need for urban trades and urban concentration made itself felt, and *Germans* moved into the Slav countries. The Germans, who after all had their heyday in the petty-bourgeois life of the imperial cities of the Middle Ages, in the sluggish inland trade conducted in caravan style, in a restricted maritime trade, and in the handicraft workshops of the fourteenth and fifteenth centuries organised on guild lines—the Germans demonstrated their vocation as the philistines of world history by the very fact that they still to this day form the core of the petty bourgeoisie throughout Eastern and Northern Europe and even in America. Many, often most of the craftsmen, shopkeepers and small middlemen in Petersburg, Moscow, Warsaw and Cracow, in Stockholm and Copenhagen, in Pest, Odessa and Jassy, in New York and Philadelphia are Germans or of German extraction. All these cities have districts where only German is spoken, and some of them, for example Pest, are almost entirely German.

This German immigration, particularly into the Slav countries, went on almost uninterruptedly since the twelfth and thirteenth centuries. Moreover, from time to time since the Reformation, as a result of the persecution of various sects large groups of Germans were forced to migrate to Poland, where they received a friendly welcome. In other Slav countries, such as Bohemia, Moravia, the Slav population was decimated by German wars of conquest, whereas the German population increased as a result of invasion.

The position is clearest in Poland. The German philistines living there for centuries never regarded themselves as politically belonging to Germany any more than did the Germans in North America; just as the "French colony" in Berlin and the 15,000 Frenchmen in Montevideo do not regard themselves as belonging to France. As far as that was possible during the days of decentralisation in the seventeenth and eighteenth centuries, they became Poles, German-speaking Poles, who had long since renounced all ties with the mother country.

But the Germans brought to Poland culture, education and science, commerce and trades.—True, they brought retail trade and guild crafts; by their consumption and the limited intercourse which they established they stimulated production to some extent. Up to 1772 Poland as a whole was not particularly well known for her high standard of education and science, and the same applies to Austrian and Russian Poland since then; of the Prussian part we shall speak later. On the other hand, the Germans prevented the formation of Polish towns with a Polish bourgeoisie. By their distinct language, their separateness from the Polish population, their numerous different privileges and urban codes, they impeded centralisation, that most potent of political means by which a country achieves rapid development. Almost every town had its own law; indeed towns with a mixed population had, and often still have, a different law for Germans, Poles and Jews. The German Poles remained at the lowest stage of industrial development; they did not accumulate large capitals; they were neither able to set up large-scale industry nor control any extensive commercial networks. The Englishman Cockerill had to come to Warsaw for industry to strike root in Poland. The entire activity of the German Poles was restricted to retail trade, the handicrafts and at most the corn trade and manufacture (weaving, etc.) on the smallest scale. In considering the merits of the German Poles it should not be forgotten that they imported German philistinism and German petty-bourgeois narrow-mindedness into Poland, and that they combined the worst qualities of both nations without acquiring their good ones.

Herr Stenzel seeks to enlist the sympathy of the Germans for the German Poles:

"When the kings ... especially in the seventeenth century, became increasingly powerless and were no longer able to protect the native Polish peasants against the severest oppression by the nobles, the German villages and towns, too, declined, and many of them became the property of the nobility. Only the larger royal cities kept some of their old liberties" (read: privileges).

Does Herr Stenzel perhaps demand that the Poles should have protected the "Germans" (i.e., German Poles, who are moreover also "natives") better than themselves? Surely it is obvious that foreigners who immigrate into any country must expect to share the good and bad with the indigenous inhabitants.

Now passing to the blessings for which the Poles are indebted to the Prussian government in particular.

Frederick II seized the Netze district in 1772, and in the following year the Bromberg canal was built, which made inland navigation between the Oder and Vistula possible.

"The region, which for centuries was an object of dispute between Poland and Pomerania, and which was largely desolate as a result of countless devastations and because of vast swamps, was now brought under cultivation and populated by numerous colonists."

Thus, the first partition of Poland was no robbery. Frederick II merely seized an area which "for centuries was an object of dispute". But since when has there no longer existed an independent Pomerania which *could* have disputed this region? For how many centuries were in fact the rights of Poland to this region no longer challenged? And in general, what meaning has this rusted and rotten theory of "disputes" and "claims", which, in the seventeenth and eighteenth centuries, served the purpose of covering up the naked commercial interests and the policy of rounding off one's lands? What meaning can it have in 1848 when the bottom has been knocked out of all historical justice and injustice?

Incidentally, Herr Stenzel ought to bear in mind that according to this junk-heap doctrine the Rhine borders between France and Germany have been "an object of dispute for millennia", and that Poland could assert her claims to suzerainty over the province of Prussia and even over Pomerania.

In short, the Netze district became part of Prussia and hence ceased to be "an object of dispute". Frederick II had it colonised by Germans, and so the "*Netze brethren*", who received such praise in connection with the Poznan affair, came into being. The state-promoted Germanisation began in 1773.

"*According to reliable information*, the Jews in the Grand Duchy are all Germans and *want* to be Germans.... The religious toleration which used to prevail in Poland and the possession of certain qualities which were lacking in the Poles, enabled the Jews in the course of centuries to develop activities which penetrated deep into Polish life", namely, into Polish purses. "As a rule they have a thorough command of both languages, although they, and their children from the earliest years, speak *German* at home."

The unexpected sympathy and recognition which Polish Jews have lately received in Germany has found official expression in this passage. Maligned wherever the influence of the Leipzig fair extends as the very incarnation of haggling, avarice and sordidness, they have suddenly become German brethren; with tears of joy honest Michael presses them to his bosom, and Herr Stenzel lays claim to them on behalf of the German nation as Germans who *want* to remain Germans.

Indeed, why should not Polish Jews be genuine Germans? Do not "they, and their children from the earliest years, speak German at home"? And what German at that!

Incidentally, we would point out to Herr Stenzel that he might just as well lay claim to the whole of Europe and half America, and even part of Asia. German, as everyone knows, is the universal language of the Jews. In New York and Constantinople, in St. Petersburg and Paris "the Jews, and their children from the earliest years, speak German at home", and some of them even a more classical German than the Poznan Jews, the "kindred" allies of the Netze brethren.

The report goes on to present the national relations in terms that are as vague as possible and as favourable as possible to the alleged half a million Germans consisting of German Poles, Netze brethren, and Jews. It says that German peasants own more land than the Polish peasants (we shall see how this has come to pass), and that since the first partition of Poland enmity between Poles and Germans, especially Prussians, reached its highest degree.

"By the introduction of its exceptionally rigidly regulated political and administrative orders" (what excellent style!) "and their strict enforcement, Prussia in particular seriously disturbed the old customs and traditional institutions of the Poles."

Not only the Poles but also the other Prussians, and especially we from the Rhine, can tell a tale about the "rigidly regulated" and "strictly enforced" measures of the worthy Prussian bureaucracy, measures which *"disturbed"* not only the old customs and traditional institutions, but also the *entire social* life, industrial and agricultural production, commerce, mining, in short all social relations without exception. But Herr Stenzel refers here not to the bureaucracy of 1807-48, but to that of 1772-1806, to the officials of genuine, dyed in the wool, Prussianism, whose baseness, corruptibility, cupidity and brutality were clearly evident in the treacherous acts of 1806. These officials are supposed to have protected the Polish peasants against the nobles and received in return nothing but ingratitude; of course the officials ought to have understood "that nothing, not even the good things granted or imposed, can compensate for the loss of national sovereignty".

We too know the way in which quite recently the Prussian officials used "to grant and impose everything". What Rhinelander, who had dealings with newly arrived officials from the old Prussian lands, did not have an opportunity to admire their inimitable, obtrusive priggishness, their impudent meddlesomeness, their overriding insolence and that combination of narrow-mindedness and infallibility. True, with us, in most cases, these old Prussian gentry soon lost some of their roughness for they had no Netze brethren, no secret inquisition, no Prussian law and no floggings—deficiency which even brought many of them to an early grave. We do not have to be told what havoc they wrought in Poland, where they could indulge in floggings and secret inquisitions to their heart's content.

In short, the arbitrary Prussian rule won such popularity that "already after the battle of Jena, the hatred of the Poles found vent in a general uprising and the ejection of the Prussian officials". This, for the time being, put an end to the bureaucratic rule.

But in 1815 it returned in a somewhat modified form. The "best", "reformed", "educated", "incorruptible" officialdom tried their hand at dealing with these refractory Poles.

"The founding of the Grand Duchy of Poznan was not conducive to the establishment of cordial relations, since ... at that time the King of Prussia could not possibly agree to have any single province set up as an entirely independent unit, thus turning his state, as it were, into a federal state."

Thus according to Herr Stenzel, the King of Prussia could "not possibly agree" to keep his own promises and the treaties of Vienna.[52]

"In 1830, when the sympathies which the Polish nobility showed for the Warsaw uprising caused anxiety, and systematic efforts were made ever since by means of various arrangements" (!)—"notably by buying up the Polish landed estates, dividing them and handing them over to the Germans—gradually to eliminate the Polish nobility altogether, the latter's resentment against Prussia increased."

"By means of various arrangements"! By prohibiting Poles from buying land brought under the hammer, and similar measures, which Herr Stenzel covers with the cloak of charity.

What would Rhinelanders say if with us, too, the Prussian government were to prohibit Rhinelanders from buying land put up for sale by order of the court. Sufficient pretexts could easily be found, namely: in order to amalgamate the population of the old and new provinces; in order that the natives of the old provinces could share in the blessings of parcellation and of the Rhenish laws; in order that Rhinelanders be induced to emigrate to the old provinces and implant their industries there as well, and so on. There are enough reasons to bestow Prussian "colonists" on us too. How would we look upon people who bought our land for next to nothing while competition was excluded, and who did it moreover with the support of the government; people who were thrust upon us for the express purpose of accustoming us to the intoxicating motto "With God for King and Country"?

After all we are Germans, we speak the same language as the people in the old provinces. Yet in Poznan those colonists were sent methodically, with unabated persistence, to the demesnes, the forests and the divided estates of the Polish nobility in order to oust the native Poles and their language from their own country and to set up a truly Prussian province, which was to surpass even Pomerania in black and white fanaticism.[53]

In order that the Prussian peasants in Poland should not be left without their natural masters, they were sent the flower of Prussian knighthood, men like *Tresckow* and *Lüttichau*, who also bought landed estates for a song, and with the aid of government loans. In fact, after the Polish uprising of 1846,[54] a joint-stock company was formed in Berlin, which enjoyed the gracious protection of the highest

personages in the land, and whose purpose was to buy up
Polish estates for German knights. The poor starvelings
from among the Brandenburg and Pomeranian aristocracy
foresaw that trials instituted against the Poles would ruin
numerous Polish squires, whose estates would shortly be
sold off dirt-cheap. This was a real godsend for many a
debt-ridden Don Ranudo[55] from the Uckermark. A fine estate
for next to nothing, Polish peasants who could be thrashed,
and what is more, a good service rendered to King and
Country—what brilliant prospects!

Thus arose the third German immigration into Poland.
Prussian peasants and Prussian noblemen settled throughout
Poznan with the declared intention, supported by the government, not of Germanising, but of *Pomeranising* Poznan.
The German Poles had the excuse of having contributed in
some measure to the promotion of commerce, the Netze
brethren could boast that they had reclaimed a few bogs,
but this last Prussian invasion has no excuse whatever. Even
parcellation was not consistently carried through, the Prussian aristocrats following hard on the heels of the Prussian
peasants.

[II]

Cologne, August 11. In the first article we have examined
the "historical foundation" of Stenzel's report in so far as
he deals with the situation in Poznan before the revolution.
Today we proceed to Herr Stenzel's history of the revolution and counter-revolution in Poznan.

"The German people, who at all times is filled with compassion
for all the unfortunate" (so long as this compassion costs nothing),
"always deeply felt how greatly its princes wronged the Poles."

Indeed, "deeply felt" within the calm German heart,
where the feelings are so "deeply" embedded that they
never manifest themselves in action. Indeed, "compassion",
expressed by a few alms in 1831 and by dinners and balls
in aid of the Poles, lasting just long enough to have a dance
and drink champagne for the benefit of the Poles, and to
sing "Poland is not yet lost".[56] But when were the Germans
prone to do something really decisive, to make a real
sacrifice!

"The Germans honestly and fraternally proffered their hand to expiate the wrongs their princes had perpetrated."

If it were possible to "expiate" anything with sentimental phrases and dull tub-thumping, then the Germans would emerge as the purest people in the world.

"Just at the moment, however, when the Poles shook hands" (that is, took the fraternally proffered hand) "the interests and aims of the two nations already diverged. The Poles' only thought was for the restoration of their old state at least within the boundaries that existed before the first partition of 1772."

Surely, only the unreasoning, confused, haphazard enthusiasm, which from time immemorial has been the principal adornment of the German national character, could have caused the Germans to be surprised by the Polish demands. The Germans wanted to "*expiate*" the injustice the Poles had suffered. What started this injustice? The earlier treacheries apart, it certainly started with the first partition of Poland in 1772. How could this be "expiated"? Of course, only by restoration of the status quo existing *before* 1772, or at least by the Germans returning to the Poles what *they* had robbed them of since 1772. But this was against the interests of the Germans? Well, if we speak of interests, then it can no longer be a question of sentimentalities like "expiation"; here the language of harsh, unfeeling practice should be used, and we should be spared rhetorical flourishes and expressions of magnanimity.

Moreover, firstly, the Poles did not "*only* think" of the restoration of the Poland of 1772. In any case what the Poles did "*think*" is hardly our concern. For the time being they *demanded* only the restoration of the *whole* of Poznan and mentioned other eventualities only in case of a German-Polish war against Russia.

Secondly, "the interests and aims of the two nations diverged" only in so far as the "interests and aims" of revolutionary Germany in the field of international relations remained exactly the same as those of the old, absolutist Germany. If Germany's "interest and aim" is an alliance with Russia, or at least peace with Russia at any price, then of course everything in Poland must remain as it was hitherto. We shall see later, however, to what extent the *real* interests of Germany are identical with those of Poland.

Then follows a lengthy, confused and disconcerted passage, in which Herr Stenzel expatiates on the fact that the German Poles were right when they wanted to do justice to Poland, but at the same time to remain Prussians and Germans. Of course it is of no concern to Herr Stenzel that the "when" excludes the "but" and the "but" the "when".

Next comes an equally lengthy and confused historical recital, in which Herr Stenzel goes into detail in an attempt to prove that, owing to the "diverging interests and aims of the two nations" and the ensuing mutual enmity which was steadily growing, a bloody clash was *unavoidable*. The Germans adhered to the *"national"* interests, the Poles merely to the *"territorial"* interests, in other words, the Germans demanded that the Grand Duchy should be divided according to nationalities, the Poles wanted the whole of their old territory.

This is again not true. The Poles asked for restoration and at the same time stated that they were quite willing to relinquish the frontier districts with a mixed population where the majority are Germans and *want* to join Germany. The inhabitants, however, should not be declared German or Polish by the Prussian *officials* at will, but according to their *own* wishes.

Herr Stenzel goes on to assert that Willisen's mission was of course bound to fail because of the (alleged, but nowhere existing) resistance of the Poles to the cession of the predominantly German districts. Herr Stenzel disposed of the statements of Willisen about the Poles and those of the Poles about Willisen. These *published* statements prove the opposite. But this happens if "one is a man who", as Herr Stenzel says, "has studied history for many years and deems it his duty never to speak an untruth and never to conceal anything".

With the same truthfulness which never conceals anything, Herr Stenzel easily passes over the cannibalism perpetrated in Poznan, the base and perfidious violation of the Convention of Jaroslawiec,[57] the massacres of Trzemeszno, Miloslaw and Wreschen, the destructive fury of a brutal soldiery worthy of the Thirty Years' War, and does not say a word about it.

Now Herr Stenzel comes to the four partitions of Poland recently effected by the Prussian government. First the Netze district and four other districts were torn away (April 14); to this were added certain parts of other districts. This territory with a total population of 593,390 was incorporated in the German Confederation on April 22. Then the city and fortress of Poznan together with the remainder of the left bank of the Warta were also included, making an additional 273,500 persons and bringing the combined population of these lands to *double* the number of Germans living in the whole of Poznan even according to *Prussian* estimates. This was effected by order in council on April 26, and already on May 2 they were admitted to the German Confederation. Now Herr Stenzel pleads with the Assembly that it is absolutely essential for Poznan to remain in German hands, that Poznan is an important, powerful fortress, with a population of over 20,000 Germans (most of them Polish Jews) who own two-thirds of all the landed property, etc. That Poznan is situated in the midst of a purely Polish territory, that it was forcibly Germanised, and that Polish Jews are not Germans, does not make the slightest difference to men who "never speak an untruth and never suppress a truth", to historians of Herr Stenzel's calibre.

In short, Poznan, for military reasons, should not be relinquished. As though it were not possible to raze the fortress, which, according to Willisen, is one of the greatest strategic blunders, and to fortify Breslau instead. But ten million (incidentally this is again not true—barely five million) have been invested, and it is of course more advantageous to keep this precious work of art with 20 to 30 square miles of Polish land into the bargain.

With the "city and fortress" of Poznan in one's hands, it will be all the easier to seize still more.

"But to keep the fortress it will be necessary to secure its approaches from Glogau, Küstrin and Thorn as well as a fortified area facing the east" (it need be only 1,000 to 2,000 paces wide, like that of Maestricht facing Belgium and Limburg). "This," continues Herr

Stenzel with a smile of satisfaction, "will at the same time ensure undisturbed possession of the Bromberg canal; but numerous areas with a predominantly Polish population will have to be incorporated into the German Confederation."

It was for all these reasons that Pfuel von Höllenstein,[58] the well-known philanthropist, carried through two new partitions of Poland, thus meeting all the desires of Herr Stenzel and incorporating three-fourths of the Grand Duchy into Germany. Herr Stenzel is the more grateful for this procedure, since the revival of Louis XIV's chambers of reunion[59] with augmented powers must evidently have demonstrated to this historian that the Germans have learned to apply the lessons of history.

According to Herr Stenzel, the Poles ought to find consolation in the fact that their share of the land is more fertile than the incorporated territory, that there is considerably less landed property in their part than in that of the Germans and that "no unbiased person will deny that the lot of the Polish peasant under a German government will be far more tolerable than that of the German peasant under a Polish government"! History provides some curious examples of this.

Finally, Herr Stenzel tells the Poles that even the small part left to them will enable them, by practising all the civic virtues,

"to befittingly prepare themselves for the moment, which at present is still shrouded in the mists of the future, and which, quite pardonably, they are trying—perhaps too impatiently—to precipitate. One of their most judicious fellow-citizens exclaimed very pertinently, 'There is a crown which is also worthy of your ambition, it is the *civic crown*!' A German would perhaps add: It does not shine, but it is solid!"

"It is solid!" But even more "solid" are the real reasons for the last four partitions of Poland by the Prussian government.

You worthy German—do you believe that the partitions were undertaken in order to deliver your German brothers from Polish rule; to have the fortress of Poznan serve as a bulwark protecting you from any attack; to safeguard the roads of Küstrin, Glogau and Bromberg, and the Netze canal? What a delusion.

You were shamefully deceived. The sole reason for the recent partitions of Poland was to *replenish the Prussian treasury*.

The earlier partitions of Poland up to 1815 were annexations of territory by force of arms; the partitions of 1848 are *robbery*.

And now, worthy German, see how you have been deceived!

After the third partition of Poland the estates of the big Polish feudal lords and those of the Catholic clergy were confiscated by Frederick William II in favour of the state. As the Declaration of Appropriation issued on July 28, 1796, says, the estates of the Church in particular "constituted a *very considerable* part of landed property as a whole". The new demesnes were either managed on the King's account or leased, and they were so extensive that 34 crown-land offices and 21 forestry divisions had to be set up for their administration. Each of these crown-land offices was responsible for a large number of villages; for example, altogether 636 villages came under the ten offices of the Bromberg district, and 127 were administered by the Mogilno crown-land office.

In 1796, moreover, Frederick William II confiscated the estates and woodlands of the convent at Owinsk and sold them to the merchant von Tresckow (forefather of the brave Prussian troop leader in the last heroic war[60]). These estates comprised 24 villages with flour mills and 20,000 morgen* of forest land, worth at least 1,000,000 thaler.

Furthermore, the crown-land offices of Krotoschin, Rozdrazewo, Orpiszewo and Adelnau, worth at least two million thaler, were in 1819 made over to the Prince of Thurn und Taxis to compensate him for the post-office privileges in several provinces which had become part of Prussia.

Frederick William II took over all these estates on the pretext that he could administer them better. Nevertheless, these estates, the property of the Polish nation, were given away, ceded or sold, and the proceeds flowed into the *Prussian* treasury.

---

* An old German land measure, varying in different localities between 0.25 and 1.23 hectares.—*Tr.*

The crown lands in Gnesen, Skorzencin and Trzemeszno were broken up and sold.

Thus 27 crown-land offices and forestry divisions, to a value of *twenty million thaler* at the very least, still remain in the hands of the Prussian government. We are prepared to prove, map in hand, that all these demesnes and forests—with very few exceptions, if any at all—are located in the incorporated part of Poznan. To prevent this rich treasure from reverting to the Polish nation it had to be absorbed into the German Confederation, and since it could not go to the German Confederation, the German Confederation had to come to it, and three-fourths of Poznan were incorporated.

That is the true reason for the four famous partitions of Poland within two months. Neither the protests of this or that nationality nor alleged strategic reasons were decisive—the frontier was determined solely by the position of the demesnes, and the rapacity of the Prussian government.

While German citizens were shedding bitter tears over the invented sufferings of their poor brothers in Poznan, while they were waxing enthusiastic about the safety of the Eastern Marches, and while they allowed themselves to be provoked to anger against the Poles by false reports about Polish barbarities, the Prussian government acted on the quiet, and feathered its nest. This German enthusiasm without rhyme or reason merely served to disguise the dirtiest deed in modern history.

That, my worthy German, is how you are treated by your responsible ministers!

Actually however you ought to have known this beforehand. Whenever Herr Hansemann has a hand in something, it is never a matter of German nationality, military necessity or suchlike empty phrases, but always a matter of cash payment and of net profit.

[III]

Cologne, August 19. We have examined in detail Herr Stenzel's report, which forms the basis of the debate. We have shown that he falsifies both the earlier and the more recent history of Poland and of the Germans in Poland, that he confuses the whole issue, and that Stenzel the historian is not only guilty of deliberate falsification but also of gross ignorance.

Before dealing with the debate itself we must take another look at the Polish question.

The problem of Poznan taken by itself is quite meaningless and insoluble. It is a fragment of the Polish problem and can only be solved in connection with and as a part of it. Only when Poland exists again will it be possible to determine the borders between Germany and Poland.

But can and will Poland exist again? This was denied during the debate.

A French historian said: *Il y a des peuples nécessaires*— there are *necessary nations*. The Polish nation is undoubtedly one of the necessary nations of the nineteenth century.

But for no one is Poland's national existence a greater necessity than it is for us Germans.

What is the main support of the reactionary forces in Europe since 1815, and to some extent even since the first French revolution? It is the Russian-Prussian-Austrian *Holy Alliance*.[61] And what holds the Holy Alliance together? The *partition of Poland*, by which all the three allies have profited.

The tearing asunder of Poland by the three powers is the tie which links them together; the robbery they jointly committed makes them support each other.

From the moment the first robbery of Polish territory was committed Germany became dependent on Russia. Russia ordered Prussia and Austria to remain absolute monarchies, and Prussia and Austria had to obey. The efforts to secure control—efforts which were in any case feeble and timid, especially on the part of the Prussian bourgeoisie—failed entirely because of the impossibility of breaking away from Russia, and because of the support which Russia offered the feudalist-absolutist class in Prussia.

Moreover, as soon as the Allies attempted to introduce the first oppressive measures the Poles not only rose to fight for their independence, but simultaneously came out in *revolutionary* action against their own internal social conditions.

The partition of Poland was effected through a pact between the big feudal aristocracy of Poland and the three partitioning powers. It was not an advance, as the ex-poet Herr Jordan contends, it was the last means the big aristocracy had to protect itself against a revolution, it was reactionary to the core.

Already the first partition led quite naturally to an alliance of the other classes, i.e., the nobles, the townspeople and to some extent the peasants, both against the oppressors of Poland and against the big Polish aristocracy. The constitution of 1791[62] shows that even then the Poles clearly understood that their independence in foreign affairs was inseparable from the overthrow of the aristocracy and from the agrarian reform within the country.

The big agrarian countries between the Baltic and the Black seas can free themselves from patriarchal feudal barbarism only by an agrarian revolution, which turns the peasants who are enthralled or liable to labour services into free landowners, a revolution which would be similar to the French Revolution of 1789 in the countryside. It is to the credit of the Polish nation that it was the first of all its agricultural neighbours to proclaim this. The first attempted reform was the constitution of 1791; during the uprising of 1830 Lelewel declared the agrarian revolution to be the only means of saving the country, but the parliament recognised this too late; during the insurrections of 1846 and 1848 the agrarian revolution was openly proclaimed.

From the day of their subjugation the Poles came out with revolutionary demands, thereby committing their oppressors still more strongly to a counter-revolutionary course. They compelled their oppressors to maintain the patriarchal feudal structure not only in Poland but in all their other countries as well. The struggle for the independence of Poland, particularly since the Cracow uprising of 1846, is at the same time a struggle of *agrarian democracy*—the only form of democracy possible in Eastern Europe—against *patriarchal feudal absolutism*.

So long, therefore, as we help to subjugate Poland, so

long as we keep a part of Poland tied to Germany, we ourselves remain tied to Russia and to the Russian policy, and
shall be unable to eradicate patriarchal feudal absolutism
in Germany. The creation of a democratic Poland is a primary condition for the creation of a democratic Germany.

But the restoration of Poland and the settlement of her
frontiers with Germany is not only necessary, it is the most
easily solvable of all the political problems which have
arisen in Eastern Europe since the revolution. The struggle
for independence of the diverse nationalities jumbled together south of the Carpathians is much more complicated and
will lead to far more bloodshed, confusion and civil wars
than the Polish struggle for independence and the establishment of the border line between Germany and Poland.

Needless to say, it is not a question of restoring a seemingly independent Poland, but of restoring the state upon a
viable foundation. Poland must have at least the dimensions
of 1772, she must comprise not only the territories but
also the estuaries of her big rivers and a large seaboard at
least on the Baltic.

The Germans could have secured all this for Poland and
at the same time protected their own interests and their
honour, if after the revolution they had had the courage,
for their own sake, arms in hand, to demand that Russia
relinquish Poland. Owing to the commingling of Germans
and Poles in the border regions and especially along the
coast, it goes without saying—and this would create no
difficulties—that both parties would have had to make some
concessions to one another, some Germans becoming Polish
and some Poles German.

After the indecisive German revolution, however, the
courage for so resolute an action was lacking. It is all very
well to make florid speeches about the liberation of Poland
and to welcome passing Poles at railway stations, offering
them the most ardent sympathies of the German people
(to whom had these sympathies not been offered?); but to
start a war with Russia, to endanger the European balance
of power and, to cap all, hand over some scraps of the
annexed territory—only one who does not know the Germans
could expect that.

4*

And what would a war with Russia have meant? A war with Russia would have meant a complete, open and effective break with the whole of our disgraceful past, the real liberation and unification of Germany, and the establishment of democracy on the ruins of feudalism, on the wreckage of the short-lived bourgeois dream of power. War with Russia would have been the only possible way of vindicating our honour and our interests with regard to our Slav neighbours, notably the Poles.

But we were philistines and have remained philistines. We made several dozen small and big revolutions, of which we ourselves took fright even before they were accomplished. We talked big, but carried nothing through. The revolution narrowed our mental horizon instead of broadening it. All problems were approached from the standpoint of the most timid, most narrow-minded, most illiberal philistinism, to the detriment, of course, of our real interests. From the angle of this petty philistinism, the major issue of Poland's liberation was reduced to the piddling slogan calling for reorganisation of a part of the Province of Poznan, while our enthusiasm for the Poles turned into shrapnel and lunar caustic.

War with Russia, we repeat, was the only possible means of upholding Germany's honour and Germany's interests. We shrank from it and the inevitable happened—the reactionary military, beaten in Berlin, raised their head again in Poznan; under the pretext of saving Germany's honour and national integrity they raised the banner of counter-revolution and crushed our allies, the revolutionary Poles—and for a moment the hoodwinked Germans exultantly cheered their victorious enemies. The new partition of Poland was accomplished, and only the sanction of the German National Assembly was still missing.

The Frankfurt Assembly still had a chance to mend matters: it should have excluded the whole of Poznan from the German Confederation and left the border question open until it could be discussed with a restored Poland *d'égal à égal*.

But that would be asking too much of our professors, lawyers and pastors who sit in the Frankfurt National

Assembly. The temptation was too great. These peaceful burghers, who had never fired a rifle, were, by simply rising or remaining seated, to conquer for Germany a country of 500 square miles and to incorporate 800,000 Netze brethren, German Poles, Jews and Poles, even though this was to be done at the expense of the honour and of the real, lasting interests of Germany—what a temptation! They succumbed to it, they endorsed the partition of Poland.

What the motives were, we shall see tomorrow.

Written by Engels
Neue Rheinische Zeitung Nos. 70,
73 and 81,
August 9, 12 and 20, 1848

CARL A. RUDISILL LIBRARY
LENOIR RHYNE COLLEGE

THE ITALIAN LIBERATION STRUGGLE
AND THE CAUSE OF ITS PRESENT FAILURE

With the same celerity with which they were expelled
from Lombardy in March, the Austrians have now returned
in triumph and have already entered Milan.

The Italian people spared no pains. They were prepared
to sacrifice life and property to complete the work they had
begun and win national independence.

But this courage, enthusiasm and readiness to make sacrifices were nowhere matched by those who stood at the helm.
Overtly or covertly, they did everything to use the means
at their disposal, not for the liberation of the country from
the harsh Austrian tyranny, but to paralyse the popular
forces and, in effect, to restore the old conditions as soon as
possible.

The Pope,* who was worked on more and more every day
and won over by the Austrian and Jesuitical politicians, put
all the obstacles in the way of the Mamiani ministry which
he, in conjunction with the "Blacks" and the "Black-
Yellows",[63] could find. The ministry itself delivered highly
patriotic speeches in both chambers, but did not have the
energy to carry out its good intentions.

The government of Tuscany distinguished itself by fine
words and even fewer deeds. But the arch-enemy of Italian
liberty among the native princes was and remains Karl
Albert. The Italians should have repeated and borne in mind
every hour of the day the saying: Heaven protect us from
our friends and we shall protect ourselves against our enemies. They hardly needed to fear Ferdinand of Bourbon,
he was unmasked long ago. Karl Albert, on the other hand,
let himself be acclaimed everywhere as *"la spada d'Italia"*

---

* Pius IX.—*Ed.*

(the sword of Italy) and the hero whose rapier was Italy's best guarantee of freedom and independence.

His emissaries went all over Northern Italy. portraying him as the only man who could and would save the country. To enable him to do this, however, it was necessary to set up a North Italian kingdom. Only this could give him the power required not only to oppose the Austrians but to drive them out of Italy. The ambition which had first made him join forces with the Carbonari,[64] whom he had afterwards betrayed, this ambition became more inflamed than ever and made him dream of a plenitude of power and magnificence before which the splendour of all the other Italian princes would very soon pale. He thought that he could appropriate the entire popular movement of 1848 and use it in the interests of his own miserable self. Filled with hatred and distrust of all truly liberal men, he surrounded himself with people more or less loyal to absolutism and inclined to encourage his royal ambitions. He placed at the head of the army generals whose intellectual superiority and political views he did not have to fear, but who neither enjoyed the confidence of the soldiers nor possessed the talent required to wage a successful war. He pompously called himself the "liberator" of Italy while making it a condition that those who were to be liberated accept his yoke. Seldom was a man so favoured by circumstances as he was. His greed, his desire to possess as much as he could led in the end to his losing everything he had gained. So long as there was no firm decision that Lombardy would join Piedmont, so long as the possibility of a republican form of government still existed, he remained in his entrenchments and did not move against the Austrians, although they were relatively weak at the time. He let Radetzky, d'Aspre, Welden, and others seize the towns and fortresses of the Venetian provinces one by one and did not stir a finger. Only when Venice sought the refuge of his crown did he deign to give his help. The same applies to Parma and Modena. Radetzky meanwhile had mustered strength and made all preparations for an attack which, in view of the inability and blindness of Karl Albert and his generals, led to a decisive victory. The outcome is well known. Henceforth Italians can and will no longer entrust their liberation to a prince or king. On the contrary, in order to save themselves they must completely discard this useless *"spada d'Italia"* as quickly as possible. If they had done this earlier, and had superannuated the King with his system and all the hangers-on, and had formed a democratic union, it is likely that by now there would have been no more Austrians in Italy. Instead, the Italians not only bore all the hardships of a war waged with fury and barbarity by their enemies and suffered the heaviest sacrifices in vain, but were left, defenceless, to the tender mercies of the vindictive Metternich-Austrian reactionaries and their soldiery. Anyone reading Radetzky's manifestos to the people of Lombardy and Welden's manifestos to the Roman legations will understand that to the Italians Attila and his Hun hordes would have appeared merciful angels. The reaction and restoration have triumphed. The Duke of Modena, called *"il carnefice"* (the hangman), who loaned the Austrians 1,200,000 florins for war purposes, has returned as well. The people, in their magnanimity, have so often made a stick for their own back, that it is time they got wiser and learned something from their enemies. Although, during his previous reign, the Duke had imprisoned, hanged and shot thousands of people for their political convictions, the Modenese let him depart unmolested. Now he has returned to discharge his sanguinary princely office with redoubled zeal.

The reaction and restoration have triumphed, but only for a time. The people are so deeply imbued with the revolutionary spirit that they cannot be held in check for long. Milan, Brescia and other towns showed in March what this spirit is capable of. The excessive suffering inflicted upon them will lead to a new rising. By taking into account the bitter experience of the past months, Italy will be able to avoid new delusions and to secure her independence under a single democratic banner.

Written by Engels
on August 11, 1848

Neue Rheinische Zeitung No. 73.
August 12, 1848

THE *ZEITUNGS-HALLE* ON THE RHINE PROVINCE

Cologne, August 26. The *Berliner Zeitungs-Halle*[65] carries the following paragraph:

"We recently had occasion to mention that the time has come when the spirit which for so long has held together the old political entities is gradually vanishing. As regards Austria hardly anyone will call this in question, but in Prussia, too, the signs of the times confirming our observation are becoming daily more manifest, and we cannot turn a blind eye to them. There is at present only one interest capable of tying the various provinces to the Prussian state, namely, that of developing liberal political institutions and jointly establishing and promoting a new and free mode of social relations. Silesia, which is making vigorous advances on the road to political and social progress, will hardly be happy in Prussia unless Prussia as a state is entirely adequate to these aspirations. As regards the Province of Saxony we know only too well that ever since its incorporation into the Prussian state it has resented it at heart. And as to the Rhineland, surely everybody will still remember the threats made by the Rhenish deputies prior to March 18, which helped to precipitate the turn of events. There is a growing spirit of alienation in this province. New evidence of this is provided in a now rather widely distributed leaflet which contains no mention of the publisher or place of publication."

The leaflet referred to by the *Zeitungs-Halle* is presumably known to all our readers.

What must please us is the view—which is at last advanced by at least *one* Berliner—that Berlin does not play the role of Paris as far as either Germany or the Rhineland in particular is concerned. Berlin is beginning to realise that it cannot govern us, cannot acquire the authority befitting a capital city. Berlin has amply proved its incompetence during the indecisive March revolution, during the storming of the armoury and during the recent disturbances.[66] To the irresolution displayed by the people of Berlin is added a complete lack of talent in all parties. Since February the whole movement has not produced a single man capable of leading his party. The spirit in this "capital of the spirit" is indeed very willing but just as weak as the flesh. The Berliners even had to import their Hansemann, their Camphausen and their Milde from the Rhine or Silesia. Far from being a German Paris, Berlin is not even a Prussian Vienna. It is not a metropolis, it is a "seat of the court".

It is, however, noteworthy that even in Berlin people are coming to the conclusion, long widespread in the Rhineland, that German unity can come about *only as a result of the disintegration* of the German so-called great powers. We have never concealed our views on this point. We are not enraptured with either the past or present glory of Germany, with either the wars of independence or the "glorious victories of German arms" in Lombardy and Schleswig. But if Germany is ever to achieve anything she must unite, she must become *one* state in deed as well as in word. And to bring this about it is necessary above all that there should be "neither an Austria nor a Prussia".[67]

Incidentally, "the spirit" which "for so long held together" us and the old Prussian provinces was a palpable, crude spirit; it was the spirit of 15,000 bayonets and a number of cannon. It was not for nothing that military units of Silesian Poles and Kasubians were stationed here on the Rhine, and that our young men had to serve in guards regiments in Berlin. This was done not in order to reconcile us with the other provinces, but to stir up hatred between the provinces and to exploit the national enmity between the Germans and Slavs, and the regional hatred of every petty German province against all the neighbouring provinces, in the interests of patriarchal feudal despotism. *Divide et impera!*

It is indeed time to put an end to the fictitious role assigned to the Berliners by "the provinces", i.e., by the junkerdom of the Uckermark and Further Pomerania, in their panic-stricken declarations, a role which the Berliners promptly accepted. Berlin is not and will never become the seat of the revolution, the capital of democracy. Only the imagination of the knights of Brandenburg, terrified at the prospect of bankruptcy, the debtor's prison and the lamppost, could ascribe to Berlin such a role, and only the coquettish vanity of the Berliners could believe that it represented the provinces. We acknowledge the March revolution, but only for what it really was. Its greatest shortcoming is that it has not revolutionised the *Berliners*.

The *Zeitungs-Halle* believes that the disintegrating Prussian state can be cemented by means of liberal institutions. On the contrary. The more liberal the institutions are, the freer will it be for the heterogeneous elements to separate, and the clearer will become the necessity of dissociation and the incompetence of the politicians of all parties in Berlin.

We repeat, the Rhineland by no means objects to remaining together with the old Prussian provinces within *Germany*, but trying to compel it to remain for ever within Prussia, whether it be an absolutist, a constitutional or a democratic Prussia, is tantamount to making Germany's unity impossible, tantamount even to losing for Germany—we express the general attitude of the people—a large and beautiful territory by attempting to keep it for Prussia.

Written by Engels
Neue Rheinische Zeitung No. 87,
August 27, 1848

MEDIATION AND INTERVENTION.
RADETZKY AND CAVAIGNAC

The armistice[68] concluded as the result of Karl Albert's treachery will expire in about three weeks (on September 21). France and Britain have offered to act as mediators. The *Spectateur républicain,* Cavaignac's paper, writes that Austria has not yet stated whether she will accept or decline the offer. France's dictator is getting annoyed over the discourtesy of the Austrians and threatens armed intervention if by a given date the Viennese cabinet does not reply, or rejects mediation. Will Austria allow a Cavaignac to prescribe the peace terms to her, especially now after the victory over democracy in Vienna and over the Italian "rebels"? Austria understands perfectly well that the French bourgeoisie wants "peace at any price", that the freedom or bondage of the Italians is altogether a matter of complete indifference to the bourgeoisie and that it will agree to anything so long as it is not openly humiliated and thus reluctantly compelled to draw the sword. It is said that Radetzky will pay a short visit to Vienna in order to say the decisive word about mediation. He does not have to travel to Vienna to do that. His policy has now prevailed, and his opinion will be none the less weighty for his remaining in Milan. If Austria were to accept the basis for peace proposed by England and France, she would do so not because she is afraid of Cavaignac's intervention but for much more pressing and compelling reasons.

The Italians were just as much deluded by the March events as the Germans. The former believed that foreign rule at any rate was now done with; the latter thought that the old system was buried for good and all. However, the foreign rule in Italy is worse than ever, and in Germany the old system has recovered from the few blows it sustained in March and it acts with greater ferocity and vindictiveness than ever before.

The Italians are now making the mistake of expecting salvation from the present government of France. Only the fall of this government could save them. The Italians are further mistaken when they regard the liberation of their country as feasible while democracy in France, Germany and other countries continues to lose ground. Reaction, to whose blows Italy has succumbed, is not merely an Italian phenomenon, it is a European phenomenon. Italy alone cannot possibly free herself from the grip of this reaction, least of all by appealing to the French bourgeoisie, which is a true pillar of reaction in Europe as a whole.

Before reaction can be destroyed in Italy and Germany, it must be routed in France. A democratic social republic must first be proclaimed in France and the French proletariat must first subjugate its bourgeoisie, before a lasting democratic victory is conceivable in Italy, Germany, Poland, Hungary and other countries.

Written by Engels
on August 31, 1848

Neue Rheinische Zeitung No. 91,
September 1, 1848

THE ANTWERP DEATH SENTENCES

Cologne, September 2. Belgium, the model constitutional state, has produced further brilliant proof of the excellence of her institutions. *Seventeen death sentences* resulting from the ridiculous Risquons-Tout affair! Seventeen death sentences to avenge the humiliation inflicted upon the prudish Belgian nation by a few imprudent men, a few hopeful fools, who attempted to raise a small corner of the constitutional cloak! Seventeen death sentences—what savagery!

The Risquons-Tout incident is well known. Belgian workers in Paris joined forces to attempt a republican invasion of their country. Belgian democrats came from Brussels to support the venture. Ledru-Rollin assisted as much as he could. Lamartine, the '"noble-minded" traitor, who was not sparing of fine words and ignoble deeds as far as both the foreign and French democrats were concerned—Lamartine, who prides himself on having conspired with the anarchists, like a lightning conductor with the lightning—Lamartine at first supported the Belgian Legion the better to be able later to betray it. The Legion set out. Delescluze, Prefect of the Department du Nord, *sold* the first column to Belgian railway officials; the train which carried them was treacherously hauled into Belgian territory right into the midst of the Belgian bayonets. The second column was led by *three Belgian spies* (we were told this by a member of the Paris Provisional Government, and the course of events confirms it), and these treacherous leaders brought it into a forest on Belgian territory, where an ambush of loaded guns was waiting for it. The column was shot down and most of its members were captured.

This tiny episode of the 1848 revolution—an episode which assumed a farcical aspect as a result of the many betrayals and the magnitude ascribed to it in Belgium— served the Brussels prosecutor as a canvas on which to embroider the most colossal plot that was ever devised. Old General Mellinet, the liberator of Antwerp, Tedesco and Ballin, in short the most resolute and most active democrats of Brussels, Liége and Ghent were implicated. Mr. Bavay would even have Mr. Jottrand of Brussels dragged into it, had not the latter known things and possessed documents whose publication would greatly compromise the entire Belgian government, the wise Leopold included.

Why were these democrats arrested, why were these monstrous proceedings started against men who knew as much about the whole thing as the jurymen who faced them? It was meant to scare the Belgian bourgeoisie and, under cover of this scare, to collect the excessive taxes and forced loans, which are the cement of the glorious Belgian political edifice, and the payments on which were rather behindhand.

In short, the accused were arraigned before the Antwerp jury, the élite of the Flemish faro-playing fraternity, who lack both the élan of French political dedication and the cool assurance of grandiose English materialism, i.e., before those dried-cod merchants who spend their whole life vegetating in philistine utilitarianism, in the most short-sighted and timid profiteering. The great Bavay knew his men and appealed to their fear.

Indeed, had anyone ever seen a republican in Antwerp? Now thirty-two of the monsters faced the terrified men of Antwerp, and the trembling jury in concert with the wise bench consigned seventeen of the accused to the tender mercies of Article 86 and others of the Code pénal, i.e., the death sentence.

Mock trials were also held during the Reign of Terror in 1793, and convictions based on other facts than those officially stated did occur, but even the fanatical Fouquier-Tinville did not conduct a trial so distinguished by clumsy barefaced lies and blind partisan hatred. Moreover, is Belgium in the grip of a civil war and are the armies of half Europe assembled at her frontiers conspiring with the rebels, as was the case in France in 1793? Is the country in danger? Has a crack appeared in the crown? On the contrary, no one intends to subjugate Belgium, and the wise Leopold still drives every day without an escort from Laeken to Brussels and from Brussels to Laeken.

What has the 81-year-old Mellinet done to be sentenced to death by jury and judges? The old soldier of the French republic saved the last spark of Belgian honour in 1831. He liberated Antwerp and in return Antwerp condemns him to death! His only sin is that he defended his old friend Becker against the insinuations of the Belgian official press and did not change his friendly attitude towards Becker even when the latter was plotting in Paris. Mellinet was in no way connected with the plot. And because of this he is without further ado sentenced to death.

As to Ballin, he was a friend of Mellinet's, often visited him, and was seen in the company of Tedesco in a coffee-house. Reason enough to sentence him to death.

And finally Tedesco. Had he not visited the German Workers' Association, did he not associate with people on whom the Belgian police had planted stage daggers? Had he not been seen with Ballin in a coffee-house? The case was established—Tedesco had provoked the great battle of Risquons-Tout—off to the scaffold with him!

And so with the others.

We are proud of being able to call many of these "conspirators", sentenced to death only because they are democrats, our friends. If the venal Belgian press slings mud at them, then we, at least, want to vindicate their honour before the face of German democracy; if their country disowns them, we want to acclaim them.

When the president of the court pronounced the sentence of death, they passionately exclaimed: "Long live the republic!" Throughout the whole procedure and the reading of the sentence they behaved with truly revolutionary steadfastness.

As against this we read in the wretched Belgian press:

"The verdict," writes the *Journal d'Anvers*, "has caused no more of a sensation in the city than the entire trial, which aroused hardly any interest. Only among the working classes" (read: the proletarian rabble) "can one find sentiments hostile to the paladins of the republic; the rest of the population hardly took any notice of it. The attempt to bring about a revolution does not cease to appear absurd even after the death sentence, which, in any case, no one believes will be executed."

To be sure, if an interesting spectacle were to be staged allowing the citizens of Antwerp to watch the guillotining of seventeen republicans headed by old Mellinet, their liberator, then they would certainly have taken notice of the trial.

The savagery of the Belgian government, the Belgian jury and law courts lies precisely in the fact that they play with death sentences.

The *Libéral Liégeois* says: "The government wanted to show its *strength*, but it has merely demonstrated its *savagery*."

But then that has always been the lot of the Flemish nation.

Written by Engels

Neue Rheinische Zeitung No. 93,
September 3, 1848

THE DANISH-PRUSSIAN ARMISTICE

Cologne, September 9. Again we revert to the Danish armistice—we are given time to do this owing to the thoroughness of the National Assembly, which, instead of taking prompt and energetic decisions and *getting* new ministers appointed, allows the committees to deliberate in the most leisurely manner and leaves the solution of the government crisis to God—a thoroughness which barely conceals "our dear friends' lack of courage".[69]

The war in Italy was always unpopular with the democratic party, and has for a long time been unpopular even with the democrats of Vienna. The storm of public indignation over the war of extermination in Poznan could be staved off only for a few weeks by means of falsifications and lies on the part of the Prussian government. The street-fighting in Prague, despite all the efforts of the national press, excited sympathy among the people towards the defeated, but not towards the victors. The war in Schleswig-Holstein, however, from the outset was popular also among the *people.* What is the reason?

Whereas in Italy, Poznan and Prague the Germans *were fighting the revolution,* in Schleswig-Holstein they *were supporting it.* The Danish war is the first *revolutionary war* waged by Germany. We therefore *advocated* a resolute conduct of the Danish war, from the very beginning, but this does not in any way denote kinship with the sea-girt bourgeois beer-garden enthusiasm.

A sad thing for Germany that her first revolutionary war is the most ridiculous war ever waged.

But come to the point. The Danish nation is in commercial, industrial, political and literary matters completely dependent on Germany. It is well known that the real capital of Denmark is not Copenhagen but Hamburg; that for a whole year the Danish government copied all the United Provincial Diet experiments conducted by the Prussian government, which passed away on the barricades; that Denmark obtains all her literary as well as material fare via Germany, and that apart from Holberg, Danish literature is a poor imitation of that of Germany.

Impotent though Germany has been from time immemorial, she has the satisfaction of knowing that the Scandinavian nations, and especially Denmark, have fallen under her sway, and that compared with *them* she is even revolutionary and progressive.

Do you require proofs? Then read the polemics carried on by the Scandinavian nations against each other ever since the concept of Scandinavianism arose. Scandinavianism is enthusiasm for the brutal, sordid, piratical, Old Norse national traits, for that profound inner life which is unable to express its exuberant ideas and sentiments in words, but can express them only in deeds, namely, in rudeness towards women, perpetual drunkenness and the wild frenzy of the Berserker alternating with tearful sentimentality.

Scandinavianism and the theory of kinship with sea-girt Schleswig-Holstein appeared simultaneously in the states of the King of Denmark. The two concepts are correlated; they evoked each other and were in conflict with each other, thereby asserting their existence.

Scandinavianism was the pattern of the Danes' appeals for Swedish and Norwegian support. But as always happens with the Christian-Teutonic nation, a dispute immediately arose as to who was the genuine Christian-Teuton, the true Scandinavian. The Swede contended that the Dane had become "Germanised" and had degenerated, the Norwegian said the same of the Swede and the Dane, and the Icelander of all three. Obviously, the more primitive a nation is, the more closely its customs and way of life resemble those of the Old Norse people, the more "Scandinavian" it must be.

The Christiania *Morgenbladet*[70] for November 18, 1846, is lying in front of us. This charming sheet contains the following amusing passages in an article on Scandinavianism.

After stating that the whole concept of Scandinavianism is nothing but an attempt by the Danes to create a movement in their own interest, the paper says:

"What have these gay vivacious people in common with the ancient, gloomy and melancholy world of warriors (*med den gamle, alvorlige og vemodsfulde Kjämpeverden*)? How can this nation, which—as even a Danish writer admits—has a docile and gentle disposition, believe itself to be spiritually related to the tough, lusty and vigorous men of a past age? And how can these people with their soft southern accent imagine that they speak a northern tongue? Although the main trait of our nation and the Swedes, like that of the ancient Northerners, is that our feelings are kept hidden in the *innermost* part of the soul, and not given *outward* expression, nevertheless these sentimental and affectionate people, who can so easily be astonished, moved and swayed and who wear their hearts upon their sleeves, nevertheless these people believe that they are of a northern cast and that they are related to the two other Scandinavian nations!"

The *Morgenbladet* attributes the degeneration of the Danes to their association with Germany and the spread of German traits in Denmark. The Germans have indeed

"lost their most sacred asset, their national character; but feeble and insipid though the German nation is, there is another nation still more feeble and insipid, namely, the Danes. While the German language is being ousted in Alsace, Vaud and on the Slav border" (!the services of the Netze brethren remained unnoticed at the time) "it has made enormous progress along the Danish border."

The Danes, we are told, now had to oppose their nationality to the Germans and for this purpose they invented Scandinavianism. The Danes were unable to resist,

"for the Danish nation, as we have said before, was *essentially Germanised*, although it did not adopt the German language. The writer of these lines has seen it admitted in a Danish paper that the *Danish* nation *does not differ essentially from the German nation*."

Thus the *Morgenbladet*.

Of course, it cannot be denied that the Danes are a more or less civilised nation. Poor Danes!

By the same right under which France took Flanders, Lorraine and Alsace, and will sooner or later take Belgium —by that same right Germany takes over Schleswig; it is the right of civilisation as against barbarism, of progress as against static stability. Even if the agreements were in Denmark's favour—which is very doubtful—this right carries more weight than all the agreements, for it is the right of historical evolution.

So long as the Schleswig-Holstein movement remained a purely legal philistine agitation of a civic and peaceful nature it merely filled well-meaning petty bourgeois with enthusiasm. When, before the outbreak of the February revolution, the present King of Denmark at his accession promised a liberal constitution for all his states, envisaging the same number of deputies for the duchies as for Denmark, and the duchies were opposed to this, the petty-bourgeois parochial nature of the Schleswig-Holstein movement became distastefully conspicuous. The issue, at that time, was not so much union with Germany—did a Germany exist at that time?—as separation from Denmark and establishment of a small independent parochial state.

But then came the revolution, which imparted to the movement a different character. The Schleswig-Holstein party was forced either to attempt a revolution or to perish. It quite correctly chose the revolution. The Danish promises, which were very favourable before the revolution, were quite inadequate after the revolution; union with Germany—formerly an empty phrase—now acquired meaning. Germany made a revolution and as usual Denmark copied it on a small provincial scale.

The Schleswig-Holstein revolution and the Provisional Government to which it gave rise behaved at first still in a rather philistine way, but the war soon compelled them to adopt a democratic course. This government, whose members are all moderate liberal worthies, formerly kindred spirits of Welcker, Gagern and Camphausen, has given Schleswig-Holstein laws which are more democratic than those of any other German state. The Kiel Provincial Assembly is the only German assembly based on universal suffrage and direct elections. The draft constitution which the government submitted to it was the most democratic constitution ever drawn up in the German language. As a result of the revolutionary war, Schleswig-Holstein, which had always trailed behind Germany in political matters, suddenly acquired more progressive institutions than the rest of Germany.

The war we are waging in Schleswig-Holstein is therefore a truly revolutionary war.

And who, from the outset, supported Denmark? The three most counter-revolutionary powers in Europe—*Russia, England* and the *Prussian government.* As long as it was possible the Prussian government merely *pretended* to be waging a *war* —this is evidenced by Wildenbruch's Note, by the alacrity with which the Prussian government, on the representations of England and Russia, ordered the withdrawal from Jutland, and finally by the two armistice agreements. Prussia, England and Russia are the three powers which have greater reason than anyone else to fear the German revolution and its first result—German unity: Prussia because she would thereby cease to exist, England because it would deprive her of the possibility of exploiting the German market, and Russia because it would spell the advance of democracy not only to the Vistula but even as far as the Dvina and the Dnieper. Prussia, England and Russia have conspired against Schleswig-Holstein, against Germany and against the revolution.

The war that may now arise from the decisions taken at Frankfurt would be a war waged by Germany against Prussia, England and Russia. This is just the kind of war that the flagging German movement needs—a war against the three great counter-revolutionary powers, a war which would *really* cause Prussia to merge into Germany, which would make an alliance with Poland an indispensable necessity and would lead to the immediate liberation of Italy; a war which would be directed against Germany's old counter-revolutionary allies of 1792-1815, a war which would "imperil the fatherland" and for that very reason save it by making the victory of *Germany* dependent on the victory of democracy.

The bourgeois and titled landowners at Frankfurt should not deceive themselves—if they decide to reject the armistice they will be setting the seal to their own downfall, just as the Girondins did during the first revolution when they took part in the events of August 10 and voted for the death of the ex-King, thereby preparing their own downfall on May 31. If, on the other hand, they accept the armistice, they will still be sealing their own downfall: they will be placing themselves under the jurisdiction of Prussia and cease to have any say in things. It is up to them to choose.

The news of Hansemann's downfall probably reached Frankfurt before the vote was taken. This may influence the vote significantly, especially since it is expected that a government of Waldeck and Rodbertus will follow who, as we know, recognise the sovereignty of the National Assembly.

The future will show. But we repeat—Germany's honour is in bad hands.

Written by Engels

Neue Rheinische Zeitung No. 99,
September 10, 1848

THE CRISIS AND THE COUNTER-REVOLUTION[71]

[I]

Cologne, September 11. Anyone reading the reports from Berlin printed below can judge for himself whether we predicted the course of the government crisis correctly. The ministers resigned and it seems that the camarilla did not approve of the government's plan to dissolve the Assembly of conciliation and to use martial law and guns in order to remain in office. The titled landowners from the Brandenburg backwoods are thirsting for a conflict with the people and a repetition of the Parisian June scenes in the streets of Berlin, but they will never fight for the Hansemann government, they will fight for a *government of the Prince of Prussia*. The choice will fall on *Radowitz, Vincke* and similar reliable men who are strangers to the Berlin Assembly and are in no way committed to it. The government of the Prince of Prussia which is to be bestowed on us will comprise the cream of the Prussian and Westphalian knights associated for form's sake with a few bourgeois worthies from the extreme Right, such as Beckerath and his like, to whom will be assigned the conduct of the prosaic commercial side of the business of state. Meanwhile hundreds of rumours are being spread, Waldeck or Rodbertus is perhaps summoned, and public opinion is misled, while at the same time military preparations are being made to come out openly at the appropriate moment.

We are facing a decisive struggle. The concurrent crises at Frankfurt and Berlin and the latest decisions of the two Assemblies compel the counter-revolution to give its last battle. If the people in Berlin dare to spurn the constitutional principle of majority rule, if they confront the 219 members of the majority with twice as many guns, if they dare to defy the majority not only in Berlin but also in Frankfurt by presenting to them a government which is quite unacceptable to either of the two Assemblies—*if they thus provoke a civil war between Prussia and Germany, then the democrats know what they have to do.*

[II]

Cologne, September 12. Although already by midday we may receive news of the definite formation of an imperial government as described by us yesterday and confirmed from other quarters, the government crisis in Berlin continues. There are only two solutions to this crisis:

Either a Waldeck government, recognition of the authority of the German National Assembly and recognition of popular sovereignty;

Or a Radowitz-Vincke government, dissolution of the Berlin Assembly, abolition of the revolutionary gains, a sham constitutionalism or even the United Provincial Diet.

Don't let us shut our eyes to the fact that the conflict which has broken out in Berlin is a conflict not between the conciliators and the ministers, but between the Assembly, which for the first time steps forth as a *constituent* assembly, and the *Crown.*

The point is whether or not it will have the courage to dissolve the Assembly.

But has the Crown the right to dissolve the Assembly?

True, in constitutional states the Crown in case of disputes has the right to dissolve the legislative chambers convened on the basis of the constitution and to appeal to the people by means of new elections.

Is the Berlin Assembly a constitutional, legislative chamber?

It is not. It has been convened "to come to an agreement with the Crown on the Prussian constitution", it has been convened not on the basis of a constitution, but on that of a *revolution*. It received its mandate by no means from the Crown or from the ministers answerable to the Crown, but from those who elected it and from the Assembly itself. The Assembly was sovereign as the legitimate expression of the revolution, and the mandate which Herr Camphausen jointly with the United Provincial Diet prepared for it in the shape of the electoral law of April 8 was nothing but a *pious wish*, and it was up to the Assembly to decide about it.

At first the Assembly more or less accepted the theory of agreement. It realised that in doing so it had been cheated by the ministers and the camarilla. At last it performed a sovereign act, stepping forth for a moment as a constituent assembly and no longer as an assembly of conciliators.

Being the sovereign Assembly of *Prussia,* it had a perfect right to do this.

A sovereign assembly, however, cannot be dissolved by anybody, and cannot be given orders by anybody.

Even as a mere assembly of conciliation, even according to Herr Camphausen's own theory, it has *equal status* with the Crown. Both parties *conclude* a political treaty, both parties have an equal share of sovereignty—that is the theory of April 8, the Camphausen-Hansemann theory, the *official* theory recognised by the Crown itself.

If the Assembly and the Crown have *equal rights, then the Crown has no right to dissolve the Assembly.*

Otherwise, to be consistent, the Assembly would also have the *right to depose the King.*

The dissolution of the Assembly would therefore be a *coup d'état.* And how people reply to a coup d'état was demonstrated on July 29, 1830, and February 24, 1848.[72]

One may say the Crown could again appeal to the same voters. But who does not know that *today* the voters would elect an entirely different assembly, an assembly which would treat the Crown with much less ceremony?

Everyone knows that after the dissolution of this Assembly it will only be possible to appeal to *voters of an entirely different kind* from those of April 8, that the only elections possible will be elections carried through under the tyranny of the sword.

Let us have no illusions—

If the Assembly wins and succeeds in setting up a Left ministry, then the power of the Crown existing *alongside* the Assembly is broken, then the King is merely a paid servant of the people and we return again to the morning of March 19—provided the Waldeck ministry does not betray us, as did many a ministry before it.

If the Crown wins and succeeds in setting up a government of the Prince of Prussia, then the Assembly will be dissolved, the right of association abolished, the press muzzled, an electoral law based on property qualifications introduced, and, as we have already mentioned, even the United Provincial Diet may be reinvoked—and all this will be done under cover of a military dictatorship, guns and bayonets.

Which of the two sides will win depends on the attitude of the people, especially that of the democratic party. It is up to the democrats to choose.

We have again the situation of July 25. Will they dare to issue the decrees being devised in Potsdam? Will the people be provoked to make the leap from July 26 to February 24 in a *single* day?

The will to do it is certainly there, but what about the courage!

[III]

Cologne, September 13. The crisis in Berlin has advanced a step further. The *conflict with the Crown*, which yesterday could still be described as inevitable, *has actually taken place*.

Our readers will find below the King's reply to the resignation of the ministers.[73] By this letter the Crown itself comes to the fore, sides with the ministers and opposes the Assembly.

It goes even further—it forms a cabinet outside the Assembly, it nominates *Beckerath*, who represents the extreme Right at Frankfurt and who, as everyone knows, will never be able to count on the support of the majority in Berlin.

The King's message is counter-signed by Herr *Auerswald*. Let Herr Auerswald, if he can, justify the fact that he thus uses the Crown to cover up his ignominious retreat, that at one and the same time he tries to hide behind the constitutional principle as far as the Chamber is concerned and tramples the constitutional principle by *compromising the Crown and invoking the republic.*

Constitutional principle! shout the ministers. Constitutional principle! shouts the Right. Constitutional principle! faintly echoes the *Kölnische Zeitung*.

"Constitutional principle!" Are these gentlemen really so foolish as to believe that it is possible to extricate the German people from the storms of 1848, and from the imminent threat of collapse of all traditional institutions, by means of the Montesquieu-Delolme worm-eaten theory of division of powers, by means of worn-out phrases and long exploded fictions.

"Constitutional principle!" But the very gentlemen who are out to save the constitutional principle at any price should realise first of all that at a provisional stage it can only be saved by energetic action.

"Constitutional principle!" But the vote of the Berlin Assembly, the clashes between Potsdam and Frankfurt, the disturbances, the reactionary attempts, the provocations of the military—has all this not shown long ago that despite all the empty talk we *are* still on *revolutionary ground*, and the pretence that we have already reached the stage of an *established,* a complete constitutional monarchy only leads to collisions, which have already brought the "constitutional principle" to the brink of the abyss?

Every provisional political set-up following a revolution calls for dictatorship, and an energetic dictatorship at that. From the very beginning we blamed Camphausen for not having acted in a dictatorial manner, for not having immediately smashed up and removed the remains of the old institutions. While thus Herr Camphausen indulged in constitutional fancies, the defeated party strengthened its positions within the bureaucracy and in the army, and occasionally even risked an open fight. The Assembly was convened for the purpose of agreeing on the terms of the constitution. It existed as an equal party alongside the Crown. Two equal powers under a provisional arrangement! It was this division of powers with the aid of which Herr Camphausen sought "to save freedom"—it was this very division of powers under provisional arrangement that was bound to lead to conflicts. The Crown served as a cover for the counter-revolutionary aristocratic, military and bureaucratic camarilla. The bourgeoisie stood behind the majority of the Assembly. The cabinet tried to mediate. Too weak to stand up for the bourgeoisie and the peasants and overthrow the power of the nobility, the bureaucracy and the army chiefs at one blow, too unskilled to avoid always damaging the interests of the bourgeoisie by its financial measures, the cabinet merely succeeded in compromising itself in the eyes of all the parties and bringing about the very clash it sought to avoid.

The one important factor in any unconstituted state of affairs is the *salut public*, the public welfare, and not this or that principle. There is only one way in which the government could avoid a conflict between the Assembly and the Crown and that is by recognising the public welfare as the sole principle, even at the risk of the government *itself* coming into conflict with the Crown. But it preferred "not to compromise" itself in Potsdam. It never hesitated to employ public welfare measures (*mesures de salut public*), dictatorial measures, against the democratic forces. What else was the application of the old laws to political crimes, even after Herr Märker had recognised that these articles of the Civil Code ought to be repealed? What else were the wholesale arrests in all parts of the kingdom?

But the cabinet carefully refrained from intervening against the counter-revolution in the name of public welfare.

It was this half-heartedness of the government in face of the counter-revolution, which became more menacing with every day, that compelled the Assembly *itself to prescribe* measures of public welfare. If the Crown represented by the ministers was too weak, then the Assembly itself had to intervene. It did so by passing the resolution of August 9.[74] It did so in a still rather mild form, by merely warning the ministers. The ministers simply took no notice of it.

Indeed, how could they have agreed to it? The resolution of August 9 flouted the constitutional principle, it is an encroachment made by the legislative power on the executive power, it undermines the division of powers and the mutual control, which are essential in the interests of freedom, it turns the Assembly of conciliation into a *National Convention*.

There follows a running fire of threats, a vociferous appeal to the fears of the petty bourgeois and the prospect of a reign of terror with guillotines, progressive taxes, confiscations and the red flag.

To compare the Berlin Assembly with the Convention. What irony!

But these gentlemen were not altogether wrong. If the government goes on the way it has been doing, we shall have a Convention before long—not merely for Prussia, but for Germany as a whole—a Convention which will have to use all means to cope with the civil war in our twenty Vendées and with the inevitable war with Russia. At present, however, we merely have a parody of the Constituent Assembly.

But how have the ministers who invoke the constitutional principle upheld this principle?

On August 9, they calmly allowed the Assembly to break up in the belief that the ministers would carry out the resolution. They had no intention of making known to the Assembly their refusal to do so, and still less of resigning their office.

They ruminated on the matter for a whole month and finally, when threatened with parliamentary questions, they curtly informed the Assembly that it was self-evident that they would not put the resolution into effect.

When the Assembly thereupon instructs the ministers, nevertheless, to put the resolution into effect, they take refuge behind the Crown, and cause a rupture between the Crown and the Assembly, thus pushing matters towards a republic.

And these gentlemen still talk about the constitutional principle!

To sum up:

The inevitable conflict between two powers having equal rights in a provisional arrangement has broken out. The cabinet was unable to govern with sufficient energy; it has failed to take the necessary measures of public welfare. The Assembly has merely performed its duty in demanding that the cabinet do its duty. The cabinet declares this to be an encroachment upon the rights of the Crown and discredits the Crown at the very moment of its resignation. The Crown and the Assembly confront each other. The "agreement" has led to disagreement, to conflict. It is possible that arms will decide the issue.

The side that has the greater courage and consistency will win.

[IV]

Cologne, September 15. The government crisis has once again entered a new phase, due, not to the arrival and vain efforts of the impossible Herr Beckerath, but to the *army revolt in Potsdam and Nauen*. The conflict between democracy and aristocracy has broken out even *within the guard regiments*. The soldiers consider that the resolution carried by the Assembly on the 7th liberates them from the tyranny of their officers; they send letters of greeting and thanks to the Assembly.

This has wrenched the sword from the hands of the counter-revolutionaries. They will not dare now to dissolve the Assembly, and since this cannot be attempted, they will have to give in, carry out the resolution of the Assembly and form a Waldeck cabinet.

It is quite possible that the soldiers in revolt at Potsdam will save us a revolution.

Written by Marx

Neue Rheinische Zeitung
Nos. 100, 101, 102 and 104,
September 12, 13, 14 and 16,
1848

FREEDOM OF DEBATE IN BERLIN

Cologne, September 16. Ever since the beginning of the crisis the counter-revolutionary press keeps alleging that the deliberations of the Berlin Assembly are not free from interference. In particular, the well-known correspondent "G" of the *Kölnische Zeitung*,[75] who also discharges his duties only "temporarily pending the appointment of a successor" [76] refers with obvious fear to the "8,000 to 10,000 strong fellows" in the Kastanienwäldchen who "morally" support their friends of the Left. The *Vossische*,[77] *Spenersche*[78] and other newspapers have set up a similar wail, and on the 7th of this month Herr Reichensperger has even tabled a motion frankly demanding that the Assembly be removed from Berlin (to Charlottenburg perhaps?).

The *Berliner Zeitungs-Halle*[79] publishes a long article in which it tries to refute these accusations. It declares that the large majority obtained by the Left was by no means inconsistent with the former irresolute attitude of the Assembly. It can be shown

"that the voting of the 7th could have taken place *without conflicting* with the former attitude even of those members who previously voted always for the cabinet, that it was indeed from their point of view in perfect harmony with their former position...." The members who came over from the centre parties "had laboured under a delusion; they *imagined* that the ministers carried out the will of the people; they had taken the endeavours of the ministers to restore law and order for an expression of their own will, i.e., that of the majority of deputies, and had not *realised* that the ministers could accede to the popular will only when it did not run counter to the will of the Crown, and not when it was opposed to it".

The *Zeitungs-Halle* thus "explains" the striking phenomenon of the sudden change in the attitude of so many deputies by ascribing it to the notions and delusions of these deputies. The thing could not be presented in a more innocent way.

The paper admits, however, that intimidations did occur. But it says,

"if outside influences did have any effect, it was only that they partially counterbalanced the ministerial misrepresentations and artful temptation, thus enabling the many weak and irresolute deputies to follow their *natural vital instinct....*"

The reasons which induced the *Zeitungs-Halle* thus morally to justify the vacillating members of the centre parties in the eyes of the public are obvious. The article is written for these gentlemen of the centre parties rather than for the general public. For us, however, these reasons do not exist, since we are privileged to speak plainly, and since we support the representatives of a party only as long and in so far as they act in a *revolutionary* manner.

Why should we not say it? The centre parties certainly were intimidated by the masses on September 7; we leave it open whether their fear was well founded or not.

The right of the democratic popular masses, by their presence, to exert a moral influence on the attitude of constituent assemblies is an old revolutionary right of the people which could not be dispensed with in all stormy periods ever since the English and French revolutions. History owes to this right almost all the energetic steps taken by such assemblies. The only reason why people dwell on the "legal basis" and why the timorous and philistine friends of the "freedom of debate" lament about it is that they do not want any energetic decisions at all.

"Freedom of debate"—there is no emptier phrase than this. The "freedom of debate" is, on the one hand, impaired by the freedom of the press, by the freedom of assembly and of speech, and by the right of the people to take up arms. It is impaired by the existing state power vested in the Crown and its ministers—the army, the police and the so-called independent judges, who depend, however, on every promotion and every political change.

The freedom of debate is always a phrase denoting simply independence of all influences that are not recognised in law. It is only the recognised influences, such as bribery, promotion, private interests and fear of a dissolution of the Assembly, that make the debates really "free". In times of revolution, however, this phrase becomes entirely meaningless. When two forces, two parties in arms confront each other, when a fight may start any moment, the deputies have only this choice:

Either they place themselves *under the protection of the people*, in which case they will put up occasionally with a small lecture;

Or they place themselves *under the protection of the Crown*, move to some small town, deliberate under the protection of bayonets and guns or even a state of siege, in which case they will raise no objections when the Crown and the bayonets dictate their decisions to them.

Intimidation by the unarmed people or intimidation by an armed soldiery—that is the choice before the Assembly.

The French Constituent Assembly transferred its sessions from Versailles to Paris. It would be quite in character with the German revolution if the Assembly of conciliation were to move from Berlin to Charlottenburg.

Neue Rheinische Zeitung No. 105,
September 17, 1848

RATIFICATION OF THE ARMISTICE

Cologne, September 19. The German National Assembly has ratified the armistice. We were not mistaken: "Germany's honour has fallen into bad hands."*

The vote was taken amidst uproar and complete darkness, when the benches of the deputies were thronged with strangers, diplomats, etc. A majority of two forced the Assembly to vote simultaneously on two entirely different questions. The armistice was carried, Schleswig-Holstein sacrificed, "Germany's honour" trampled under foot and the *merging of Germany in Prussia* decided by a majority of 21 votes.

On no other issue has there been such a clear expression of public opinion. On no other issue have the gentlemen of the Right so openly admitted that they uphold a cause which is *indefensible*. In no other issue were Germany's interests so unequivocal and so obvious as in this. The National Assembly has made its decision—it has pronounced the *death sentence* upon itself and upon the so-called central authority created by it. If Germany had a Cromwell it would not be long before he would say: "You are no Parliament. . . . Depart, I say. . . . In the name of God,—go!"[80]

There is talk of the impending withdrawal of the Left. If it had courage, this poor derided Left, which has been fisted by the majority and called to order on top of it by the noble Gagern. Never has a minority been so insolently and consistently maltreated as has been the Frankfurt Left by the noble Gagern and his 250 champions of the majority. If only it had courage!

Lack of courage is ruining the entire German movement.

---

* See this volume, p. 119.—*Ed.*

The counter-revolution as well as the revolutionary party lack the courage for the decisive blows. All Germans, whether on the right or on the left, know now that the present movement must lead to terrible clashes, to bloody battles, fought either to suppress it or to carry it through. But instead of courageously facing these unavoidable battles and fighting them out with a few rapid and decisive blows, the two parties—the party of the counter-revolution and that of movement—have virtually come to an agreement to put them off as long as possible. It is due to this constant resort to petty expedients, to trivial concessions and palliatives, to these attempts at mediation, that the unbearable and uncertain political situation has led everywhere to numerous isolated uprisings, which can only be liquidated by way of bloodshed and the curtailment of rights already won. It is this fear of struggle that gives rise to thousands of minor clashes making the year 1848 exceptionally sanguinary and so complicating the position of the contending parties that in the end the struggle will be the more violent and destructive. But "our dear friends' lack of courage"!

The crucial struggle for Germany's centralisation and democratic organisation cannot possibly be avoided. Every day brings it nearer despite all attempts to play it down and compromise. The complex situation in Vienna, Berlin and Frankfurt demands a decision, and if *everything* should fail because of German timidity and indecision, we shall be saved by France. The consequences of the June victory are now taking shape in Paris—the royalists are getting the better of Cavaignac and his "pure republicans" in the National Assembly, in the press and in the clubs; a general uprising is threatening to break out in the legitimist South; Cavaignac has to resort to Ledru-Rollin's revolutionary remedies, i.e., to departmental commissioners invested with extraordinary powers; it was with the greatest difficulty that he managed to defend himself and his government in Parliament last Saturday. Another such division, and Thiers, Barrot and company, the men in whose interests the June victory was won, will possess a majority, Cavaignac will be thrown into the arms of the red republic, and the struggle for the republic's existence will start.

If Germany's irresoluteness should persist, the new phase of the French revolution will also be a signal for a fresh outbreak of open struggle in Germany, a struggle which we hope will take us a little further and will at least free Germany from the traditional fetters of her past.

Written by Engels

Neue Rheinische Zeitung No. 107,
September 20, 1848

THE UPRISING IN FRANKFURT

[I]

Cologne, September 19, 7 p.m. The German-Danish armistice has raised a storm. A sanguinary revolt has begun in Frankfurt. The workers of Frankfurt, Offenbach and Hanau, and the peasants of the surrounding districts, have staked their life to defend Germany's honour betrayed by the National Assembly to a Prussian government which has ignominiously resigned.

The outcome of the struggle is still uncertain. Until yesterday evening the soldiers apparently made little progress. In Frankfurt, apart from the Zeil and perhaps a few other streets and squares, artillery is of little use, and cavalry of hardly any use. In this respect the people are in an advantageous position. Citizens of Hanau, armed with weapons from the arsenal they had stormed, have come to their assistance, as have also peasants from numerous villages in the vicinity. Yesterday evening the military probably numbered about 10,000 men and very little artillery. Large reinforcements of peasants must have arrived during the night, and considerably smaller ones of soldiers, the immediate vicinity being denuded of troops. The revolutionary temper of the peasants in the Odenwald, Nassau and the Electorate of Hesse precluded further withdrawals; it is likely that communications have been interrupted. If today the insurgents are still holding out, then the whole of the Odenwald, Nassau, the Electorate of Hesse and Rhenish Hesse will take up arms, the entire population between Fulda, Koblenz, Mannheim and Aschaffenburg will be in arms, and there are insufficient troops available to crush the uprising. And who will answer for Mainz, Mannheim, Marburg, Cassel and Wiesbaden—towns in which hatred of the army has reached its highest pitch as a result of the bloody excesses of the so-called Federal troops? Who will answer for the peasants on the Rhine, who can easily prevent troop movements along the river?

We admit, nevertheless, that we have little hope of the courageous insurgents being able to win the day. Frankfurt is too small a town, the number of troops is disproportionately large, and the well-known counter-revolutionary sentiments of the local petty bourgeoisie are too great to allow us to be very hopeful.

But even if the insurgents are defeated, this will settle nothing. The counter-revolution will become arrogant, it will enslave us for a time by introducing martial law, by suppressing freedom of the press, and banning the clubs and public meetings; but before long the crowing of the Gallic cock[81] will announce the hour of liberation, the hour of revenge.

[II]

Cologne, September 20. The news from Frankfurt is beginning to confirm our fears of yesterday. It seems certain that the insurgents have been ejected from Frankfurt, and that now they are holding only Sachsenhausen, where they are said to be strongly entrenched. A state of siege has been declared in Frankfurt; anyone caught carrying weapons or resisting the "Federal Authority" is to be court-martialed.

Thus the gentlemen in the Paulskirche are now on an equal footing with their colleagues in Paris. They can now at their leisure and under the rule of martial law reduce the fundamental rights of the German people to a "minimum".

The railway line to Mainz is torn up in many places, and the post arrives either late or not at all.

It appears that artillery decided the outcome of the fight in the wide streets and enabled the army to attack the fighters on the barricades from the rear. Additional factors were the zeal with which the petty bourgeois of Frankfurt opened their houses to the soldiers, thus giving them every advantage in the street-fighting, and the superior strength of the troops, swiftly brought up by rail, over the peasant contingents, who arrived slowly on foot.

But even if the fight has not been renewed in Frankfurt itself, it certainly does not mean that the rising has been crushed. The angry peasants are not likely to put their weapons down forthwith. Though they may not be able to break up the National Assembly, they still have enough at home that has to be cleared away. The storm that was repelled outside the Paulskirche can spread to six or eight petty residences and to hundreds of manor-houses. The peasant war begun this spring will not come to an end until its goal, the liberation of the peasants from feudalism, has been achieved.

What is the reason for the persistent victory of "order" throughout Europe and for the series of recurrent defeats of the revolutionary party from Naples, Prague and Paris to Milan, Vienna and Frankfurt?

All parties know that the struggle impending in all civilised countries is quite different from, infinitely more significant than, all previous revolutions; in Vienna and Paris, in Berlin and Frankfurt, in London and Milan the point at issue is the *overthrow of the political rule of the bourgeoisie*, an upheaval whose immediate consequences horrify all portly, stockjobbing bourgeois.

Is there a revolutionary centre anywhere in the world where the red flag, the emblem of the militant, united proletariat of Europe, has not been found flying on the barricades during the last five months?

The fight in Frankfurt against the Parliament of the combined landowners and the bourgeoisie was likewise waged under the red flag.

The reason for all these defeats is that every uprising that now takes place is a direct threat to the political existence of the bourgeoisie, and an indirect threat to its social existence. The people, largely unarmed, have to fight not only the well-armed bourgeoisie but also the organised power of the bureaucratic and military state which the bourgeoisie has taken over. The people, who are unorganised and poorly armed, are confronted by all the other social classes, who are well organised and fully armed. That is the reason why up to now the people have been defeated and will continue to be defeated until their opponents are weakened either through dissension, or because the army is engaged in war—or until some important event impels the people to begin a desperate fight and demoralises their opponents.

Such an event is impending in France.

Hence we need not give up hope, even though during the last four months the barricades everywhere have been defeated by grape-shot. On the contrary, every victory of our opponents was at the same time a defeat for them, for it divided them and, ultimately, gave control not to the conservative party that was victorious in February and March, but in each case to *the* party that had been *overthrown* in February and March. Only for a short time did the victory won in Paris in June establish the rule of the petty bourgeoisie, the *pure* republicans; hardly three months have passed and the big bourgeoisie, the constitutional party, is threatening to overthrow Cavaignac and drive the "pure ones" into the arms of the "reds". This will happen in Frankfurt too—the victory will benefit, not the respectable gentlemen from the centre parties, but those of the *Right*. The bourgeoisie will have to give pride of place to the gentlemen representing the military, bureaucratic and aristocratic state and will very soon taste the bitter fruit of victory.

May it do them good! Meanwhile we shall await the moment when the hour of liberation for Europe will have struck in Paris.

Written by Engels

Neue Rheinische Zeitung
Nos. 107 (supplement) and 108,
September 20 and 21, 1848

REVOLUTION IN VIENNA

Cologne, October 11. In its *first* issue (for June 1) the *Neue Rheinische Zeitung* wrote of a revolution (on May 25) in Vienna. Today, when we resume publication for the *first* time after the break caused by the declaration of martial law in Cologne, we bring news of the much more important Viennese revolution of October 6 and 7. Detailed reports on the events in Vienna compel us today to omit all analytical articles. Only a few words of comment, therefore, on the revolution in Vienna. Our readers will see from the reports of our Vienna correspondent* that the bourgeoisie's distrust of the working class threatens, if not to wreck the revolution, at least to hamper its development. However that may be, the repercussions of this revolution in Hungary, Italy and Germany completely upset the plan of campaign devised by the counter-revolution. The flight from Vienna of the Emperor and of the Czech deputies[82] compels the Viennese bourgeoisie to continue the fight unless it is prepared to surrender unconditionally. The dreams of the Frankfurt Assembly, which is just now engaged in presenting us Germans with

a national jail and a common whip,[83]

have been rudely interrupted by the events in Vienna, and the government at Berlin is beginning to doubt the efficacy of *martial law* as a panacea. Martial law, like the revolution, is making a round-the-world tour. A large-scale experiment has just been made to impose martial law on a whole country, Hungary. This attempt has called forth a revolution in Vienna instead of a counter-revolution in

---

* Müller-Tellering.—*Ed.*

Hungary. Martial law will not recover from this setback. Its reputation has been permanently ruined. By an irony of fate, simultaneously with Jellachich, *Cavaignac*, the hero of martial law in the West, has been singled out for attack by all the factions who were saved in June by his grape-shot. Only by resolutely going over to the revolution will he be able to hold out for some time.

Following the latest news from Vienna, we publish several reports sent on October 5, because they reflect the hopes and fears current in Vienna about the fate of Hungary.

Written by Marx

Neue Rheinische Zeitung No. 114,
October 12, 1848

THE PARIS *RÉFORME* ON THE SITUATION
IN FRANCE

Cologne, November 2. Even *before* the June uprising we repeatedly exposed the illusions of the republicans who cling to the traditions of 1793, the republicans of the *Réforme* (of Paris). Under the impact of the June revolution and the movement to which it gave rise the utopian republicans gradually had their eyes opened.

A leading article in the *Réforme* for October 29 reflects the conflict between the old delusions of the party and the new facts.

The *Réforme* says:

"In our country the fights waged to seize the reins of government have long been *class wars*, struggles of the bourgeoisie and the people against the nobility when the first republic came into being; the sacrifices of the armed people without, and rule of the bourgeoisie within during the empire; the attempt to restore feudalism under the older branch of the Bourbons; finally, in 1830, the triumph and rule of the bourgeoisie—that is our history."

The *Réforme* adds with a sigh:

"We certainly regret that we have to speak of *classes*, of ungodly and hateful divergences, but these divergences exist and we cannot overlook this fact."

That is to say: up to now the *Réforme* in its republican optimism saw only *"citoyens"* but it has been so hard pressed by history that the splitting up of the *"citoyens"* into *"bourgeois"* and *"prolétaires"* can no longer be dismissed by any effort of imagination.

The *Réforme* continues:

"The despotism of the bourgeoisie was broken in February. What did the people demand? Justice for all and equality. That was its primary slogan, its primary desire. The wishes of the bourgeoisie, whose eyes had been opened by the flash of lightning, were at first the same as those of the people."

The paper's views on the February revolution are still based on the speeches of that time. The despotism of the bourgeoisie, far from having been broken during the February revolution, was completed by it. The Crown, the last feudal aureole, which concealed the rule of the bourgeoisie, was cast aside. The rule of capital emerged unadulterated. Bourgeoisie and proletariat fought against a common enemy during the February revolution. As soon as the common enemy was eliminated, the two hostile classes held the field of battle alone and the decisive struggle between them was bound to begin. People may ask, why did the bourgeoisie fall back into royalism, if the February revolution brought bourgeois rule to its completion? The explanation is a simple one. The bourgeoisie would have liked to return to the period when it ruled without being responsible for its rule; when a puppet authority standing between the bourgeoisie and the people had to act for it and to serve it as a cloak. A period when it had, as it were, a crowned scapegoat, which the proletariat hit whenever it aimed at the bourgeoisie, and against which the bourgeoisie could join forces with the proletariat whenever that scapegoat became troublesome and attempted to establish itself as an authority in its own right. The bourgeoisie could use the King as a kind of lightning-conductor protecting it from the people, and the people as a lightning-conductor protecting it from the King.

Since the illusions, some of them hypocritical, some honest, which became widespread immediately after the defeat of Louis Philippe, are mistakenly accepted by the *Réforme* as facts, the developments *following* those days in February appear to it as a series of errors, awkward accidents, that a great man adequate to the needs of the moment could have avoided. As though Lamartine, the jack-o'-lantern, had not been the true man of the moment.

The *Réforme* bemoans the fact that the true man, the great man, has not yet appeared, and the situation gets worse every day.

"On the one hand the industrial and commercial crisis grows; on the other hand hatred grows and all strive towards contradictory goals. Those who were oppressed before February 24 seek their ideal of happiness and freedom in the conception of an entirely new society. The only concern of those who governed under the monarchy is to regain their realm in order to exploit it with redoubled harshness."

Now what is the attitude of the *Réforme* towards these sharply antagonistic classes? Does it realise even vaguely that class contradictions and class struggle will disappear only with the disappearance of classes?

No. Just now it admitted that class contradictions exist. But class contradictions are based on economic foundations, on the existing mode of material production and the conditions of commerce resulting from it. The *Réforme* knows no better way of changing and abolishing these contradictions than to disregard their real basis, that is, these very material conditions, and to withdraw into the hazy blue heaven of republican ideology, in other words, into the poetic February period, from which it was violently ejected by the June events. It writes:

"The saddest aspect of these internal dissensions is the obliteration, the loss of the patriotic, national sentiments", i.e., of just that patriotic and national enthusiasm which enabled both classes to veil their distinct interests, their conditions of life. When they did that in 1789, their real contradictions were not yet developed. What at that time was an adequate expression of the real position, is today merely an escape from the existing situation. What had substance then, is today just a relic.

"France," concludes the *Réforme*, "evidently suffers from a deep-seated malady, but it is curable. It is caused by a confusion of ideas and morals, by a neglect of justice and equality in social relations, and by depravity resulting from egoistical teaching. The means for reorganisation must be sought in this sphere. Instead people have recourse to material means."

The *Réforme* presents the whole case as a matter of "conscience", and moral twaddle is then used as a means to solve everything. The antithesis of bourgeoisie and proletariat accordingly derives from the ideas of these two classes. And where do these ideas derive from? From the social relations. And where do these relations derive from? From the material, economic conditions of life of the hostile classes. According to the *Réforme*, if the two classes are *no longer conscious* of their real position and their real contradictions, and become intoxicated with the opium of the "patriotic" sentiments and phrases of 1793, then their difficulties will be solved. What an admission of helplessness!

Written by Marx

Neue Rheinische Zeitung No. 133,
November 3, 1848

THE LATEST NEWS FROM VIENNA, BERLIN AND PARIS

Cologne, November 4. *The outlook brightens.*

There is no direct news yet from *Vienna*. But even according to the official *Prussian papers*, it is clear that *Vienna* has not surrendered and that *Windischgrätz* deliberately or as a result of a *misunderstanding* had given to the world a *false telegram*. The "good" press, like an orthodox, multilingual echo, has willingly repeated the message although it has tried hard to mask its malicious glee behind a woebegone countenance. Stripped of all their fantastic and self-contradictory trash, the reports from Silesia and Berlin bring out the following facts. By October 29 the imperial bandits had obtained control only of a few suburbs. The reports received up till now do *not* show that they have gained a foothold in Vienna itself. The whole story of Vienna's surrender boils down to a few *treasonable proclamations of the Vienna town council*. The advanced guard of the Hungarian army attacked Windischgrätz on October 30, and *was said* to have been driven back. On October 31 Windischgrätz resumed the shelling of Vienna—without result. His army is now between the Viennese and the over 80,000-strong Hungarian army. Windischgrätz's infamous manifestos called forth uprisings or at least very threatening movements in all provinces. Even the Czech fanatics in Prague, the neophytes of Slovanská Lípa,[84] have awakened from their wild dreams and declared *for Vienna* against the imperial Schinderhannes.[85] *Never* before has the counter-revolution dared to proclaim its plans with such fatuous brazenness. Even at *Olmütz*, that Austrian Koblenz,[86] the crowned idiot can feel the ground shaking beneath his feet. The fact that the troops are led by the world-famed

Sipehsalar* Jellachich—whose name is so great that "*at the flash of his sabre the frightened moon hides behind the clouds*" and "the roar of cannon" always "points the way" in which he must hurriedly decamp—leaves no doubt that the people of Hungary and Vienna

> Horsewhip that scum into the Danube River,
> Go castigate that overweening rabble,
> Those starveling beggars, all so tired of living,
> That horde of miscreants, rogues and vagabonds,
> Croatian riff-raff, abject peasant hirelings,
> That vomit, spewed up by a glutted homeland
> For desperate ventures and for *certain doom.*

Later reports will give appalling details of the crimes perpetrated by Croats and other knights "of law and order and constitutional freedom". The European bourgeoisie ensconced in stock exchanges and other convenient observation posts will loudly acclaim the gory spectacle; the same wretched bourgeoisie that broke into screams of moral indignation because of a few harsh acts of popular justice and with a thousand voices unanimously anathemised the "murderers" of honest Latour and noble Lichnowski.

The *Poles*, avenging the Galician murders, are once more advancing at the head of the liberators of Vienna, just as they march at the head of the Italian people and everywhere act as high-minded *generals of the revolution.* Three cheers for the *Poles!*

The *Berlin camarilla*, intoxicated with the blood of Vienna, blinded by the pillars of smoke rising from the burning suburbs, stunned by the Croats' and Hungarians' shouts of victory, has dropped its cloak. "Peace has been restored in Berlin." We shall see.

Finally, from *Paris* come the first subterranean rumbles announcing the earthquake that will bury the genteel republic under its own ruins.

The outlook brightens.

Written by Marx

Neue Rheinische Zeitung No. 135,
November 5, 1848

---

* Commander-in-Chief.—*Ed.*

THE VICTORY OF THE COUNTER-REVOLUTION IN VIENNA

Cologne, November 6. *Croatian freedom and order has won the day,* and this victory was celebrated with arson, rape, looting and other atrocities. *Vienna is in the hands of Windischgrätz, Jellachich and Auersperg.* Hecatombs of victims are sacrificed on the grave of the aged traitor Latour.

The gloomy forecasts of our Vienna correspondent* have come true, and by now he himself may have become a victim of the butchery.

For a while we hoped Vienna could be liberated by Hungarian reinforcements, and we are still in the dark regarding the movements of the Hungarian army.

Treachery of every kind prepared the way for Vienna's fall. The entire performance of the *Imperial Diet* and the *town council* since October 6 is a tale of continuous treachery. Who are the people represented in the Imperial Diet and the town council?

The *bourgeoisie.*

A part of the Viennese *National Guard* openly sided with the camarilla from the very beginning of the October revolution. Towards the end of the October revolution another part of the National Guard in collusion with the imperial bandits fought against the proletariat and the Academic Legion. To which strata do these groups of the National Guard belong?

To the *bourgeoisie.*

The bourgeoisie in *France,* however, *headed* the counter-revolution only after it had broken down all obstacles to the rule of its own class. The bourgeoisie in *Germany*

---

* Müller-Tellering. See *Neue Rheinische Zeitung* No. 127, October 27, 1848.—*Ed.*

meekly joins the *retinue* of the absolute monarchy and of feudalism before securing even the first conditions of existence necessary for its own civic freedom and its rule. In France it played the part of a tyrant and made its own counter-revolution. In Germany it acts like a slave and carries out the counter-revolution for its own tyrants. The bourgeoisie in France won its victory in order to humble the people. In Germany it humbled itself to prevent the victory of the people. History presents no example of *greater wretchedness* than that of the *German bourgeoisie.*

Who fled from Vienna in large numbers leaving their wealth to be watched over by the magnanimous people, the people whom, in reward for their watchman's duties, they maligned while away and whose massacre they witnessed on their return?

The *bourgeoisie.*

Whose innermost secrets were revealed by the thermometer which dropped whenever the people of Vienna showed signs of life, and rose whenever the people were in the throes of death? Who used the runic script of the *stock exchange quotations*?

The *bourgeoisie.*

The "German National Assembly" and its "central authority" have betrayed Vienna. Whom do they represent?

Mainly the *bourgeoisie.*

The victory of "Croatian order and freedom" at Vienna depended on the victory of the "genteel" republic in Paris. Who won the day in June?

The *bourgeoisie.*

European counter-revolution began its debaucheries with its victory in Paris.

In February and March armed force was beaten everywhere. Why? Because it represented only the *government.* After June it was everywhere victorious because the *bourgeoisie* everywhere had come to a secret understanding with it, while retaining official leadership of the revolutionary movement and introducing all those half measures which by the very nature of things were bound to miscarry.

The national fanaticism of the Czechs was the most powerful instrument the Viennese camarilla possessed. *The allies are already at loggerheads.* In this issue our readers will find the protest of the Prague delegation against the insolent rudeness with which it was greeted in Olmütz.

This is the *first symptom of the struggle which is going to break out between the Slav party and its hero Jellachich on the one hand, and the party of the plain camarilla, which stands above all nationality, and its hero Windischgrätz on the other.* Moreover the German peasants in Austria are not yet pacified. Their voice will be loudly heard above the caterwauling of the Austrian nationalities. And from a third quarter the voice of the Tsar, the friend of the people, reaches as far as Pest; his henchmen are waiting for the word of command in the Danubian principalities.

Finally, the last decision of the German National Assembly at Frankfurt, which incorporates German Austria into the German empire, should lead to a gigantic conflict, unless the German central authority and the German National Assembly see it as their task to enter the arena in order to be hissed off the boards by European public. For all their pious resignation the struggle in Austria will assume gigantic dimensions such as world history has never yet witnessed.

The second act of the drama has just been performed in *Vienna*, its first act having been staged in Paris under the title of *The June Days.* In Paris the Guarde mobile, in Vienna "Croats"—in both cases lazzaroni, lumpen-proletariat hired and armed—were used against the working and thinking proletarians. We shall soon see the third act performed in *Berlin*.

Assuming that *arms* will enable the counter-revolution to establish itself in the whole of Europe, *money* would then kill it in the whole of Europe. European *bankruptcy, national bankruptcy* would be the fate nullifying the victory. Bayonets crumble like tinder when they come into contact with the salient "economic" facts.

But developments will not wait for the bills of exchange drawn by the European states on European society to expire. The crushing counter-blow of the June revolution will be struck in *Paris*. With the victory of the "red republic" in Paris, *armies* will be rushed from the *interior* of their countries to the frontiers and across them, and the *real strength* of the fighting parties will become evident. We shall then remember this June and this October and we too shall exclaim:

Vae victis!

The purposeless massacres perpetrated since the June and October events, the tedious offering of sacrifices since February and March, the very cannibalism of the counter-revolution will convince the nations that there is only one way in which the murderous death agonies of the old society and the bloody birth throes of the new society can be *shortened*, simplified and concentrated, and *that way* is *revolutionary terror.*

Written by Marx

Neue Rheinische Zeitung No. 136,
November 7, 1848

THE CRISIS IN BERLIN[87]

Cologne, November 8. The situation looks very complicated, but it is very simple.

The *King*, as the *Neue Preussische Zeitung*[88] correctly notes, stands "*on the broad foundation*" of his "*hereditary divine*" rights.

On the other side, the *National Assembly* has *no foundation whatever*, its purpose being to constitute, to lay the foundation.

Two sovereign powers.

The connecting link between the two is *Camphausen*, and the *theory of agreement*.

When these two sovereign powers are no longer able to agree or do not want to agree, they become two inimical sovereign powers. The *King* has the *right* to throw down the gauntlet to the Assembly, the *Assembly* has the *right* to throw down the gauntlet to the King. The *greater right* is on the side of the *greater might*. Power is tested in *struggle*. The test of the struggle is *victory*. Each of the two powers can prove that it is right only by its *victory*, that it is wrong only by its *defeat*.

The King until now has not been a *constitutional* king. He is an *absolute* monarch who decides for or against constitutionalism.

The Assembly until now has not been a *constitutional* but a *constituent* assembly. It has so far attempted to constitute constitutionalism. It can continue or discontinue its *attempts*.

Both the King and the Assembly temporarily acquiesced in the constitutional ceremonial.

The King's demand that a Brandenburg cabinet be appointed at his pleasure in refiance of the majority of the Chamber, is the demand of an *absolute monarch*.

The Chamber's presumption to send a deputation *straight* to the King forbidding the formation of a Brandenburg cabinet, is the presumption of an *absolute Chamber*.

The King and the Assembly have sinned against constitutional convention.

The King and the Chamber have both retreated to their original sphere, the King deliberately, the Chamber unwittingly.

The King is at an advantage.

Right is on the side of *might*.

Legal phrases are on the side of *impotence*.

A *Rodbertus* cabinet would be the cipher in which plus and minus neutralise each other.

Written by Marx

Neue Rheinische Zeitung No. 138,
November 9, 1848

NEW INSTITUTIONS—PROGRESS
IN SWITZERLAND

Berne, November 9. The new legislative Federal Assembly, consisting of the Swiss National Council and the Council of States, has been meeting here since the day before yesterday. The city of Berne has gone out of its way to give them brilliant and fascinating reception. There has been music, festive processions, illuminations, the boom of cannon and the peal of bells—nothing has been forgotten. The sessions began the day before yesterday. In the National Council, which is elected by universal suffrage and according to the number of inhabitants (Berne has returned 20 deputies, Zurich 12, the smallest cantons two or three), the great majority of deputies are liberals of a radical hue. The decidedly radical party is strongly represented, and the conservatives have only six or seven seats out of over a hundred. The Council of States, which is made up of two deputies from each canton and one deputy from each demicanton, on the whole resembles the last Diet as regards composition and character. The old cantons have once again returned several true separatists,[89] and as a result of the indirect elections, the reactionary element, though definitely in a minority, is nevertheless more strongly represented in this Council than it is in the National Council. As a matter of fact, by abolishing binding mandates[90] and invalidating half votes, the Council of States has been turned into a rejuvenated version of the Diet and has been pushed into the background by the creation of the National Council. It plays the thankless role of a senate or a chamber of peers, the role of heir to the mature wisdom and sober judgment of the forefathers, acting as a drag on the National Council which is assumed to be excessively fond of innovation. This dignified and sedate institution already shares the fate of similar bodies in England and America, and the now defunct one in France. Even before it has shown any signs of life it is looked down upon by the press and overshadowed by the National Council. Practically no one talks about the Council of States, and if it did make itself talked about it would be still worse for it.

Although the National Council is supposed to represent the entire Swiss "nation", it has already at its first session given proof of typically Swiss discord and hair-splitting, even if not of petty cantonal spirit. Three votes had to be taken to elect a president, although there were only three candidates with any serious chances, and all three of them from Berne. The three gentlemen in question were Ochsenbein, Funk and Neuhaus; the first two represent the moderate radical party of Berne, the third the moderate liberal, semi-conservative party. In the end Ochsenbein was elected by 50 votes out of 93, that is, with a very narrow majority. One can understand the Zurich and other *Moderados*[91] preferring the wise and very experienced Herr Neuhaus to Herr Ochsenbein, but the fact that Herr Funk, who represents exactly the same political colouring as Herr Ochsenbein, should have been put forward as a competing candidate and received support in two votings, shows how unorganised and undisciplined the parties still are. At any rate the election of Ochsenbein means that the Radicals gained a victory in the first contest of the parties. In the subsequent election of a vice-president, five votes had to be taken to produce an absolute majority. On the other hand, the staid and experienced Council of States almost unanimously elected the *Moderado* Furrer from Zurich as its president in the first round of voting. These two elections amply illustrate how different a spirit obtains in the two Chambers and that they will soon move in different directions and enter into conflict with each other.

The choice of a federal capital will be the next interesting issue to be debated. It will be interesting for the Swiss because the financial interests of many of them are involved, and interesting for people abroad because this debate will reveal most clearly to what extent the old parochial patriotism, the petty cantonal narrow-mindedness has been finished with. The competition is most intense between Berne, Zurich and Lucerne. Berne would like to see Zurich satisfied with the federal university, and Lucerne with the federal court of law, but in vain. Berne at any rate is the only suitable city, being the point where German and French Switzerland merge, the capital of the largest canton and the rising centre of the whole Swiss movement. But in order to become a real centre, Berne must also possess the university and the federal court. But try and explain that to the Swiss, whose fanaticism for their cantonal town has been roused! It is quite possible that the more radical National Council will vote for radical Berne, the sedate Council of States for the sedate, wise and prudent Zurich. An extremely difficult situation will then arise.

There has been considerable unrest in *Geneva* during the last three weeks. The reactionary patricians and bourgeois, who, from their villas, keep the villages around Geneva in almost feudal dependence, managed with the help of their peasants to push through all their three candidates in the elections to the National Council. But the [local] authorities declared the elections invalid, as more ballot-papers were returned than had been issued. Only this measure was able to pacify the revolutionary workers of Saint-Gervais, groups of whom were already marching through the streets and shouting "*Aux armes!*" The attitude of the workers in the course of the week that followed was so menacing that the bourgeois preferred not to vote at all rather than provoke a revolution with the inevitable scenes of horror; especially since the government threatened to resign if the reactionary candidates were once more elected. The Radicals meanwhile altered their list of candidates, to which they added some more moderate names, made up for lost canvassing time, and obtained 5,000 to 5,500 votes in the new elections, that is, almost a thousand more than the reactionaries had received in the previous round. The three reactionary candidates got hardly any votes; General Dufour, who received the highest number, managed to poll 1,500 votes. Elections to the Great Council were held a week later. The city elected 44 Radicals, and the countryside, which had to return 46 councillors, elected almost exclusively reactionaries. The *Revue de Genève*[92] is still arguing with the bourgeois papers as to whether all 46 are reactionary or half a dozen of them will vote for the Radical government. We shall soon know. Still greater confusion may reign in Geneva; for if the government, which is here elected directly by the people, is forced to resign, then a situation similar to that obtaining during the second elections to the National Council might easily result, and a Radical government would be confronted by a reactionary majority in the Great Council. It is moreover certain that the workers of Geneva are only waiting for an opportunity to secure the threatened gains of 1847[93] by a new revolution.

On the whole, compared with the early forties, Switzerland has made considerable progress. This is nowhere so striking as among the working class. Whereas this old spirit of parochial narrow-mindedness and pedantry still holds almost undivided sway among the bourgeoisie and especially in the old patrician families, or has, at best, assumed more modern forms, the Swiss workers have developed to a remarkable degree. Formerly they kept aloof from the Germans and displayed the most absurd "free Swiss" national arrogance, complained about the "foreign rogues" and showed no interest whatever in the contemporary movement. Now this has changed. Ever since working conditions have deteriorated, ever since Switzerland has been democratised, and especially since the minor riots have given place to European revolutions and battles such as those waged in Paris in June and in Vienna in October—ever since then the Swiss workers have been drawn more and more into the political and socialist movements, have fraternised with foreign workers, especially German workers, and have abandoned their "free Swiss attitude". In the French part of Switzerland and in many of her German districts, Germans and German Swiss are members of the same workers' association on an equal footing, and associations consisting mainly of Swiss workers have decided to join the proposed organisation of German Democratic Associations which has partially been set up. Whereas the extreme Radicals of official Switzerland dream at best of the one and indivisible Helvetian republic, Swiss workers often express the view that the whole of little Switzerland's independence will go to the dogs in the impending European storm. And this is said quite calmly and indifferently, without a word of regret, by these proletarian traitors! All the Swiss I have met expressed great sympathy for the Viennese, but among the workers it amounted to real fanaticism. No one speaks about the National Council, the Council of States, the riot of the priests in Fribourg,[94] but Vienna is on everybody's lips all day long. One would think that Vienna were again the capital of Switzerland as it was in the days before Wilhelm Tell, that Switzerland belonged again to Austria. Hundreds of rumours were bruited about, dilated upon, called in question, believed, refuted, and all possible aspects were thoroughly discussed. And when, at last, the news of the defeat of the heroic Viennese workers and students and of Windischgrätz's superior strength and barbarity was definitely confirmed, the effect on these Swiss workers was as great as though their own fate had been decided in Vienna and their own country had succumbed. Though this feeling is not yet a universal one, it is steadily gaining ground among the Swiss proletariat, and the fact that it already exists in many localities is, for a country like Switzerland, a great advance.

Written by Engels

Neue Rheinische Zeitung No. 143,
November 15, 1848

COUNTER-REVOLUTION IN BERLIN

[I]

Cologne, November 11. The *Pfuel cabinet* was a *"misunderstanding"*; its real meaning was the *Brandenburg cabinet*. The Pfuel cabinet was the *table of contents*, the Brandenburg cabinet the *content* itself.

Brandenburg in the Assembly and the Assembly in Brandenburg.[95]

Thus runs the epitaph of the House of Brandenburg.[96]

The Emperor Charles V was admired because he had had himself buried while still alive.[97] To have a bad joke engraved on one's tombstone is to go one better than Charles V and his criminal code.[98]

Brandenburg in the Assembly and the Assembly in Brandenburg!

A King of Prussia once put in an appearance in the Assembly. That was not the real Brandenburg. The Marquis of Brandenburg who appeared in the Assembly the day before yesterday was the real King of Prussia.

The guardroom in the Assembly, the Assembly in the guardroom—that means: *Brandenburg in the Assembly, the Assembly in Brandenburg!*

Or will the *Assembly in Brandenburg*—Berlin, as is well known, is situated in the Province of Brandenburg—be master of the *Brandenburg in the Assembly*? Will Brandenburg seek the protection of the Assembly as a Capet once did in another Assembly.[99]

Brandenburg in the Assembly and the Assembly in Brandenburg is an ambiguous expression, which is equivocal and portentous.

As we know, it is much easier for nations to get the better of *kings* than of *legislative assemblies*. History gives us a whole list of abortive revolts of the people against national assemblies. It knows only two important exceptions to this rule. The English people in the person of *Cromwell* dissolved the *Long Parliament*, and the French people in the person of *Bonaparte* dissolved the legislative body. But the Long Parliament had long ago become a *Rump*, and the legislative body a *corpse*.

Have the *kings* been more fortunate in their *revolts against legislative assemblies* than the people?

Charles I, James II, Louis XVI, and Charles X are hardly promising progenitors.

There are luckier ancestors in *Spain* and *Italy* however. And recently in *Vienna*?

But one must not forget that a *Congress of Nations* was in session in Vienna and that the *representatives of the Slavs*, apart from the Poles, went over to the imperial camp with flying colours.[100]

The struggle of the camarilla in Vienna against the Diet was at the same time a struggle of the *Slav* Diet against the *German* Diet. It was not *Slavs*, however, who seceded in the Berlin Assembly, it was *slaves*, and slaves do not constitute a party; at best they are camp-followers of a party. The members of the Right[101] who left the Berlin Assembly have not strengthened the enemy camp, they have infected it with a fatal malady called *treason*.

The *Slav* party *carried the day* in Austria together with the camarilla. It will now *fight* the camarilla over the spoils. If the Berlin camarilla wins it will not have to share the victory with the *Right* or to defend it against the *Right*; the Right will be given a *tip*—and *kicks*.

The Prussian Crown is *right* when it confronts the Assembly as an *absolute Crown*. But the Assembly is *wrong* because it does not confront the Crown as an *absolute assembly*. To begin with it should have *arrested* the ministers as *traitors, traitors to the sovereignty of the people*. It should have *proscribed* and *outlawed* all officials who obey orders others than those of the Assembly.

But the *political* weakness characterising the actions of the National Assembly in *Berlin* may become a source of *civic* strength in the *provinces*.

The bourgeoisie would have liked to transform the *feudal monarchy* into a *bourgeois monarchy by peaceful* means. After depriving the feudal party of armorial bearings and titles, which are offensive to its civic pride, and of the dues appertaining to feudal property, which violate the bourgeois mode of appropriation, the bourgeoisie would have liked to unite with the feudal party and together with it enslave the people. But the old bureaucracy does not want to be reduced to the status of a servant of a bourgeoisie for whom, until now, it had been a despotic tutor. The feudal party does not want to see its marks of distinction and interests burnt at the altar of the bourgeoisie. Finally, the Crown sees in the elements of the old feudal society—a society of which it is the crowning excrescence—its true, native social ground, whereas it regards the bourgeoisie as alien artificial soil which bears it only under the condition that it withers away.

The bourgeoisie turns the intoxicating *"divine right"* into a sober *legal title*, the rule of blood into the rule of paper, the royal sun into a plebeian gas lamp.

Royalty, therefore, was not taken in by the bourgeoisie. Its reply to the partial revolution of the bourgeoisie was a full-fledged counter-revolution. Its cry: *Brandenburg in the Assembly and the Assembly in Brandenburg* drove the bourgeoisie once more into the *arms of the revolution, into the arms of the people.*

While admitting that we do not expect the bourgeoisie to answer in a manner befitting the occasion, we must say, on the other hand, that in its rebellion against the National Assembly the Crown, too, resorts to hypocritical half measures and hides its head under the constitutional veil at the very moment when it tries to cast off this irksome veil.

Brandenburg makes the *German central authority give* him the *order* for his *coup d'état. The regiments of the Guards marched into Berlin by order of the central authority.* The Berlin counter-revolution is carried out by order of the German central authority. Brandenburg orders the Frankfurt [Assembly] to give him this order. It denies its sovereignty at the very moment when it wants to establish it. Herr Bassermann of course jumped at the opportunity to play the servant as master. But he has the satisfaction of seeing the master in his turn play the servant.

Whatever the outcome in Berlin may be, the *dilemma* is: either the *King* or the *people*, and with the cry, *Brandenburg in the Assembly and the Assembly in Brandenburg*, the people will be victorious.

We may have to go through a hard school, but it is a preparatory school for a *full-fledged revolution*.

[II]

Cologne, November 11. *European revolution* is taking a *circular course*. It started in Italy and assumed a European character in Paris; the first repercussion of the February revolution followed in Vienna; the repercussion of the Viennese revolution took place in Berlin. European *counterrevolution* struck its first blow in Italy, at Naples; it assumed a European character in Paris in June; the first repercussion of the June counter-revolution followed in Vienna; it comes to a close and discredits itself in Berlin. *The crowing of the Gallic cock in Paris will once again rouse Europe.*

But in *Berlin the counter-revolution is bringing itself into disrepute. Everything becomes disreputable in Berlin, even counter-revolution.*

In *Naples* the lazzaroni are leagued with the monarchy against the bourgeoisie.

In *Paris* the greatest struggle ever known in history is taking place. The bourgeoisie is leagued with the lazzaroni against the working class.

In *Vienna* we have a flock of nationalities who imagine that the counter-revolution will bring them emancipation. In addition—the secret spite of the bourgeoisie against the workers and the Academic Legion; discord within the Civil Guard itself; finally, attacks by the people supplying a pretext for the attacks by the Court.

Nothing like that is happening in Berlin. The bourgeoisie and the people are on one side and the drill-sergeants on the other.

Wrangel and *Brandenburg*, two men who have no head,

no heart, no opinions, nothing but moustaches*—such is the antithesis of the querulous, self-opinionated, irresolute National Assembly.

Will-power—be it even that of an ass, an ox, a police-man—is all that is needed to tackle the weak-willed grumblers of the March revolution. And the *Prussian Court, which has just as little will-power as the National Assembly,* seeks out the *two most stupid men* in the monarchy and tells these lions: *represent will-power.* Pfuel still had a few grains of brain. But *absolute stupidity* makes even the grumblers of the March achievements flinch.

> *"With stupidity the gods themselves struggle in vain,"*[102]

exclaims the perplexed National Assembly.

These Wrangels and Brandenburgs, these blockheads who can *want* because they have no will of their own, because they only want what they are *ordered,* and who are too stupid to question the orders they are given with a faltering voice and trembling lips—they, too, have *discredited* themselves because they did not get down to *skull-breaking,* the only job these *battering-rams* are good for.

Wrangel does not go beyond confessing that he recognises only a National Assembly that obeys orders. *Brandenburg* is given a lesson in parliamentary behaviour, and after having shocked the Chamber with his crude, repulsive jargon appropriate to a drill-sergeant, he allows the National Assembly "to tyrannise the tyrant" and carries out its orders by humbly *begging* for permission to speak, though he had just attempted to *usurp* this right.

> *I had rather be a tick in a sheep*
> *Than such a valiant ignorance.*[103]

Berlin's calm attitude *delights* us; the ideals of the Prussian drill-sergeants prove unavailing against it.

But the National Assembly? Why does it not use its power to proscribe? Why does it not outlaw the Wrangels? Why does not one of the deputies step into the midst of Wrangel's bayonets to outlaw him and address the soldiers?

---

* The term *"Schnurrbart"* (moustache) in eighteenth-century student slang stood also for policeman.—*Ed.*

Let the Berlin National Assembly turn over the leaves of the *Moniteur*,[104] the *Moniteur* for 1789-95.

And what should *we* do at the present time?

We should refuse to pay taxes. A Wrangel and a Brandenburg understand—for these creatures learn Arabic from the Hyghlans[105]—that they wear a sword and get a uniform and a salary. But *where* the sword, the uniform and the salary come from—that they do not understand.

There is only one means for securing the defeat of the monarchy, and that is to do it before the *advent of the anti-June revolution*, which will take place *in Paris* in December.[106]

The monarchy defies not only the people, but the bourgeoisie as well.

Defeat it therefore in a bourgeois manner.

How can one defeat the monarchy in a bourgeois manner?

By starving it into surrender.

And how can one starve it into surrender?

By refusing to pay taxes.

Consider it well. No princes of Prussia, no Brandenburgs and Wrangels produce the *bread for the army*. It is you who produce even the bread for the army.

[III]

Cologne, November 13. Just as once the French National Assembly, on finding its official meeting place closed, had to hold its session in the *tennis-court*, so now the Prussian National Assembly has to meet in the *shooting-gallery*.[107]

A resolution passed in the shooting-gallery declares *Brandenburg a traitor*. The text, as received from our Berlin correspondent (who signs his articles ⊙), is contained in our special edition issued this morning, but it is not mentioned in the report published in the *Kölnische Zeitung*.[108]

However, we have just received a letter from a *member of the National Assembly* in which he writes:

"*The National Assembly (i.e., 242 members) unanimously declared that by introducing this measure (dissolution of the Civil Guard) Brandenburg has committed high treason, and every person who actively or passively assists in carrying through this measure is to be regarded as a traitor."*

Dumont's reliability is well known.

Since the National Assembly has declared *Brandenburg a traitor*, the *obligation to pay taxes* ceases *automatically. No taxes are due to a government that commits high treason.* Tomorrow we shall tell our readers in greater detail *how in England, the oldest constitutional country*, a *refusal to pay taxes* operated during a similar conflict.[109] Incidentally, the *traitorous government itself* has shown the people the right way *when it immediately refused to pay taxes* (allowances, etc.) to *the National Assembly* in order to *starve it into submission.*

The aforementioned deputy writes further:

"The Civil Guard will not hand over their arms."

A fight therefore seems inevitable, and it is the *duty of the Rhineland to hasten to the assistance of the Berlin National Assembly with men and weapons.*

Written by Marx

Neue Rheinische Zeitung Nos. 141, 141 (second edition) and 142, November 12 and 14, 1848

6*

APPEAL
OF THE DEMOCRATIC DISTRICT COMMITTEE
OF THE RHINE PROVINCE[110]

Proclamation

Cologne, November 14. The Rhenish District Committee of Democrats calls upon all democratic associations in the Rhine Province immediately to convene their associations and organise everywhere popular meetings in order to encourage the entire population of the Rhine Province to refuse to pay taxes, since this is the most effective measure of protest against the arbitrary acts committed by the government against the assembly of Prussian elected representatives.

It is necessary to advise against any violent resistance in the case of taxes collected under a writ of execution, but it can be recommended that at public sales people should refrain from bidding.

In order to agree on further measures, the District Committee is of the opinion that a congress of deputies from all associations should be held, and herewith invites them to meet on Thursday, November 23, at 9 a.m. (in Eiser's Hall, Komödienstrasse, Cologne).

Cologne, November 14, 1848

For the District Committee
Karl Marx   *Schneider II*

Neue Rheinische Zeitung No. 143,
November 15, 1848

IMPEACHMENT OF THE GOVERNMENT

The town of Brandenburg refuses to have anything to do with the Brandenburg cabinet and has sent a letter of thanks to the National Assembly.

Statements issued throughout the country recognise only the government of the National Assembly.

The cabinet has again committed high treason by defying the Habeas Corpus Act[111] and proclaiming a state of siege without the assent of the National Assembly and by expelling the National Assembly from the shooting-gallery at the point of the bayonet.

The seat of the National Assembly is the people and not this or that heap of stones. If it is driven out of Berlin it will meet elsewhere, in Breslau, Cologne, or any other place it thinks fit. It has declared this in the resolution it passed on the 13th.

The Berliners scoff at the state of siege and are in no way intimidated by it. Nobody is handing over his arms.

Armed men from various parts of the country are hurrying to the assistance of the National Assembly.

The Guard regiments have refused to obey orders. More and more soldiers are fraternising with the people.

Silesia and Thuringia are in revolt.

We, however, appeal to you, citizens—send money to the democratic Central Committee in Berlin. But pay no taxes to the counter-revolutionary government. The National Assembly has declared that refusal to pay taxes is justified in law. It has not yet passed a resolution on this out of consideration for the civil servants. A *starvation diet* will make these officials realise the power of the citizenry and will make good citizens of them.

Starve the enemy and refuse to pay taxes! Nothing is sillier than to supply a traitorous government with the means to fight the nation, and the means of all means is *money*.

Written by Marx
on November 15, 1848

Neue Rheinische Zeitung No. 143
(special edition),
November 15, 1848

NO TAX PAYMENTS!

Cologne, November 16. All the Berlin newspapers, with the exception of the *Preussische Staats-Anzeiger*,[112] *Vossische Zeitung*,[113] and *Neue Preussische Zeitung*,[114] have failed to arrive.

The Civil Guard in the wealthy south-western district of Berlin has been disarmed, but only there. It is the same battalion that dastardly murdered the engineering workers on October 31.[115] The disarming of this battalion strengthens the popular cause.

The National Assembly was again driven out of the Köllnische Rathaus[116] by force of arms. It assembled then in the Mielenz Hotel, where finally it unanimously (by *226 votes*) passed the following resolution on the *non-payment of taxes*:

"*So long as the National Assembly is not at liberty to continue its sessions in Berlin, the Brandenburg cabinet has no right to dispose of government revenues and to collect taxes.*

"*This decree comes into force on November 17.*

The National Assembly, November 15."

From today, therefore, taxes are abolished! It is high treason to pay taxes. Refusal to pay taxes is the primary duty of the citizen!

Written by Marx

Neue Rheinische Zeitung No. 145
(special supplement),
November 17, 1848

APPEAL[117]

Cologne, November 18. The Rhenish District Committee of Democrats calls upon all democratic associations in the Rhine Province to have the following measures decided upon and carried through:

1. Since the Prussian National Assembly itself has ruled that taxes are not to be paid, their forcible collection must be resisted everywhere and in every way.

2. In order to repulse the enemy the local militia must be organised everywhere. The cost of weapons and ammunition for impecunious citizens is to be defrayed by the community or by voluntary contributions.

3. The authorities are to be asked everywhere to state publicly whether they recognise the decisions of the National Assembly and intend to carry them out. In case of refusal committees of public safety are to be set up, and where possible this should be done with the consent of the local councils. Local councils opposed to the Legislative Assembly should be re-elected by a universal vote.

Cologne, November 18

For the Rhenish District Committee of Democrats
Karl Marx   Karl Schapper   Schneider II

Neue Rheinische Zeitung No. 147
(second edition),
November 19, 1848

THE ASSEMBLY AT FRANKFURT

Cologne, November 22. The resolution of the Berlin Assembly regarding the refusal to pay taxes has been declared unlawful and void by the Frankfurt Parliament. It has thus sided with Brandenburg, with Wrangel, with specific Prussianism. Frankfurt has moved to Berlin, and Berlin to Frankfurt. The German Parliament is in Berlin, and the Prussian Parliament in Frankfurt. The Prussian Parliament has become a German Parliament, and the German one has become Brandenburg's Prussian Parliament. Prussia was to have merged into Germany, now the German Parliament at Frankfurt wants Germany to be merged into Prussia.

German Parliament! Whoever spoke of a German Parliament after the grave events in Berlin and Vienna. After the death of Robert Blum no one gave another thought to the life of the noble Gagern. Who cared a hang about a Schmerling after the setting up of the Brandenburg-Manteuffel ministry! The professors who "made history" for their own amusement had to allow the shelling of Vienna, the murder of Robert Blum and the barbarity of Windischgrätz! The gentlemen who were so greatly concerned about the cultural history of Germany left the practical application of culture in the hands of a Jellachich and his Croats! While the professors were evolving the theory of history, history ran its stormy course without bothering about the professorial history.

The resolution passed the day before yesterday has destroyed the Frankfurt Parliament. The resolution has driven it into the arms of the traitor Brandenburg. The Parliament at Frankfurt is guilty of high treason, it must be brought to trial. If a whole people rises to protest against an arbitrary act of a king, and if this protest is made in an entirely legal way—by refusing to pay taxes—and an assembly of professors declares—without being at all competent to do so—that the refusal to pay taxes, this revolt of the whole people, is unlawful, then this assembly places itself outside the law, it commits high treason.

It is the duty of all members of the Frankfurt Assembly who voted against this resolution to resign from this "deceased Federal Diet". It is the duty of all democrats to elect these resigned "Prussians" to the German National Assembly at Berlin in place of the "Germans" who have left. The National Assembly in Berlin is not a "fragment", it is a complete entity, for it constitutes a quorum. But the Brandenburg Assembly at Frankfurt will become a "fragment", for the inevitable resignation of the 150 deputies will surely be followed by many others who do not wish to set up a Federal Diet at Frankfurt. The Frankfurt Parliament! It fears a red republic and decrees a *red monarchy*. We do not want a *red* monarchy, we do not want the crimson crown of Austria to extend its sway over Prussia, and we therefore declare that the German Parliament is guilty of high treason. Nay, we do it too much honour; we impute to it a political importance which it has long since lost. The severest judgment has already been passed upon it—disregard of its rulings and total oblivion.

Written by Marx

Neue Rheinische Zeitung No. 150,
November 23, 1848

THE REVOLUTIONARY MOVEMENT IN ITALY

Cologne, November 29. After six months of democracy's almost uninterrupted defeats, after a series of unprecedented triumphs for the counter-revolution, there are at last indications of an approaching victory of the revolutionary party. Italy, the country whose uprising was the prelude to the European uprising of 1848 and whose collapse was the prelude to the fall of Vienna—Italy rises for the second time. Tuscany has succeeded in establishing a democratic government, and Rome has just won a similar government for itself.

London, April 10; Paris, May 15 and June 25; Milan, August 6; Vienna, November 1[118]—these are the four important dates of the European counter-revolution, the four milestones marking the stages of its latest triumphal march.

Not only was the revolutionary power of the Chartists broken in *London on April 10,* but the *revolutionary propaganda impact of the February victory was* for the first time *broken.* Those who correctly assess the position of England and the role she plays in modern history were not surprised that the continental revolutions passed over her without leaving a trace for the time being. England, a country which, through her industry and commerce, dominates all those revolutionary nations of the Continent and nevertheless remains relatively independent of her customers because she dominates the Asian, American and Australian markets; a country in which the contradictions of present-day bourgeois society, the class struggle of the bourgeoisie and the proletariat, are most strongly developed and are most acute, England more than any other country follows her own, independent, course of development. The fumbling approach of continental provisional governments to the solution of problems and the abolition of contradictions is not required in England, for *she* is more competent in dealing with and solving them than any other country. England does not accept the revolution of the Continent; when the time comes England will *prescribe the revolution to the Continent*. That is England's position and the necessary consequence of her position, and hence the victory of "order" on April 10 was quite understandable. But who does not remember that this victory of "order", this first counter-blow to the blows of February and March, gave fresh support to the counter-revolution everywhere and raised daring hopes in the hearts of those known as conservatives. Who does not remember that everywhere throughout Germany the action of London's special constables was immediately accepted as a model by the entire Civil Guard. Who does not remember the impression made by this first proof that the movement which had broken out was not unconquerable,

On *May 15, Paris* promptly provided its counterpart to the victory of the English party that wants to maintain the status quo. The outermost waves of the revolutionary flood were stemmed on April 10; on May 15 its force was broken at its very source. April 10 demonstrated that the February movement was not irresistible; May 15 demonstrated that the insurrection could be checked in Paris. The revolution defeated at its centre was of course bound to succumb at the periphery as well. And this happened to an increasing extent in Prussia and the smaller German states. But the revolutionary current was still strong enough to secure two victories of the people in Vienna, the first also on May 15, the second on May 26, while the victory of absolutism in Naples, likewise won on May 15, acted because of its excesses rather as a counterbalance to the victory of order in Paris. Something was still missing, though. Not only had the revolutionary movement to be defeated in Paris, but armed insurrection had to be divested of the spell of its invincibility in Paris itself; only then could the counter-revolution feel safe.

And that happened at *Paris* in a battle lasting four days,

from *June* 23 to 26. Four days of gun-fire put an end to the impregnability of the barricades and the invincibility of the armed people. What did Cavaignac demonstrate by his victory if not that the laws of warfare are more or less the same in a street and in a défilé, when faced by a barricade or by an entanglement or bastion? That 40,000 undisciplined armed workers, without guns or howitzers and without deliveries of ammunition, can withstand a well-organised army of 120,000 experienced soldiers and 150,000 men of the National Guard supported by the best and most numerous artillery and abundantly supplied with ammunition for no more than four days? Cavaignac's victory was the most brutal suppression of the smaller force by a force numerically seven times as big; it was the most inglorious victory ever won, the more inglorious for the blood that it cost despite the overwhelmingly superior forces. Nevertheless it was regarded with amazement as if it were a wonder, for this victory won by superior forces divested the people of Paris and the Paris barricades of the aura of invincibility. By defeating 40,000 workers, Cavaignac's 300,000 men defeated not only the 40,000 workers, but, without realising it, defeated the European revolution. We all know that from that day an impetuous storm of reaction set in. There was nothing now to restrain it; the people of Paris were defeated with shell and grape-shot by conservative forces, and what could be done in Paris could be repeated elsewhere. Nothing remained to democracy after this decisive defeat but to make as honourable a retreat as possible and defend its positions foot by foot in the press, at public meetings and in parliaments—positions which could no longer be held.

The next great blow was the *fall of Milan*. The recapture of Milan by Radetzky was indeed the first European event following the June victory in Paris. The double-headed eagle on the spire of the Milan Cathedral signified not only the fall of Italy as a whole, it also signified the restoration of *Austria*, the restoration of the stronghold of European counter-revolution. Italy crushed and Austria resurrected—what more could the counter-revolution demand! Indeed, with the fall of Milan there was a slackening of revolutionary energy in Italy for a time, Mamiani was over-thrown in Rome, the democrats were defeated in Piedmont; and simultaneously the reactionary party raised its head again in Austria and from its centre, Radetzky's headquart-ers, it began with renewed courage to spread the net of its intrigues over all provinces. Only then did Jellachich assume the offensive, only then was the great alliance of the counter-revolution with the Austrian Slavs completed.

I say nothing of the brief intermezzi in which the counter-revolution gained local victories and conquered separate provinces, of the setback in Frankfurt, and so on. They are of local, perhaps national, but not European significance.

Finally, the work that was begun on the day of Custozza[119] was completed on November 1—just as Radetzky had marched into Milan so did Windischgrätz and Jellachich march into Vienna. Cavaignac's method was employed, and employed successfully, against the largest and most active focus of German revolution. The revolution in Vienna, like that in Paris, was smothered in blood and smoking ruins.

But it almost seems as if the victory of November 1 also marks the moment when the retrogressive movement reaches the turning point and a crisis occurs. The attempt step by step to repeat the bold exploit of Vienna in Prussia has failed. Even if the country should forsake the Constituent Assembly, the most the Crown can expect is merely a partial victory which will decide nothing, and at any rate the first discouraging effect of the Viennese defeat has been miti-gated by the crude attempt to copy it in every detail.

While Northern Europe has either been forced back again into the servitude of 1847 or is struggling to make safe the gains won during the first months against the at-tacks of the counter-revolution, Italy is suddenly rising again. Leghorn, the only Italian city which the fall of Milan spurred on to a victorious revolution, Leghorn has at last imparted its democratic élan to the whole of Tuscany and has succeeded in setting up a radically democratic cabinet, more radical than any that ever existed under a monarchy, and more radical even than many a government formed in a republic. This government responded to the fall of Vienna and the restoration of Austria by proclaiming an Italian

Constituent Assembly. The revolutionary fire-brand which this democratic government has thus hurled into the midst of the Italian people has kindled a fire: in Rome the people, the National Guard and the army have risen to a man, have overthrown the evasive, counter-revolutionary cabinet and secured a democratic cabinet, and first among the demands they succeeded in putting through is a government based on the principle of Italian nationality, namely, the sending of delegates to the Italian Constituent Assembly as proposed by Guerazzi.

Piedmont and Sicily will undoubtedly follow suit. They will follow just as they did last year.

And then? Will this second resurrection of Italy within three years—like the preceding one—herald the dawn of a new upsurge of European democracy? It almost looks as if it will. For the time of counter-revolution has expired. France is about to throw herself into the arms of an adventurer in order to escape the rule of Cavaignac and Marrast; Germany is more divided than ever; Austria is overwhelmed; Prussia is on the eve of civil war. All the illusions of February and March have been ruthlessly crushed beneath the swift tread of history. Indeed, the people have nothing more to learn from any further victories of the counter-revolution!

It is up to the people, when the occasion arises, to apply the lessons of the past six months *at the right moment* and *fearlessly*.

Written by Marx
Neue Rheinische Zeitung No. 156,
November 30, 1848

THE COUP D'ÉTAT
OF THE COUNTER-REVOLUTION

Cologne, December 7. *The National Assembly has been dissolved. The representatives of the people have been dispersed "by the grace of God".*

The reason given by the government for this act of violence adds bitter contempt to the coup d'état carried through with such insolence.[120]

The National Assembly now reaps the fruits of its perennial weakness and cowardice. For months it allowed the conspiracy against the people to do its work unmolested, to grow strong and powerful, and hence it has now become its first victim.

The people, too, is now suffering for its sins, committed out of magnanimity, or rather stupidity, in March and even in April and May, and finally for its so-called "passive resistance". It is now to be hoped that it has learned its lesson. Its next victory will put an end to the policy of "agreement" and to all other phrases and hypocrisies.

Written by Marx

Neue Rheinische Zeitung No. 163,
December 8, 1848

THE BOURGEOISIE
AND THE COUNTER-REVOLUTION

[I]

Cologne, December 9. We have never concealed the fact that we do not proceed from a *legal basis*, but from a *revolutionary basis*. Now the government has for its part abandoned the false pretence of a legal basis. It has taken its stand on a revolutionary basis, for the *counter-revolutionary* basis, too, is *revolutionary*.

§ 6 of the law of April 6, 1848, ordains:

"The right to approve all *laws* as well as to determine the national budget and to pass *taxes* must in any case belong to the future representatives of the people."

§ 13 of the law of April 8, 1848, reads:

"The Assembly convened on the basis of this law is called upon *to establish* the *future Constitution* by agreement with the Crown and during its lifetime to exercise the prerogatives of the former Imperial Diet, in particular regarding the passing of taxes."

The government sends this Assembly of conciliators to the devil, imposes a so-called constitution[121] upon the country and levies taxes which the representatives of the people had refused to grant it.

The Camphausen epic, a sort of pompous *legal Jobsiad,*[122] was brought to an abrupt end by the Prussian government. In retaliation the great *Camphausen*, the author of this epic, continues coolly to deliberate in Frankfurt as envoy of this same Prussian government, and goes on scheming with the Bassermanns in the interests of that same Prussian government. This Camphausen, who invented the theory of agreement in order to preserve the legal basis, that is, in order first of all to cheat the revolution of the respect that is due to it, at the same time invented the mines which were later to blow up the legal basis together with the theory of agreement.

This man provided for *indirect* elections, which produced an assembly to which, at a moment of sudden revolt, the government could shout: *Trop tard!* He recalled the Prince of Prussia, the head of the counter-revolution, and even resorted to an official lie to transform Prince's flight into an educational journey.[123] He abolished neither the old Prussian laws dealing with political crimes nor the old courts. Under his government the old bureaucracy and the old army gained time to recover from their fright and to reorganise their whole structure. All the leading personalities of the old regime were left untouched in their positions. Under Camphausen the camarilla carried on a war in Poznan, while he himself carried on a war in Denmark. The Danish war was intended as a channel to draw off the superabundant patriotism[124] of the German youth, on whom after their return the police inflicted fitting disciplinary punishment. This war was to give some popularity to General Wrangel and his infamous regiments of the Guards and in general to rehabilitate the Prussian army. This purpose achieved, the sham war had to be ended at any price by a disgraceful armistice, which was once again negotiated at Frankfurt between the same Camphausen and the German National Assembly. The outcome of the Danish war was the appointment of the *"Commander-in-Chief of the two Brandenburgs"*[125] and the return to Berlin of the regiments of the Guards which had been driven out in March.

And the war which the Potsdam camarilla waged in *Poznan* under the auspices of Camphausen!

The war in Poznan was more than a war against the Prussian revolution. It was the fall of Vienna, the fall of Italy, the defeat of the heroes of June. It was the first decisive victory gained by the Russian Tsar over the European revolution. And all this was done under the auspices of the great *Camphausen*, the thinking friend of history,[126] the knight of the great debate, the champion of negotiation.

Under *Camphausen* and with his help the counter-revolution seized all important positions; it prepared an army ready for action while the Assembly of conciliators debated.

Under *Hansemann-Pinto*,[127] the Minister of Action, the old police force was fitted out with new uniforms, and the bourgeoisie waged a war—as bitter as it was petty—against the people. The conclusion from these premises was drawn under *Brandenburg*'s rule. The only things needed for this were a moustache and sword instead of a head.

When Camphausen resigned we exclaimed:

He has sown reaction as interpreted by the bourgeoisie, he will reap reaction as interpreted by the aristocracy and absolutism.

We have no doubt that His Excellency, the Prussian envoy *Camphausen*, at this moment regards himself a feudal lord and has come to a peaceable agreement with his "misunderstanding".

One should not, however, commit the error of ascribing initiatives of world historical significance to such mediocrities as a Camphausen and a Hansemann. They were nothing but the instruments of a class. Their language, their actions, were merely the official echo of the class which brought them to the forefront. They were simply the big bourgeoisie placed in the forefront.

The members of this class formed the *liberal opposition* in the late *United Provincial Diet* of blessed memory, which Camphausen resurrected for a moment.

The gentlemen of this liberal opposition have been reproached with having deserted their principles after the March revolution. This is a fallacy.

The big landowners and capitalists—and they were the only ones to be represented in the United Provincial Diet— in short the money-bags, became wealthier and more educated. With the development of bourgeois society in Prussia, in other words, with the development of industry, trade and agriculture, the old class distinctions had, on the one hand, lost their material basis.

The aristocracy itself was largely bourgeoisified. Instead of dealing in loyalty, love and faith, it now dealt primarily in beetroot, liquor and wool. Its tournaments were held on the wool market. On the other hand, the absolutist state, which in the course of development lost its old social basis, became a restrictive fetter for the new bourgeois society with its changed mode of production and its changed requirements. The bourgeoisie had to claim its share of political power, if only by reason of its material interests. Only the bourgeoisie itself could legally assert its commercial and industrial requirements. It had to wrest the administration of these, its "most sacred interests" from the hands of an antiquated bureaucracy which was both ignorant and arrogant. It had to demand control over the national wealth, whose creator it considered itself. Having deprived the bureaucracy of the monopoly of so-called education and conscious of the fact that it possesses a far superior knowledge of the real requirements of bourgeois society, the bourgeoisie had also the ambition to secure for itself a political status in keeping with its social status. To attain this aim it had to be able freely to debate its own interests and views and the actions of the government. It called this *"freedom of the press"*. The bourgeoisie had to be able to *enter* freely into *associations*. It called this the *"right of free association"*. As the necessary consequence of *free competition*, it had likewise to demand *religious liberty* and so on. Before March 1848 the Prussian bourgeoisie was rapidly moving towards the realisation of all its aims.

The Prussian state was in financial difficulties. Its borrowing power was exhausted. This was the secret reason for the convocation of the United Provincial Diet. Although the government struggled against its fate and ungraciously dissolved the United Provincial Diet, lack of money and of credit facilities would inevitably have driven it gradually into the arms of the bourgeoisie. Those who are kings by the grace of God have always bartered their privileges for hard cash, as did the feudal barons. The first great act of this historic deal in all Christian Germanic states was the emancipation of the serfs; the second act was the constitutional monarchy. *"L'argent n'a pas de maître"*, but the *maîtres* cease to be *maîtres* as soon as they are demonetised.

And so the liberal opposition in the United Provincial Diet was simply the bourgeoisie in opposition to a political form that was no longer appropriate to its interests and needs. In order to oppose the Court, the bourgeoisie had to court the people.

It may have really imagined that its opposition was *for* the people.

Obviously, the rights and liberties which the bourgeoisie sought *for itself* could be demanded from the government only under the slogan: *popular rights* and *popular liberties*.

This opposition, as we have said, was rapidly moving towards its goal when the *February storm* broke.

[II]

Cologne, December 11. When the March flood—a flood in miniature—subsided it left on the surface of Berlin no prodigies, no revolutionary giants, but traditional creatures, thickset bourgeois figures—the liberals of the United Provincial Diet, the representatives of the conscious Prussian bourgeoisie. The main contingents for the new ministries were supplied by the *Rhineland* and *Silesia*, the provinces with the most advanced bourgeoisie. They were followed by a whole train of Rhenish lawyers. As the bourgeoisie was pushed into the background by the feudal aristocracy, the Rhineland and Silesia were replaced in the cabinets by the old Prussian provinces. The only link of the Brandenburg cabinet with the Rhineland is through a single Elberfeld Tory. *Hansemann* and *von der Heydt!* These two names exemplify the whole difference between March and December 1848 for the Prussian bourgeoisie.

The Prussian bourgeoisie reached the political summit, not by means of a *peaceful deal with the Crown*, as it had desired, but as the result of a *revolution*. It was to defend, not its own interests, but *those of the people*—for a *popular movement* had prepared the way for the bourgeoisie—against the Crown, in other words, against *itself*. For the bourgeoisie regarded the Crown simply as a cloak provided by the grace of God, a cloak that was to conceal its own profane interests. The inviolability of *its* own interests and of the political forms appropriate to these interests, expressed in constitutional language, is *inviolability of the Crown*. Hence the enthusiasm of the German bourgeoisie and in particular of the Prussian bourgeoisie for the *constitutional monarchy*. Although the February revolution together with its repercussions in Germany was welcomed by the Prussian bourgeoisie, because the revolution had placed the helm of state into its hands, it also upset the plans of the bourgeoisie, because its rule was thus bound by conditions which it neither wanted nor was able to fulfil.

The bourgeoisie did not raise a finger; it simply allowed the people to fight for it. Hence the rule it was called upon to exercise was not the rule of a commander who has defeated his adversary, but the rule of a committee of public safety which has been entrusted by the victorious people with the protection of its interests.

Camphausen was still clearly aware of this embarrassing position, and the weakness of his cabinet was entirely due to this feeling and the circumstances that gave rise to it. Even the most shameless actions of his government are therefore tinctured by a sort of shamefaced blush. Open *shamelessness* and *insolence* were *Hansemann*'s privileges. The red *complexion* is all that distinguishes these two artists from one another.

The *March revolution in Prussia* should not be confused either with the *English* revolution of 1648 or with the *French* one of 1789.

In 1648 the bourgeoisie was allied with the modern aristocracy against the monarchy, the feudal aristocracy and the established church.

In 1789 the bourgeoisie was allied with the people against the monarchy, the aristocracy and the established church.

The model for the revolution of 1789 (at least in Europe) was only the revolution of 1648; that for the revolution of 1648 only the revolt of the Netherlands against Spain.[128] Both revolutions were a century ahead of their model not only in time but also in substance.

In both revolutions the bourgeoisie was the class that *really* headed the movement. The *proletariat* and the *non-bourgeois strata of the middle class* had either not yet evolved interests which were different from those of the bourgeoisie or they did not yet constitute independent classes or class divisions. Therefore, where they opposed the bourgeoisie, as they did in France in 1793 and 1794, they fought only for the attainment of the aims of the bourgeoisie, albeit in a non-bourgeois *manner*. The *entire French terrorism* was just a *plebeian way* of dealing with the *enemies of the bourgeoisie,* absolutism, feudalism and philistinism.

The revolutions of 1648 and 1789 were not *English* and *French* revolutions, they were revolutions in the *European* fashion. They did not represent the victory of a *particular* social class over the *old political system*; they *proclaimed the political system of the new European society.* The bourgeoisie was victorious in these revolutions, but the *victory of the bourgeoisie* was at that time the *victory of a new social order*, the victory of bourgeois ownership over feudal ownership, of nationality over provincialism, of competition over the guild, of partitioning [of the land] over primogeniture, of the rule of the landowner over the domination of the owner by the land, of enlightenment over superstition, of the family over the family name, of industry over heroic idleness, of bourgeois law over medieval privileges. The revolution of 1648 was the victory of the seventeenth century over the sixteenth century; the revolution of 1789 was the victory of the eighteenth century over the seventeenth. These revolutions reflected the needs of the world at that time rather than the needs of those parts of the world where they occurred, that is, England and France.

There has been nothing of this in the *Prussian March revolution.*

The February revolution actually *abolished* the constitutional monarchy and nominally *abolished* the rule of the bourgeoisie. The Prussian March revolution ought to have nominally *established* a constitutional monarchy and actually *established* the rule of the bourgeoisie. Far from being a *European revolution* it was merely a weak repercussion of a European revolution in a backward country. Instead of being ahead of its century, it was over half a century behind its time. From the very outset it was a *secondary* phenomenon, and it is well known that secondary diseases are harder to cure and are liable to cause more harm than the primary diseases do. It was not a question of establishing a new society, but of resurrecting in Berlin a society that had expired in Paris. The Prussian March revolution was not even a *national, German* revolution; from the very start it was a *provincial Prussian* revolution. In Vienna, Cassel, Munich and various other towns provincial uprisings took place alongside it and competed with it.

Whereas 1648 and 1789 gained boundless self-confidence from the knowledge that they were leading the universe, it was the ambition of the Berlin [revolution] of 1848 to constitute an anachronism. Its light is like that of the stars which reaches us, the inhabitants of the Earth, only after the bodies from which it had emanated have been extinct for a hundred thousand years. The March revolution in Prussia was, on a small scale—just as it did everything on a small scale—such a star for Europe. Its light was that of a social body which had long since disintegrated.

The German bourgeoisie developed so sluggishly, timidly and slowly that at the moment when it menacingly confronted feudalism and absolutism, it saw menacingly pitted against itself the proletariat and all sections of the middle class whose interests and ideas were related to those of the proletariat. The German bourgeoisie found not just one class *behind* it, but all Europe hostilely *facing* it. Unlike the French bourgeoisie of 1789, the Prussian bourgeoisie, when it confronted monarchy and aristocracy, the representatives of the old society, was not a class speaking for the *whole* of modern society. It had been reduced to a kind of *estate* as clearly distinct from the Crown as it was from the people, with a strong bend to oppose both adversaries and irresolute towards each of them individually because it always saw both of them either in front of it or behind it. From the first it was inclined to betray the people and to compromise with the crowned representatives of the old society, for it already belonged itself to the old society; it did not advance the interests of a new society against an old one, but represented refurbished interests within an obsolete society. It stood at the helm of the revolution not because it had the people behind it but because the people drove it forward; it stood at the head because it merely represented the spleen of an old social era and not the initiatives of a new one. A stratum of the old state that had failed to break through and was thrown up on the surface of the new state by the force of an earthquake; without faith in itself, without faith in the people, grumbling at those above, frightened of those below, egoistical towards both and aware of its egoism; revolutionary with regard to the conservatives and conservative with regard to the revolutionaries. It did not trust its own slogans, used phrases instead of ideas, it was intimidated by the world storm and exploited it for its own ends; it displayed no energy anywhere, but resorted to plagiarism everywhere, it was vulgar because unoriginal, and original in its vulgarity; haggling over its own demands, without initiative, without faith in itself, without faith in the people, without a historic mission, an abominable dotard finding himself condemned to lead and to mislead the first youthful impulses of a virile people so as to make them serve his own senile interests—sans eyes, sans ears, sans teeth, sans everything—this was the *Prussian bourgeoisie* which found itself at the helm of the Prussian state after the March revolution.

[III]

Cologne, December 15. The *theory of agreement*, which the bourgeoisie, on attaining power in the person of the *Camphausen* cabinet, immediately publicised as the "broadest" basis of the Prussian *contrat social*, was by no means an empty theory; on the contrary, it grew on the tree of "*golden*" life.

The sovereign by the grace of God was by no means vanquished by the sovereignty of the people as a result of the March revolution. The Crown, the absolute state, was merely compelled to *come to an agreement* with the bourgeoisie, its old rival.

The Crown offers the aristocracy as a sacrifice to the bourgeoisie, the bourgeoisie offers the people as a sacrifice to the Crown. Under these circumstances the monarchy becomes bourgeois and the bourgeoisie monarchical.

Only these two powers exist since the March revolution. They use each other as a sort of lightning-conductor against the revolution. Always, of course, on the "*broadest democratic basis*".

Herein lay the *secret of the theory of agreement*.

The oil and wool merchants[129] who formed the first cabinet after the March revolution took pleasure in protecting the exposed Crown with their plebeian wings. They were highly delighted at having gained access to the Court and reluctantly driven by pure magnanimity to abandon their austere Roman pose, i.e., the Roman pose of the United Provincial Diet, to use the corpse of their former popularity to fill the chasm that threatened to engulf the throne. *Camphausen* plumed himself on being the *midwife* of the constitutional throne. The worthy man was evidently deeply moved by his own action, his own magnanimity. The Crown and its followers reluctantly suffered this humiliating protection and made *bonne mine à mauvais jeu*, hoping for better days to come.

The *bourgeois gentilhomme* was easily taken in by a few honeyed words and curtsies from the partly disintegrated army, the bureaucracy that trembled for its positions and salaries, and the humiliated feudals, whose leader was engaged in a constitutional educational journey.

The Prussian bourgeoisie was *nominally* in control and did not for a moment doubt that the powers of the old state had placed themselves unreservedly at its disposal and had become offshoots of its own omnipotence.

Not only in the cabinet but throughout the monarchy the bourgeoisie was intoxicated with this delusion.

Did not the army, the bureaucracy and even the feudal lords act as willing and obedient accomplices in the only heroic deeds the Prussian bourgeoisie performed after the March revolution, namely, the often sanguinary machinations of the Civil Guard against the unarmed proletariat? Did not the subdued district governors and penitent major-generals listen with admiration to the stern patriarchal admonitions which the *local councillors* addressed to the people—the only efforts, the only heroic deeds of which these local councillors, the local representatives of the bourgeoisie (whose obtrusive servile vulgarity the Windischgrätzes, Jellachiches and Weldens afterwards repaid with kicks), were capable after the March revolution? Could the Prussian bourgeoisie have doubted after this that the former ill-will of the army, bureaucracy and feudal aristocracy had been transformed into respectful loyalty to the bourgeoisie, the magnanimous victor who had put a curb both upon itself and upon anarchy?

Clearly the Prussian bourgeoisie now had only one duty—
to settle itself comfortably in power, get rid of the troublesome anarchists, restore "law and order" and retrieve the
profit lost during the storms of March. It was now merely a
question of reducing to a minimum the *costs* of its rule and of
the March revolution which had brought it about. The
weapons which, in its struggle against the feudal society
and the Crown, the Prussian bourgeoisie had been compelled
to demand in the name of the people, such as the right
of association and freedom of the press, were they not bound
to be broken in the hands of a deluded people who no longer
needed to use them to fight *for* the bourgeoisie and who
revealed an alarming inclination to use them *against* the
bourgeoisie?

The bourgeoisie was convinced that evidently only one
obstacle stood in the way of its *agreement* with the Crown,
in the way of a deal with the old state, which was resigned
to its fate, and that obstacle was the people—*puer robustus
sed malitiosus*,[130] as Hobbes says. The *people* and the *revolution*!

The *revolution* was the *legal title of the people*; the vehe-
ment claims of the people were based on the revolution. The
revolution was the bill drawn by the people on the bourgeoisie. The bourgeoisie came to power through the revolution. The day it came to power was also the day this bill
became due. The bourgeoisie had to *protest* the bill.

Revolution in the mouth of the people meant: you, the
bourgeois, are the *Comité du salut public*, the Committee of
Public Safety, to whom we have entrusted the government
in order that you should defend our interests, the interests
of the people, *in face of* the Crown, but not in order that
you should *come to an agreement with* the Crown regarding
your own interests.

Revolution was the people's protest against an arrangement between the bourgeoisie and the Crown. The bourgeoisie that was making arrangements with the Crown *had
therefore to protest* against the *revolution*.

And that was done under the great *Camphausen. The
March revolution was not recognised.* The National Representatives at Berlin set themselves up as *representatives of*

the Prussian bourgeoisie, as the *Assembly of conciliators*, by *rejecting* the motion recognising the March revolution.

The Assembly sought to undo what had been done. It vociferously declared to the Prussian people that the people did not come to an agreement with the bourgeoisie in order to make a revolution against the Crown, but that the purpose of the revolution was to achieve an agreement between the Crown and the bourgeoisie against the people! Thus was the *legal title* of the revolutionary people annulled and a *legal basis* secured for the conservative bourgeoisie.

The legal basis!

Brüggemann, and through him the *Kölnische Zeitung*, have prated, fabled and moaned so much about the "legal basis", have so often lost and recovered, punctured and mended that "legal basis", tossed it from Berlin to Frankfurt and from Frankfurt to Berlin, narrowed and widened it, turned the simple basis into an inlaid floor and the inlaid floor into a false bottom (which, as we know, is the principal device of performing conjurors), and the false bottom into a bottomless trapdoor, so that in the end the legal basis has turned for our readers into the basis of the *Kölnische Zeitung*; thus, they could confuse the shibboleth of the Prussian bourgeoisie with the private shibboleth of Herr Joseph Dumont, a necessary invention of the *Prussian* world history with the arbitrary hobby-horse of the *Kölnische Zeitung*, and regard the legal basis simply as the basis on which the *Kölnische Zeitung* arises.

The *legal basis*, namely, the *Prussian legal basis*!

The *legal basis* on which Camphausen, the knight of the great debate, the resurrected phantom of the United Provincial Diet and the Assembly of conciliators, moved *after* the March revolution—is it the constitutional law of 1815[131] or the law of 1820 regarding the Provincial Diet,[132] or the edict of 1847,[133] or the electoral and agreement law of April 8, 1848[134]?

It is none of these.

"Legal basis" simply meant that the revolution failed to gain firm ground and the old society did not lose its ground; that the March revolution was an "occurrence" that acted merely as a "stimulus" towards an "agreement" between the throne and the bourgeoisie, preparations for which had long been made within the old Prussian state, and the need for which the Crown itself had expressed in its royal decrees, but had not, prior to March, considered as *"urgent"*. In short, the "legal basis" meant that *after* the March revolution the bourgeoisie wanted to negotiate with the Crown on the same footing as *before* the March events, as though no revolution had taken place and the United Provincial Diet had achieved its goal without a revolution. The "legal basis" meant that the *revolution*, the legal title of the people, was to be ignored in the *contrat social* between the government and the bourgeoisie. *The bourgeoisie deduced its claims from the old Prussian legislation, in order that the people should not deduce any claims from the new Prussian revolution.*

Naturally, the *ideological cretins* of the bourgeoisie, its journalists, and such like, had to pass off this palliative of the bourgeois interests as the real interests of the bourgeoisie, and persuade themselves and others to believe this. The phrase about the legal basis acquired real substance in the mind of a *Brüggemann*.

The *Camphausen* government fulfilled its task, the task of being an *intermediate link* and a *transitional stage*. It was the *intermediate link* between the bourgeoisie which had risen on the shoulders of the people and the bourgeoisie which no longer required the shoulders of the people; between the bourgeoisie which apparently represented the people in face of the Crown and the bourgeoisie which really represented the Crown in face of the people; between the bourgeoisie emerging from the revolution and the bourgeoisie which had emerged as the core of the revolution.

In keeping with its role, the Camphausen government coyly and bashfully confined itself to *passive resistance* against the revolution.

Although it rejected the revolution in theory, in practice it *resisted* only its encroachments and *tolerated* only the reestablishment of the old political authorities.

The bourgeoisie in the meantime believed that it had reached the point where *passive resistance* had to turn into *open attack*. The *Camphausen* cabinet resigned not because it had committed some blunder or other, but simply because it was the *first* cabinet following the March revolution, because it was the *cabinet of the March revolution* and by virtue of its origin it had to conceal that it represented the bourgeoisie under the guise of a dictatorship of the people. Its dubious beginnings and its ambiguous character still imposed on it certain conventions, restraints and considerations with regard to the sovereign people which were irksome to the bourgeoisie, and which a second cabinet originating directly from the Assembly of conciliators would no longer have to reckon with.

Its resignation therefore puzzled the arm-chair politicians. It was followed by the *Hansemann* government, the *government of action*, as the bourgeoisie intended to proceed from the period when it *passively* betrayed the people to the Crown to the period of *active* subjugation of the people to its own rule in agreement with the Crown. The *government of action* was the *second* government *after* the March revolution; that was its whole secret.

[IV]

Cologne, December 29.

"Gentlemen, business is business!"[135]

In these few words Hansemann epitomised the whole liberalism of the United Provincial Diet. This man was bound to become the head of a government based on the Assembly of conciliators, a government which was to turn *passive resistance* to the people into an *active attack* on the people, the *government of action*.

No Prussian government contained so many *middle-class* names. Hansemann, Milde, Märker, Kühlwetter, Gierke! Even *von Auerswald*, the label presentable at Court, belonged to the liberal aristocracy of the Königsberg opposition which paid homage to the bourgeoisie. *Roth von Schreckenstein* alone represented the old bureaucratic Prussian feudal nobility among this rabble. *Roth von Schreckenstein!* The surviving title of a vanished novel about robbers and knights by the late *Hildebrandt*.[136] But *Roth von Schreckenstein* was merely the feudal setting for the bourgeois jewel. *Roth von Schreckenstein* in a middle-class government meant this, spelled out in capital letters: the Prussian feudalists, the army and bureaucracy are guided by the newly arisen star, the Prussian middle class. These powerful figures have placed themselves at its disposal, and the middle class has set them up in front of its throne, just as bears were placed in front of the rulers of the people on old heraldic emblems. Roth von Schreckenstein is merely intended to be the bear of the middle-class government.

On *June 26* the Hansemann government presented itself to the National Assembly. Its actual existence began in *July*. The *June revolution* was the background of the government of action, just as the *February revolution* formed the background of the government of mediation.

The bloody victory of the Paris bourgeoisie over the proletarians of Paris was used against the people by the Prussian bourgeoisie, just as the bloody victory of the Croats at Vienna was used against the bourgeoisie by the Prussian Crown. The suffering of the Prussian bourgeoisie after the Austrian November was *retribution* for the suffering of the Prussian people after the French June. In their short-sighted narrow-mindedness the German philistines mistook themselves for the French bourgeoisie. They had overturned no throne, they had not abolished feudal society, still less its last vestiges, they did not have to uphold a society they themselves had created. After the June events, as after those of February, they believed, as they had since the beginning of the sixteenth century and during the eighteenth century, that they would be able in their traditional crafty money-making manner to pocket three-quarters of the profit produced by someone else's labour. They had no inkling of the fact that behind the French June lurked the Austrian November and behind the Austrian November, the Prussian December. They did not suspect that whereas in France the throne-shattering bourgeoisie was confronted by only one enemy, the proletariat, the Prussian bourgeoisie, grappling with the Crown, possessed only one ally—the people. Not because these two groups have no hostile and contradictory interests, but because they are still welded together by *the same* interests in face of a third power which oppresses them both equally.

The Hansemann government regarded itself as a *government of the June revolution*. In contrast to the "red robbers", the philistines in every Prussian town turned into "respectable republicans", without ceasing to be worthy royalists, and occasionally overlooking the fact that the "reds" wore *white-and-black* cockades.[137]

In his speech from the throne on June 26, Hansemann gave short shrift to Camphausen's mysteriously nebulous "monarchy on *the broadest democratic basis*".

"*Constitutional monarchy based on the two-chamber system* and the joint exercise of legislative power by the two chambers and the Crown"—that was the dry formula to which he reduced the portentous motto of his enthusiastic predecessor.

"Modification of the most essential conditions that are incompatible with the new constitution, liberation of property from the fetters that hamper its most *advantageous utilisation* in a large part of the monarchy, reorganisation of the administration of justice, reform of fiscal legislation and particularly *annulment of tax exemptions*, etc." and above all "*strengthening of the state* which is necessary for safeguarding the *freedom* which has been won" (by the citizens) "against reaction" (i.e., using the freedom in the interests of the feudal aristocracy) "and anarchy" (i.e., using the freedom in the interests of the people) "and for *restoring the shaken trust*"

—such was the government's programme, the programme of the Prussian bourgeoisie in office, whose classical representative is *Hansemann*.

In the United Provincial Diet Hansemann was the most bitter and the most cynical adversary of trust, for—"*gentlemen, business is business!*" Hansemann in office proclaimed the "*restoration of the shaken trust*" a foremost necessity, for—this time he addressed the *people* as previously he had addressed the *throne*—for

"*Gentlemen, business is business!*"

Previously it was a question of the trust that *gives* money, this time it was of the trust that *makes* money; then it was a matter of *feudal* trust, the sincere trust in God, King and Country, now it was *bourgeois* trust, trust in trade and commerce, in interest-bearing capital, in the solvency of one's commercial friends, that is, commercial trust; it is not a matter of faith, love or hope, but of *credit*.

Hansemann's words: *"restoration of the shaken trust"*, expressed the fixed idea of the Prussian bourgeoisie.

Credit depends on the confidence that the exploitation of wage labour by capital, of the proletariat by the bourgeoisie, of the petty bourgeois by the big bourgeois, will continue in the traditional manner. Hence any political move of the proletariat, whatever its nature, unless it takes place under the direct command of the bourgeoisie, shakes this trust, impairs credit. "Restoration of the shaken trust" when uttered by Hansemann signifies:

Suppression of every political move of the proletariat and of all social strata whose interests do not completely coincide with the interests of the class which believes itself to be standing at the helm of state.

Hansemann accordingly placed the *"strengthening of the state"* side by side with the "restoration of the shaken trust". But he mistook the character of this "state". He sought to strengthen the state which served credit and bourgeois trust, but he strengthened the state which demands trust and if necessary extorts this trust with the help of grape-shot, because it has no credit. He wanted to economise on the costs of bourgeois rule but has instead burdened the bourgeoisie with the exorbitant millions which the restoration of Prussian feudal rule costs.

He told the workers quite laconically that he had an excellent remedy for them. But before he could produce it the "shaken trust" must first of all be restored. To restore this trust the working class had to give up all political activity and interference in the business of state and revert to its former habits. If it followed his advice and trust were restored, this mysterious potent remedy would prove effective if only because it would no longer be required or applicable, since in this case the malady itself—the upset of bourgeois law and order—would have been eliminated. And what need is there of a medicine when there is no malady? But if the people obstinately stuck to their purpose, very well, then he would *"strengthen* the state", the police, the army, the courts, the bureaucracy, and would set his bears on them, for "trust" had become a "business question", and:

"Gentlemen, business is business!"

Hansemann's programme, even though he may smile about it, was an *honest* programme, a well-intentioned programme.

He wanted to strengthen the power of the state not only against anarchy, that is, against the people, he wanted to strengthen it also against reaction, that is, against the Crown and feudal interests in case they attempted to assert themselves against the bourgeoisie's purse and their *"most essential"*, that is, their most modest, political claims.

The very composition of the government of action expressed a protest against this "reaction".

It differed from all previous Prussian cabinets in that its real *Prime Minister* was the *Minister of Finance.* For centuries the Prussian state had carefully concealed the fact that the departments of war, internal and foreign affairs, church and educational matters and even the treasury of the royal household as well as faith, hope and charity depended on profane *financial* matters. The government of action placed this tiresome bourgeois truth uppermost by placing Herr Hansemann at its head, a man whose ministerial programme like his opposition programme may be summarised in the words:

"Gentlemen, business is business!"

The monarchy in Prussia became a "money affair".

Now let us pass on from the programme of the government of action to its actions.

It really carried out its threat of *"strengthening the state"* against *"anarchy"*, that is, against the working class and all sections of the middle class who did not stick to the programme of Herr Hansemann. It can even be said that, apart from increasing the tax on beet-sugar and spirits, this *reaction* against so-called *anarchy*, i.e., against the revolutionary movement, was the only serious action of this government of action.

Numerous lawsuits against the press based on Prussian law or, where it did not exist, on the Code pénal,[138] numerous arrests on the same "sufficient grounds" (Auerswald's formula), introduction of a system of constables in Berlin[139] at the rate of one constable per every two houses, police interference with the freedom of association, the use of soldiers against unruly citizens and of the Civil Guard against unruly workers, and the introduction, by way of deterrent, of martial law—all these events of Hansemann's Olympiad are still vividly remembered. No details need be mentioned.

This aspect of the efforts of the government of action was summarised by *Kühlwetter* in the following words:

"A state that wants to be really free must have a really large police force as its executive arm",

to which Hansemann muttered one of his usual remarks:

"This would also greatly help to *restore trust* and *revive the rather slack commercial activity.*"

The government of action accordingly "*strengthened*" the old Prussian police force, the judiciary, the bureaucracy and the army, who, since they receive their *pay* from the bourgeoisie, also *serve* the bourgeoisie, as Hansemann thought. At any rate, they were "*strengthened*".

On the other hand, the temper of the proletariat and bourgeois democrats is expressed by *one* event. Because a few reactionaries maltreated a few democrats in Charlottenburg, the people stormed the residence of the Prime Minister in Berlin. So popular had the government of action become. The next day Hansemann tabled a law against riotous gatherings and public meetings. This shows how cunningly he intrigued against reaction.

Thus the actual, tangible, popular activity of the government of action was purely *policemanic* in character. In the eyes of the proletariat and the *urban* democrats this cabinet and the Assembly of conciliators, whose majority was represented in the cabinet, and the Prussian bourgeoisie, the majority of whom constituted the majority in the Assembly of conciliation, represented the *old*, refurbished *police and bureaucratic state.* To this was added resentment against the bourgeoisie, because it governed and had set up the *Civil Guard* as an integral part of the police.

The "achievement of the March events", as the people saw it, was that the liberal gentlemen of the bourgeoisie, too, took *police* duties upon themselves. There was thus a twin police force.

Not the actions of the government of action, but the drafts of its organic laws show clearly that it "*strengthened*" the "*police*"—the ultimate expression of the old state—and spurred it into action only in the interest of the bourgeoisie.

In the bills relating to *local government, jury,* and *Civil Guard,* introduced by the Hansemann cabinet, *property* in one form or another always forms the demarcation line between *lawful* and *unlawful* territory. All these bills contain the most servile concessions to royal power, for the bourgeois cabinet believed that the wings of royalty had been clipped and that it had become its ally; but as a consolation the ascendancy of capital over labour is all the more ruthlessly emphasised.

The Civil Guard Law approved by the Assembly of conciliation was turned against the bourgeoisie and had to provide a legal pretext for disarming it. According to the fancy of its authors, however, it was to become valid only after the promulgation of the Law on Local Government and of the constitution, that is, after the consolidation of the rule of the bourgeoisie. The experience which the Prussian bourgeoisie gained in connection with the Civil Guard Law may contribute to its enlightenment and show it that for the time being all its actions that are meant to be directed against the people are only directed against itself.

As far as the people are concerned, the Hansemann ministry is in *practice* epitomised by the old Prussian policeman, and in *theory* by the offensive *Belgian* differentiation[140] between bourgeois and non-bourgeois.

Now let us pass on to another section of the ministerial programme, to *anarchy against reaction.*

In this respect the ministry can boast more pious wishes than real deeds.

Among the pious *bourgeois* wishes are the partition and sale of demesnes to private owners, the abandonment of banking to free competition, the conversion of the *Seehand-lung*[141] into a private institution, etc.

It was unfortunate for the government of action that all its economic attacks against the feudal party took place under the aegis of a *forced loan*, and that in general its attempts at reformation were seen by the people merely as financial expedients devised to replenish the treasury of the strengthened "state". Hansemann thus won the hatred of one party without winning the approval of the other. And it has to be admitted that he only ventured to attack feudal privileges when *money matters* closest to the Minister of Finance, when *money matters as understood by the Ministry of Finance*, became pressing. In this narrow sense he told the feudal lords:

"Gentlemen, business is business!"

Thus even his positive middle-class efforts directed against the feudalists reveal the same police taint as his negative measures designed to *"revive commercial activity"*. For in the language of political economy the *police* is called *exchequer*. The increase in the beet-sugar and liquor duties which Hansemann passed through the National Assembly roused the indignation of the money-bags standing with God for King and Country in Silesia, Brandenburg, Saxony, East and West Prussia, etc. But while this measure angered the industrial landowners in the old Prussian provinces, it caused no less displeasure among the middle-class distillers in the Rhine Province, who perceived that their conditions of competition compared with those of the old Prussian provinces had become even more unfavourable. And to crown all, it angered the workers in the old provinces, for whom it simply meant, and could only mean, a *rise in the price of a prime necessity*. This measure therefore merely amounted to replenishing the treasury of the "strengthened state". This example suffices, since it is the only action against the feudalists *actually* taken by the government of action, the only bill of this nature which really became law.

Hansemann's "bills" abrogating all *exemptions* from graduated and *land taxes*,[142] and his projected income-tax caused the landowning votaries of "God, King and Country" to rave as if stung by the tarantula. They denounced him as a *communist* and even today the Prussian Knight of the Cross* crosses itself three times at the mention of Hansemann's name. That name sounds like Fra Diavolo[143] to it. The repeal of all exemptions from the land-tax, the only important measure to be introduced by a Prussian minister during the glorious reign of the Assembly of conciliators, failed because of the *principled narrow-mindedness of the Left*. Hansemann himself had justified this narrow-mindedness. Was the Left to provide new financial resources for the cabinet of the *"strengthened state"* before the completion and promulgation of the constitution?

The bourgeois cabinet *par excellence* was so unlucky that its most radical measure had to be frustrated by the radical members of the Assembly of conciliators. It was so barren that its whole crusade against feudalism merely resulted in a *tax increase*, which was equally odious to all classes, and its entire financial acumen brought forth a *forced loan*: two measures, which ultimately only provided *subsidies for the campaign of the counter-revolution against the bourgeoisie*. But the *feudal* aristocrats were convinced of the "nefarious" intentions of the *bourgeois* cabinet. Thus even the financial struggle of the Prussian bourgeoisie against feudalism merely proved that owing to its unpopularity and impotence it was only able to collect *money against itself* and—*gentlemen, business is business!*

Just as the bourgeois cabinet succeeded in equally offending the urban proletariat, the middle-class democrats and the feudal nobility, so did it manage to alienate and antagonise even the *peasants* oppressed by feudalism, and in this it was eagerly supported by the *Assembly of conciliators*. It has to be remembered after all that during half of its existence the Assembly was appropriately represented by the Hansemann cabinet and that the bourgeois martyrs of today were yesterday the train-bearers of Hansemann.

During Hansemann's rule Patow introduced a bill abolishing feudal obligations (see the criticism of it we published earlier). It was a most wretched concoction of the helpless

---

* An allusion to the *Kreuz-Zeitung.—Ed.*

bourgeois desire to abolish feudal privileges, those "conditions that are incompatible with the new constitution", and of bourgeois fear of revolutionarily infringing on any kind of property whatever. Wretched, timid and narrow-minded egoism blinded the Prussian bourgeoisie to such an extent that it repulsed the *peasantry, its most needed ally.*

On *June 3* deputy *Hanow* moved

"that all pending proceedings which concern landowner-peasant relations and the commutation of services be immediately discontinued at the request of one of the sides until the promulgation of a new law based on just principles."

Not until the *end of September*, that is, four months later, under the Pfuel cabinet, did the Assembly of conciliation pass a bill designed to discontinue pending proceedings between landowners and peasants, after rejecting all liberal amendments and retaining the "reservation about the provisional establishment of current obligations" and the "collection of dues and arrears in dispute".

In *August*, if we are not mistaken, the Assembly of conciliators declared that *Nenstiel's* motion that *"labour services be abolished immediately"* was *not urgent.* Could the peasants be expected to consider it an urgent matter for them to take up the cudgels for this Assembly of conciliators, which had thrown them back into conditions worse than those they had actually won after the March events?

The French bourgeoisie began by emancipating the peasants. Together with the peasants it conquered Europe. The Prussian bourgeoisie was so preoccupied with its *most narrow,* immediate interests that it foolishly lost even this ally and turned it into a tool of the feudal counter-revolutionaries.

The *official* history of the dissolution of the middle-class cabinet is well known.

Under its protective arm, the "state" was "strengthened" to such an extent and the popular energy so weakened that even on July 15 the Dioscuri Kühlwetter and Hansemann were obliged to send a warning against reactionary machinations of civil servants, and especially chiefs of rural districts, to all district governors in the monarchy; that later an *"Assembly of the nobility and big landowners for the protection*" of their privileges[144] met in Berlin alongside the Assembly of conciliators; and that finally, in opposition to the so-called Berlin National Assembly, a "diet of local communities for the protection of the threatened property rights of landlords", a body originating in the Middle Ages, was convoked in Upper Lusatia on September 4.

The energy expended by the government and the so-called National Assembly against these increasingly menacing counter-revolutionary symptoms found adequate expression in paper admonitions. The bourgeois cabinet reserved bayonets, bullets, prisons and constables exclusively for the people *"so as to restore the shaken trust and revive commercial activity"*.

The incidents at *Schweidnitz*,[145] where the troops in fact murdered the bourgeoisie in the person of the Civil Guard, finally roused the National Assembly from its apathy. On August 9 it braced itself for a heroic deed, that of the Stein-Schultze army order,[146] whose most drastic measure of coercion was an appeal to the *tact* of the Prussian officers. A measure of coercion indeed! Did not royalist honour forbid the officers to follow the dictates of bourgeois honour?

On *September 7*, a month after the Assembly of conciliators had passed the Stein-Schultze army order, it once more decided that its resolution was a real resolution and should be carried out by the ministers. Hansemann refused to do this and resigned on September 11, after having appointed himself a bank director at a yearly salary of 6,000 thaler, for—*gentlemen, business is business!*

Finally, on *September 25*, the Assembly of conciliators gratefully agreed to *Pfuel's* thoroughly watered-down formula of acceptance of the Stein-Schultze army order, which by that time Wrangel's parallel army order[147] and the large number of troops concentrated around Berlin had turned into a *bad joke*.

A mere glance at these dates and the history of the Stein-Schultze army order suffices to show that the army order was not the *real* reason for Hansemann's resignation. Is it likely that Hansemann, who did not shy at recognising the revolution, should have shied at this paper proclamation? Are we to believe that Hansemann, who, whenever the portfolio slipped from his fingers, always picked it up again, has this time, in a fit of virtuous exasperation, left it on the ministerial benches to be hawked about? No, our Hansemann is no fanatic. Hansemann was simply deceived, just as in general he was the representative of the deceived bourgeoisie. He was given to understand that on no account would he be dropped by the Crown. He was made to lose his last semblance of popularity in order that the Crown should at last be able to sacrifice him to the malice of the country squires and get rid of this middle-class tutelage. Moreover, the plan of campaign agreed upon with Russia and Austria required that the cabinet should be headed by a general appointed by the camarilla from outside the Assembly of conciliators. The old "state" had been sufficiently "strengthened" under the bourgeois cabinet to venture on this coup.

Pfuel was a mistake. The victory of the Croats at Vienna made even a Brandenburg a useful tool.

Under the Brandenburg cabinet the Assembly of conciliators was ignominiously dispersed, fooled, derided, humiliated and hunted, and the *people*, at the decisive moment, remained *indifferent*. The *defeat* of the Assembly was the *defeat of the Prussian bourgeoisie*, of the *constitutionalists*, hence a *victory for the democratic party*, however dear it had to pay for that victory.

And the *imposed* constitution?

It had once been said that never would a "piece of paper" be allowed to come between the King and *his* people.[148] Now it is said, there shall *only* be *a piece of paper* between the King and *his* people. The *real* constitution of Prussia is the *state of siege*. The imposed French constitution had only one article—the 14th, which invalidated it.[149] Every article of the imposed Prussian constitution is an article 14.

By means of this constitution the Crown imposes new privileges—that is, upon *itself*.

It permits itself to dissolve the Chambers indefinitely. It permits ministers in the interim to issue any desired law (even those affecting property and so forth). It permits deputies to impeach ministers for such actions, but at the risk, under martial law, of being classed as "internal enemies". Finally, it permits itself, should the stock of the counter-revolution go up in the spring, to replace this nebulous "piece of paper" by a Christian-Germanic Magna Charta *organically* growing out of the distinctions of the medieval estates, or to drop the constitutional game altogether. Even in this case the conservative bourgeois would fold their hands and pray:

"The Lord gave, and the Lord hath taken away; blessed be the name of the Lord!"

The history of the Prussian middle class, and that of the German middle class in general between March and December shows that a purely *middle-class revolution* and the establishment of *bourgeois rule* in the form of a *constitutional monarchy* is impossible in Germany, and that the only alternatives are either a feudal absolutist counter-revolution or a *social republican revolution*.

The viable section of the bourgeoisie is bound to awake again from its apathy—this is guaranteed above all by the *staggering bill* which the counter-revolution will present it with in the spring and, as our Hansemann so thoughtfully says:

Gentlemen, business is business!

Written by Marx

Neue Rheinische Zeitung Nos.
165, 169, 170 and 183,
December 10, 15, 16 and 31,
1848

THE REVOLUTIONARY MOVEMENT

Cologne, December 31. Never was a revolutionary movement opened with such an edifying overture as the revolutionary movement of 1848. The Pope gave it the blessing of the Church, and Lamartine's aeolian harp vibrated with tender philanthropical tunes on the words of *fraternité*, the brotherhood of members of society and nations.

> Welcome all ye myriad creatures!
> Brethren, take the kiss of love![150]

Driven out of Rome, the Pope at present is staying at Gaeta under the protection of the tigerish idiot Ferdinand; Italy's *"iniciatore"*[151] conspires against Italy with Austria, Italy's traditional mortal enemy, whom in happier days he threatened to excommunicate. The recent French presidential elections have given statistical proof of the unpopularity of Lamartine, the traitor. There has been no event more philanthropic, humane, and weak than the February and March revolutions, nothing more brutal than the inevitable consequences of this *humanity of weakness*. The proofs are Italy, Poland, Germany, and above all, those who were defeated in June.

But the defeat of the French workers in June was the defeat of the June victors themselves. Ledru-Rollin and the other men of the Mountain[152] were ousted by the party of the *National,* the party of the bourgeois republicans; the party of the *National* was ousted by Thiers-Barrot, the dynastic opposition; these in turn would have had to make way for the legitimists if the cycle of the three restorations had not come to an end, and if Louis Napoleon was something more than an empty ballot-box by means of which the

French peasants announced their entry into the revolutionary social movement, and the French workers their condemnation of all leaders of the preceding periods—Thiers-Barrot, Lamartine and Cavaignac-Marrast. But let us note the fact that the inevitable consequence of the defeat of the revolutionary French working class was the defeat of the republican French bourgeoisie, to which it had just succumbed.

The defeat of the working class in France and the victory of the French bourgeoisie at the same time signified the renewed suppression of the nationalities, who had responded to the crowing of the Gallic cock with heroic attempts to liberate themselves. Prussian, Austrian and English *Sbirri* once more plundered, ravished and murdered in Poland, Italy and Ireland. The defeat of the working class in France and the victory of the French bourgeoisie was at the same time the defeat of the middle classes in all European countries where the middle classes, united for the moment with the people, responded to the crowing of the Gallic cock with sanguinary insurrections against feudalism. Naples, Vienna, Berlin. The defeat of the working class in France and the victory of the French bourgeoisie was at the same time a victory of East over West, the defeat of civilisation by barbarism. The suppression of the Romanians by the Russians and their tools, the Turks, began in Wallachia; Croats, pandours, Czechs, serezhans* and similar rabble throttled German liberty in Vienna, and the Tsar is now omnipresent in Europe. The overthrow of the bourgeoisie in France, the triumph of the French working class, and the liberation of the working class in general is therefore the rallying-cry of European liberation.

But *England,* the country that turns whole nations into her proletarians, that spans the whole world with her enormous arms, that has already once defrayed the cost of a European Restoration, the country in which class contradictions have reached their most acute and shameless form—*England* seems to be the rock which breaks the revolution-

---

* Mounted troops in the Austrian army who were notorious for their cruelty.—*Ed.*

ary waves, the country where the new society is stifled before it is born. England dominates the world market. Any upheaval in economic relations in any country of the European continent, in the whole European continent without England, is a storm in a teacup. Industrial and commercial relations within each nation are governed by its intercourse with other nations, and depend on its relations with the world market. But the world market is dominated by England and England is dominated by the bourgeoisie.

Thus, the liberation of Europe, whether brought about by the struggle of the oppressed nationalities for their independence or by overthrowing feudal absolutism, depends on the successful uprising of the French working class. Every social upheaval in France, however, is bound to be thwarted by the English bourgeoisie, by Great Britain's industrial and commercial domination of the world. Every partial social reform in France or on the European continent as a whole, if designed to be lasting, is merely a pious wish. Only a *world war* can break old England, as only this can provide the Chartists, the party of the organised English workers, with the conditions for a successful rising against their powerful oppressors. Only when the Chartists head the English government will the social revolution pass from the sphere of utopia to that of reality. But any *European war* in which England is involved is a world war, waged in Canada and Italy, in the East Indies and Prussia, in Africa and on the Danube. A European war will be the first result of a successful workers' revolution in France. England will head the counter-revolutionary armies, just as she did during the Napoleonic period, but the war itself will place her at the head of the revolutionary movement and she will repay the debt she owes to the revolution of the eighteenth century.

The table of contents for 1849 reads: *Revolutionary rising of the French working class, world war.*

Written by Marx

Neue Rheinische Zeitung No. 184,
January 1, 1849

A BOURGEOIS DOCUMENT

Cologne, January 4. In England, where the rule of the bourgeoisie has reached the highest stage of development, public charity too, as we know, has assumed the most noble and magnanimous forms. In England's workhouses—those public institutions where the redundant labour population is allowed to vegetate at the expense of bourgeois society— charity is cunningly combined with the *revenge* which the bourgeoisie wreaks on the wretches who are compelled to appeal to its charity. Not only do the poor devils receive the bare and most meagre means of subsistence, hardly sufficient for physical reproduction, their activity, too, is restricted to a form of revolting, unproductive, meaningless drudgery, such as work at the treadmill, which deadens both mind and body. These unfortunate people have committed the crime of having ceased to be an object of exploitation yielding a profit to the bourgeoisie—as is the case in ordinary life—and having become instead an object of expenditure for those born to derive benefit from them; like so many barrels of alcohol which, left unsold in the warehouse, become an object of expenditure to the dealer. To bring home to them the full magnitude of their crime, they are deprived of everything that is granted to the lowest criminal—association with their wives and children, recreation, talk—everything. Even this *"cruel charity"* is due not to enthusiasm but to thoroughly practical and rational reasons. On the one hand, if all the paupers in Great Britain were suddenly thrown into the street, bourgeois order and commercial activity would suffer to an alarming extent. On the other hand, British industry has alternate periods of feverish over-production, when the demand for hands can hardly be satisfied, and the hands are nevertheless to be obtained as cheaply as possible, followed by periods of slack business, when production is far larger than consumption and it is difficult to find useful employment even at half pay for half the labour army. Is there a more ingenious device than the workhouse for maintaining a reserve army in readiness for the favourable periods while converting them in these pious institutions during unfavourable commercial periods into unresisting machines without will, without aspirations and requirements?

The Prussian bourgeoisie differs favourably from the English bourgeoisie, since it opposes British political arrogance reminiscent of pagan Rome with Christian humility and meekness and cringes in worshipful reverence before throne, altar, army, bureaucracy and feudalism; instead of displaying the commercial energy which conquers whole continents, it engages in Chinese pedantry appropriate to imperial citizens, and tries to confound the impetuous titanic spirit of inventiveness in industry by clinging staunchly and virtuously to the traditional semi-guild routine. But the Prussian bourgeoisie approaches its British ideal in one respect—in its *shameless maltreatment of the working class.* That, as a body, it in general lags behind the British bourgeoisie, is due simply to the fact that, on the whole, as a *national class,* it has never achieved anything of importance and never will, because of its lack of courage, intelligence and energy. It does not exist on a national scale, it exists only in *provincial, municipal, local, private* forms, and in *these* forms it confronts the working class even more ruthlessly than the English bourgeoisie. Why is it that since the Restoration the people longed for Napoleon, whom they had just before that chained to a lonely rock in the Mediterranean? Because it is easier to endure the tyranny of a genius than that of an idiot. Thus the English worker can feel a certain national pride in face of the German worker, because the master who enslaves him enslaves the whole world, whereas the master of the German worker, the German bourgeois, is himself *everybody's servant,* and nothing is more galling and humiliating than to be the *servant of a servant.*

We publish here without any alterations the *"Worker's Card"*, which proletarians engaged on municipal works have to sign in the good city of Cologne; this historical document shows the impudence with which our bourgeoisie treats the working class.

WORKER'S CARD

§ 1. Every worker must *strictly obey* the instructions and orders of *all municipal supervisors*, who have been sworn in as *police officers. Disobedience and insubordination will entail immediate dismissal.*

§ 2. No worker is allowed to move from one section to another or to leave the building-site *without the special permission of the supervisor.*

§ 3. Workers purloining wheelbarrows, carts or other equipment from another section in order to use them in their work will be dismissed.

§ 4. Drunkenness, disturbance of the peace, and the starting of squabbles, quarrels and fights entail immediate dismissal.—In *appropriate cases* moreover legal proceedings will be taken against the culprits.

§ 5. A worker arriving *ten minutes late* at his place of work will be given no work on that *particular half day*; if this should occur three times he *may* be debarred from work.

§ 6. If workers are dismissed at their own request or by way of punishment, they will receive their wages at the next regular pay-day in accordance with the work done.

§ 7. A worker's dismissal is noted in the Worker's Card.—Should the dismissal be by way of punishment, the worker, *according to the circumstances*, is barred from re-employment either at the same place of work or at all municipal works.

§ 8. The *police* are always to be informed when workers are dismissed by way of punishment and of the reasons for their dismissal.

§ 9. Should workers have any *complaints* to make *against the building-site supervisor*, these are to be lodged with the *town surveyor* through an elected delegation of three workers. This officer will examine the cause of the complaint on the spot and *give his decision.*

§ 10. The working hours are from six thirty in the morning to twelve noon and from one o'clock in the afternoon till evening darkness sets in. (Wonderful style!)

§ 11. The worker is employed on these conditions.

§ 12. Payment is made on the building-site on Saturday afternoon.

The sworn building-site supervisor, for the present [...] whose instructions have to be obeyed.

Cologne

Signature or sign } of the worker   { Assigned to section of ...
                                            and has, etc.
                                            Signature of the building-site
                                            supervisor

Could the *Russian* edicts of the Autocrat of all the Russias be couched in more Asiatic terms?

The municipal, and even "*all municipal* supervisors, who have been sworn in as *police officers*", must be "strictly obeyed". "*Disobedience* and *insubordination* will entail *immediate* dismissal." That is first of all *passive obedience*. Then, according to § 9, the workers have the right to complain to "the *town surveyor*". The decisions of this pasha are irrevocable and directed, of course, *against the workers*, if only for hierarchical reasons. And once this decision has been taken and the municipal interdict laid upon the workers, woe to them, for they will then be placed under *police surveillance*. The last semblance of bourgeois freedom disappears, for, according to § 8, "the *police* are always to be informed when workers are dismissed by way of punishment and of the reasons for their dismissal".

But gentlemen, if you dismiss a worker, if you terminate a contract by which he gives *his labour* for *your wages*, what on earth has the *police* to do with this cancellation of a *civil agreement*? Is the municipal worker a convict? Have you *denounced* him to the *police* because he did not pay due deference to you, his hereditary, most wise and noble-minded masters? Would you not deride the citizen who *denounced* you to the *police* for having broken some delivery contract, or failed to pay a bill when it was due, or drunk too much on New-Year's eve? Of course you would! But as regards the worker you are bound by no civil agreement, you lord it over him with the caprice of the *lords by the grace of God!* You make the police, on your behalf, keep a record of his conduct.

Under § 5, a worker arriving *ten minutes* late is punished with the loss of *half a day's labour*. What a punishment in comparison with the offence! You are *centuries* late, but the worker is not allowed to arrive *ten minutes* after half past six without losing *half a working day*.

Finally, in order that this patriarchal arbitrariness should not be in any way restricted and the worker be entirely dependent on your whim, you have left the mode of punishment, as far as possible, to the discretion of your uniformed servants. Dismissal and denunciation to the police is, according to § 4, to be followed in *"appropriate* cases", that is, in cases which you will be pleased to regard as appropriate, by "legal proceedings against the culprits". Under § 5, the worker who arrives late for the third time, i.e., ten minutes after half past six, *"may"* be debarred altogether. In case of dismissal by way of punishment, § 7 states, the worker, *"according to the circumstances,* is barred from re-employment either at the *same* place of work or at *all* municipal works", and so on and so forth.

What scope for the whims of the annoyed bourgeois is given in this criminal code of our municipal Catos, these great men who grovel before Berlin!

This model law shows *what sort of Charter our bourgeoisie,* if it stood at the helm of state, *would impose on the people.*

Written by Marx

Neue Rheinische Zeitung No. 187,
January 5, 1849

MONTESQUIEU LVI

[I]

Cologne, January 20. The "honourable" *Joseph Dumont* allows an anonymous writer, who is not paid by him but pays him and who in the feuilleton seeks to work upon the *primary voters,* to address the *Neue Rheinische Zeitung* in the following way:

"The *Neue Rheinische Zeitung,* the *Organ of Democracy,* has been pleased to take notice of the articles published in this paper under the title "*To the Primary Voters*", and to state that they were borrowed from the *Neue Preussische Zeitung.*

"In face of this *lie,* we simply declare that these articles are paid for *as advertisements,* and that, with the exception of the first one borrowed from the *Parlaments-Korrespondenz,* they were written in Cologne and their author has up to now not even seen, let alone read, the *Neue Preussische Zeitung.*"

We understand how important it is for Montesquieu LVI to authenticate his *property.* We also understand how important for Herr Dumont is the statement that he is "*paid*" even for the leaflets and advertisements which he sets up, prints and distributes in the interest of his class, the *bourgeoisie.*

As for the anonymous writer, he is aware of the French saying: "*Les beaux esprits se rencontrent.*" It is not his fault that his own intellectual products and those of the *Neue Preussische Zeitung* and of the "Prussian Associations"[153] are as alike as two peas.

We *have never read* his advertisements in the *Kölnische Zeitung,* but the leaflets produced by Dumont's printing-house and sent to us from various quarters, we deemed worthy of a casual glance. Now, however, comparison has shown us that the same stuff plays the simultaneous role of advertisement and leaflet.

In order to atone for the injustice we have done to the anonymous Montesquieu LVI we have imposed upon ourselves the harsh penance of reading all his advertisements in the *Kölnische Zeitung* and making his intellectual private property available to the German public as "common property".

Here is wisdom!

Montesquieu LVI is chiefly concerned with the *social* question. He has found the "easiest and simplest way" to *solve* it, and he extols his Morrison pill with the unctuous, naively shameless pathos of a quack.

> " The easiest and simplest way to achieve this however" (that is, the solution of the social question) "is to accept the constitution imposed on December 5, 1848, revise it, then make everyone swear allegiance to it, and thus to establish it. *This is our only way to salvation.* Consequently, any man who has a sympathetic heart for the misery of his poor brothers, who wants to feed the hungry and clothe the naked... anyone, in short, who *wants to solve the social question... should not vote for anyone who is opposed to the constitution*" (Montesquieu LVI).

Vote for Brandenburg, Manteuffel, Ladenberg, and the *social question* will be solved in the "simplest" and "easiest way"! Vote for Dumont, Camphausen, Wittgenstein or else for minor gods such as Compes and Mevissen—and the *social question* will be solved! The "social question" for *a vote*! He who "wants to feed the hungry and clothe the naked" should vote for Hansemann and Stupp! One social question less for each vote! Acceptance of the imposed constitution—that is the *solution of the social problem*!

We do not for a moment doubt that neither Montesquieu LVI nor his patrons in the Citizens' Associations[154] will wait for the imposed constitution to be accepted, revised,[155] sworn, and promulgated before "feeding the hungry and clothing the naked". Appropriate measures have already been taken.

During the last few weeks circulars have been distributed in which capitalists inform craftsmen, shopkeepers, and others that, considering the present state of affairs and the revival of credit, the rate of interest, for philanthropical reasons, has been raised from 4 to 5 per cent. First solution of the social question!

The municipal council of Cologne has in the same spirit

drawn up a *"Worker's Card"* for the unfortunate people who must either starve or sell their hands to the city (cf. No. 187 of the *Neue Rheinische Zeitung**). It will be remembered that under this Charter, imposed on the workers, the worker who has lost his job is bound by contract to place himself under *police surveillance.* Second solution of the social question!

Shortly after the March events, the municipal council established an eating-house in Cologne at cost prices, beautifully furnished, with fine rooms that could be heated, etc. *After* the imposition of the constitution other premises were substituted for this, premises managed by the poor-law administration, where there is no heating, no crockery, where food may not be consumed on the spot and where a quart of indescribable gruel costs eight pfennigs. Third solution of the social question!

While they ruled Vienna the workers guarded the banks, the houses and the wealth of the bourgeois, who had fled. These same bourgeois, on their return, denounced these workers to Windischgrätz as "robbers" who ought to be *hanged.* Unemployed who applied to the municipal council were put into the army to fight Hungary. Fourth solution of the social question!

In Breslau the wretched people who were obliged to seek refuge in the poor house were calmly exposed to cholera by the municipal council and the government who deprived them of the most essential physical necessaries of life, and took notice of the victims of their cruel charity only when they themselves were attacked by the disease. Fifth solution of the social question!

In the Berlin association "with God for King and Country", a supporter of the imposed constitution declared that it was distressing that in order to further one's interests and plans one still had to pay compliments to the *"proletariat".*

That is the solution of the "solution of the social question"!

"The Prussian spies are so dangerous because they are

never paid but are always hoping to be paid," says our friend Heine. And the Prussian bourgeois are so dangerous because they never pay but always promise to pay.

An election costs the English and French bourgeois quite a lot of money. Their corrupt practices are well known. The Prussian bourgeoisie are very shrewd! They are much too virtuous and upright to dip into their pocket; they pay with the *"solution of the social question"*. And that costs nothing. Montesquieu LVI, however, as Dumont officially assures us, pays at least for the advertisements in the *Kölnische Zeitung* and appends—gratis—the solution of the *"social question"*.

The practical part of our Montesquieu's *petites oeuvres* thus boils down to the following: vote for Brandenburg, Manteuffel, Ladenberg! Elect Camphausen and Hansemann! Send us to Berlin, let our people establish themselves there. That is the *solution of the social question.*

The immortal *Hansemann* has solved these problems. First, the establishment of law and order to revive credit. Then, the solution of the "social question" with powder and shot, as in 1844, when "my dear Silesian weavers ought to be helped".

Hence, vote for the advocates of the imposed constitution!

But Montesquieu LVI accepts the imposed constitution only to be able afterwards to "revise" and "swear allegiance to it"!

Montesquieu, my good man! Once you have accepted the constitution you can revise it only on its own basis, that is, in so far as it suits the King and the second Chamber consisting of country squires, financial magnates, high-ranking officials and clerics. The only possible revision has been judiciously indicated in the imposed constitution itself. It consists in abandoning the constitutional system and restoring the former Christian-Germanic *system of estates.*

After the acceptance of the imposed constitution this is the only possible and only permitted revision, which cannot have escaped the shrewd Montesquieu.

Thus the essays of Montesquieu LVI, in their practical part, amount to this: vote for Hansemann and Camphausen! Vote for Dumont and Stupp! Vote for Brandenburg and Manteuffel! Accept the imposed constitution! Elect delegates who accept the imposed constitution—and all this under the pretext of solving the "social question".

What the hell does the pretext matter to us, when it is a question of the imposed constitution.

But our Montesquieu of course prefaces his practical instructions for the solution of "the social question", the quintessence of his monumental work, with a theoretical part. Let us examine this theoretical part.

The profound thinker explains first *what the "social questions" are*.

"And so, what, in effect, is the social question?

"Human beings must and want to live.

"To live they need dwellings, clothes and food.

"Dwellings and clothes are not produced by nature at all, and only a scanty and by no means sufficient amount of food grows naturally.

"Hence man himself must procure everything to satisfy these needs.

"This he does by labour.

"*Labour, therefore, is the first condition of our life; without labour we cannot live.*

"Among primitive peoples everybody built his own hut, made his own clothes from animal skins and gathered fruit for his meals. That was the primitive state.

"But if man needs nothing beyond shelter, clothes and food, if he satisfies merely his *physical* wants, then he remains at the same level as the animals, for animals can do this too.

"But man is a higher being than an animal, he needs more, he needs joy, he must raise himself to moral values. But he can do that only if he lives in society.

"But when men began to live in societies entirely new conditions arose. They soon perceived that work was much easier when each individual performed only one particular job. Thus, one made clothes, another built houses, a third provided food, and the first gave the second what he lacked. The various estates of men thus developed automatically, one becoming a hunter, another a craftsman, and a third a cultivator. But men did not stop at this, for humanity must go forward. People began to invent. They invented spinning and weaving, they learned to forge iron and tan hides. The more inventions were made the more diverse did the crafts become, and the easier did farming become with the aid of the plough and spade which the handicrafts gave it. All helped each other and co-operated. Then intercourse started with neighbouring peoples; one people had what the other needed, and the latter possessed things which the former lacked. These were exchanged. Thus *trading* arose, that is, a new branch of human activity. Thus culture advanced step by step; from the first clumsy inventions through the centuries down to the inventions of our day.

"Thus, science and art arose among men and life became richer and more varied.. The physician treated the sick, the clergyman preached, the merchant traded, the farmer tilled the land, the gardener grew flowers, the mason built houses, for which the carpenter made the furniture, the miller ground flour from which the baker baked bread. Everything was interconnected, no one could live in isolation, nobody could satisfy all his needs himself.

"These are the social relations.

"They have arisen quite naturally of their own accord. And if today you make a revolution which destroys the very foundations of these relations, and if tomorrow you start life anew, *then relations exactly the same as the present ones will arise again.* This was so for thousands of years among all the nations on earth. And if anyone draws a distinction between the workers and the bourgeoisie this is a *big lie. We all work,* each in his own way, each according to his strength and abilities. The physician works when he visits the sick, the musician when he plays a dance tune, the merchant when he writes his letters. Everyone works, each at his job."

Here is wisdom! He that hath ears to hear, let him hear. What, then, in effect is the physiological question?

Every material being presupposes a certain weight, density, etc. Every organic body consists of various component parts, each of which performs its own special function, and reciprocal interaction takes place between the organs.

"These are physiological relations."

Montesquieu LVI cannot be denied an original talent for simplifying science. He ought to be granted a patent (without government guarantee).

The products of labour cannot be produced without labour. One cannot reap without sowing, one cannot have yarn without weaving, etc.

Europe will bend in admiration before the great genius who here, in Cologne, without any aid from the *Neue Preussische Zeitung* has himself brought these truths to light.

In their work men enter into certain relations with one another. There takes place a *division of labour* which may be more or less diversified. One person bakes, another forges iron, one person agitates, another howls,[156] Montesquieu LVI writes and Dumont prints. *Adam Smith,* acknowledge thy master!

The discoveries that *labour* and the *division of labour* are essential conditions of every human society enable Montesquieu LVI to draw the conclusion that the existence of *"various estates"* is quite natural, that the distinction between "bourgeoisie and proletariat" is a *"big lie"*, that even if a *"revolution"* were completely to destroy the existing "social relations" today, *"relations exactly the same as the present ones will arise again"*, and finally that for anyone who has "a sympathetic heart for the misery of his poor brothers" and who wishes to gain the respect of Montesquieu LVI, it is absolutely necessary to elect delegates in keeping with the ideas of Manteuffel and the imposed constitution.

"This was so for thousands of years among all the nations on earth"!! In Egypt there was labour and division of labour—and *castes*; in Greece and Rome labour and division of labour—and *free men and slaves*; in the Middle Ages labour and division of labour—and *feudal lords* and *serfs, guilds, estates*, etc. In our day there is labour and division of labour—and *classes,* one of which owns all means of production and all means of subsistence, while the other lives only so long as it sells its labour, and it sells its labour only so long as the employing class enriches itself by purchasing this labour.

Is it not obvious, therefore, that *"for thousands of years the same conditions existed among all the nations on earth"* as in *Prussia* today, since *labour and division of labour* always existed in one form or another? Or is it, on the contrary, not evident that it is the continuously changing method of labour and division of labour which is constantly transforming social relations and property relations?

In 1789 the bourgeois did not tell feudal society that an aristocrat should remain an aristocrat, a serf a serf and a guildsman a guildsman—because there is no society without labour and division of labour. There is no life without breathing of air. Hence, argues Montesquieu LVI, breathe the stuffy air and do not open any window.

One must possess the naively clumsy insolence of a German imperial philistine grown grey in crass ignorance to contribute oracular pronouncements upon problems on

which our century is breaking its teeth, after having
rammed the first elements of political economy—labour and
division of labour—in a superficial and distorted manner into
his inert head.

"There is no society without labour and division of
labour.

"Hence

"Elect advocates of the imposed Prussian constitution,
and only advocates of the imposed constitution, as delegates."

This epitaph will be inscribed in large letters on the
walls of the magnificent marble mausoleum which a grateful
posterity will feel obliged to erect for Montesquieu LVI (not
to be confused with Henry CCLXXXIV of Reuss-Schleiz-
Greiz-Lobenstein-Eberswalde*) who solved the social question.

Montesquieu LVI does not conceal from us *"where the
difficulty lies"* and what he intends to do as soon as he is
proclaimed a lawgiver.

"The state," he teaches, *"must see to it that everybody receives sufficient education to be able to learn something useful in this world."*

Montesquieu LVI has never heard that under existing
conditions the division of labour replaces complex labour
by simple labour, the labour of adults by that of children,
the labour of men by that of women, the labour of the
independent workers by automatons; that, with the development of modern industry, the education of workers becomes
unnecessary and impossible. We refer the Montesquieu of
Cologne neither to *Saint-Simon* nor to *Fourier* but to
Malthus and *Ricardo*. This worthy should first acquaint
himself with the rudiments of present-day conditions before
trying to improve them and making oracular utterances.

*"The community must take care of people who have been reduced to
poverty as a result of illness or old age."*

And if the community itself is reduced to poverty which
will be the inevitable result of the 100-million tax and the

---

* An allusion to Henry LXXII, Prince of Reuss-Lobenstein-Ebers-
dorf.—*Ed.*

recurrent imposition of martial law together with the new constitution?

"When new inventions or commercial crises destroy entire industries the state must come to their assistance and find remedies."

Though he may be little versed in the things of this world, it can hardly have escaped the Montesquieu of Cologne that "new inventions" and commercial crises are features just as permanent as Prussian ministerial decrees and legal basis. New inventions, especially in Germany, are only introduced when competition with other nations makes it vital to introduce them; and should the newly arising branches of industry be expected to ruin themselves in order to render assistance to the declining ones. The new industries that come into being as a result of inventions come into being precisely because they can produce more cheaply than the declining industries. What the deuce would be the advantage if they had to feed the declining industries? But it is well known that the state, the government, only seems to give. It has to be given first in order to give. But who should do the giving, Montesquieu LVI? The declining industry, so that it decline even faster? Or the rising industry, so that it wither on the stem? Or those industries that have not been affected by the new inventions, so that they go bankrupt because of the invention of a new tax? Think it over carefully, Montesquieu LVI!

And what about the commercial crises, my dear man? When a European commercial crisis occurs the Prussian state is above all anxious to extract the last drops, by means of distraint, etc., from the usual sources of revenue. Poor Prussian state! In order to neutralise the effect of commercial crises, the Prussian state would have to possess, in addition to national labour, a third source of income in Cloud-Cuckoo-Land. If royal New-Year's greetings, Wrangel's army orders or Manteuffel's ministerial decrees could indeed conjure up money, then the *"refusal to pay taxes"* would not have caused such panic among the Prussian "trusty and well-beloved subjects", and the social question, too, would have been solved without an imposed constitution.

It will be remembered that the *Neue Preussische Zeitung*

called our *Hansemann* a *communist* because he intended to
do away with exemption from taxation. In Cologne our
Montesquieu, who has never read the *Neue Preussische Zeitung*, has *all by himself* conceived the idea of calling everyone a "communist" and "red republican" who endangers the
imposed constitution. Therefore, vote for Manteuffel, or you
are not only personal enemies of labour and the division of
labour, but also communists and red republicans. Acknowledge Brüggemann's latest "legal basis" or renounce the Code
civil.[157]

    Figaro, tu n'aurais pas trouvé ça!
More about Montesquieu LVI tomorrow.

[II]

    Cologne, January 21. With the sly petty cunning of an
experienced *horse-dealer, Montesquieu LVI* seeks to sell the
"gift horse", the imposed constitution, to the primary voters.
He is the Montesquieu of the horse-fair.

Anyone not wanting the imposed constitution wants a
republic, and not just a republic, but a red republic! Unfortunately, the issue in our elections is least of all a republic, or a red republic; it is simply this:

Do you want the old *absolutism* together with a refurbished *system of social estates*, or do you want a bourgeois
system of representation? Do you want a political constitution in keeping with the "existing social relations" of past
centuries, or do you want a political constitution in keeping
with the "existing social relations" of your century?

In this case, therefore, it is least of all a matter of fighting
against bourgeois property relations similar to the struggle
that is taking place in France and is in the offing in
England; rather it is a question of a struggle against a
political constitution which endangers "*bourgeois* property
relations" by surrendering the helm of state to the representatives of "*feudal* property relations", to the King by the
grace of God, the army, the bureaucracy, the country
squires, and a few financial magnates and philistines who
are allied with them.

Beyond a doubt, the imposed constitution has solved the social question in keeping with the views of these gentlemen.

What is the *"social question"* as understood by the *civil servant*? It is the maintenance of his salary and his present position, which is superior to the people.

What is the *"social question"* as understood by the nobility and its big landowners? It is the maintenance of the hitherto existing feudal rights of the landowners, seizure of the most lucrative posts in the army and civil service by the families of the landed nobility, and finally direct alms from the public purse. Apart from these palpable *material* and therefore *"most sacred"* interests of the gentlemen "with God for King and Country", it is for them, of course, also a question of preserving those social privileges which distinguish their species from the inferior species of the bourgeois, peasants and plebeians. The old National Assembly was dispersed because it dared to touch these "most sacred interests". As we have already indicated, these gentlemen, by "revision" of the imposed constitution, understand simply the introduction of a *system of social estates,* that is to say, a form of political constitution representing the "social" interests of the feudal aristocracy, the bureaucracy and the monarchy by the grace of God.

We repeat, there is not the slightest doubt that the imposed constitution solves the "social question" according to the ideas of the aristocracy and bureaucracy, in other words, it presents these gentlemen with a form of government which ensures the exploitation of the people by these demigods.

But has the imposed constitution solved the "social question" from the standpoint of the *bourgeoisie*? In other words, does the bourgeoisie receive a political form enabling it freely to run matters concerning its class as a whole, i.e., the interests of commerce, industry and agriculture, to make the most productive use of public funds, to manage the state apparatus as cheaply as possible, to protect national labour effectively abroad, and within the country to open up all springs of national wealth silted by feudal mud?

Does history provide a single example showing that under a king imposed by the grace of God, the bourgeoisie ever succeeded in attaining a form of government in keeping with its material interests?

In order to establish a constitutional monarchy it was twice compelled to get rid of the Stuarts in Britain, and the hereditary Bourbons in France and to expel William of Orange from Belgium.[158]

What is the reason?

A hereditary king by the grace of God is not a particular individual but the physical representative of the old society within the new society. Political power in the hands of a king by the grace of God is political power in the hands of the old society existing now merely as a ruin; it is political power in the hands of the feudal estates, whose interests are profoundly antagonistic to those of the bourgeoisie.

But it is the *"King by the grace of God"* who forms the basis of the imposed constitution.

Just as the feudal strata of society regard the monarchy by divine right as their *political apex*, so does the monarchy by divine right regard the feudal estates as its *social foundation*, the well-known *"monarchical wall"*.

Therefore, whenever the interests of the feudal lords and of the army and bureaucracy controlled by them clash with the interests of the bourgeoisie, the monarchy by divine right will invariably be impelled to a coup d'état and a revolutionary or counter-revolutionary crisis will arise.

Why was the National Assembly ejected? Only because it upheld the interests of the bourgeoisie as against the interests of feudalism; because it wanted to abolish feudal relations, which impede agriculture, to subordinate the army and bureaucracy to trade and industry, to stop the squandering of public funds and abolish aristocratic and bureaucratic titles.

All these matters *chiefly* and *directly* affected the *interests of the bourgeoisie.*

Thus, *coup d'états* and *counter-revolutionary crises* are vital to the existence of the monarchy by the grace of God, which the March and similar events compelled to eat humble pie and reluctantly to accept a pseudo-bourgeois monarchy.

Can *credit* ever revive again under a form of government

whose inevitable climax are coup d'états, counter-revolutionary crises and states of siege?

What a delusion!

Bourgeois industry *must* burst the chains of absolutism
and feudalism. A revolution against both only demonstrates
that bourgeois industry has reached a level when it must
either secure an appropriate political form or perish.

The system of bureaucratic tutelage consolidated by the
imposed constitution spells *death* for industry. It is sufficient to look at the Prussian administration of mines, the
factory regulations, etc. When an English manufacturer
compares his costs of production with those of a Prussian
manufacturer, he will always first of all note the time losses
which the Prussian manufacturer incurs because he has to
observe bureaucratic rules.

What sugar-refiner does not remember the Prussian trade
agreement with the Netherlands in 1839?[159] What Prussian
factory owner does not blush at the memory of 1846, when
the Prussian government in deference to the Austrian government banned exports to Galicia for a whole province, and
when one bankruptcy after another occurred in Breslau the
Prussian government declared with astonishment that it
had had no idea that so important an export trade was
carried with Galicia, etc.!

Men of the same type are placed at the helm of state
by the imposed constitution, and this "gift" itself comes
from the same men. Consequently, examine it twice.

The Galicia adventure draws our attention to another
point.

At that time the counter-revolutionary Prussian government in league with Austria and Russia sacrificed Silesian
industry and Silesian trade. This manoeuvre will be constantly repeated. The banker of the Prussian-Austrian-
Russian counter-revolution, from which the monarchy by
the grace of God with its monarchical walls will always
have to seek *outside* support, is *England*. The same *England*
is German industry's most dangerous opponent. These two
facts, we believe, speak for themselves.

At home, an industry fettered by bureaucracy and an
agriculture fettered by feudal privileges; abroad, a trade

sold by the counter-revolution to England—such is the fate
of Prussia's national wealth under the aegis of the imposed
constitution.

The report of the "Financial Commission" of the dispersed
National Assembly has thrown sufficient light on the divine
management of national wealth.

The report however mentions only by way of example
the sums taken from the treasury to support the tottering
monarchical walls and gild foreign pretenders to the absolute monarchy (Don Carlos). But this money, purloined from
the pockets of the rest of the citizens to enable the aristocracy to live in appropriate style and to keep the "pillars"
of the feudal monarchy well buttressed, is only of secondary importance compared with the state budget imposed simultaneously with Manteuffel's constitution. The main features of the imposed state budget are, first of all, a *strong army*
to enable the minority to rule the majority; as large an
army as possible of officials so that as many of them as
possible, by virtue of their private interests, are alienated
from the common interest; unproductive employment of
public funds in order that wealth, as the *Neue Preussische
Zeitung* says, should not make the *subjects* presumptuous;
immobilisation wherever possible of public funds instead of
employing them in industry in order that at predictable
moments of crisis the government by divine right independently confront the people. The basic principle of the imposed Prussian constitution is to use the taxes for maintaining the state as an oppressive, independent and sacred force
contraposed to industry, commerce and agriculture, instead
of *degrading* it by turning it into a profane *tool* of bourgeois society.

The gift is worthy of the donor. The constitution is of a
piece with the present Prussian government that presented
it. To get an idea of *this government's hostility towards the
bourgeoisie* it is sufficient to point to its proposed *trade regulations.* On the pretext of *advancing towards association*
the government attempts to *return to the guild system.*
Competition compels the manufacturer to produce as cheaply
as possible and therefore on a constantly increasing scale,
i.e., with *more capital*, with a continuously *expanding divi-*

sion of labour and constantly *increasing use of machinery.*
Every new division of labour depreciates the traditional
skill of the craftsmen, every new machine ousts hundreds of
workers, production on a larger scale, that is, with more
capital, ruins small trade and petty-bourgeois enterprise.
The government promises to protect the handicrafts against
the factories, acquired skills against division of labour, and
small capital against big capital, by means of *feudal guild
practices.* Thus, the German nation, particularly the Prussian, which is barely able to withstand English competition,
is to become its defenceless prey, forced to accept a form
of trade organisation that is incompatible with modern
means of production and is already burst wide open by
modern industry.

We are certainly the last people to desire the rule of the
bourgeoisie. We were the first in Germany to raise our
voice against the bourgeoisie when today's "men of action"
were spending their time complacently in petty squabbles.

But we say to the workers and the petty bourgeois: it is
better to suffer in the contemporary bourgeois society,
whose industry creates the means for the foundation of a
new society that will liberate you all, than to revert to a
bygone society, which, on the pretext of saving your classes,
thrusts the entire nation back into medieval barbarism.

But medieval estates and conditions are, as we have seen,
the *social foundation* of the government by the grace of
God. This government is unsuitable for modern bourgeois
society. It necessarily tries to create a society in its own
image. It is *entirely consistent,* when it attempts to replace
free competition by the guild system, mechanical spinning
by the spinning-wheel and the steam plough by the hoe.

Why is it then that, under these circumstances, the Prussian bourgeoisie, in contrast to its French, English and
Belgian predecessors, proclaims as its shibboleth the imposed
constitution (and with it the monarchy by divine right, the
bureaucracy and the landowning nobility)?

The commercial and industrial sections of the bourgeoisie throw themselves into the arms of the counter-revolution for fear of the revolution. As though counter-revolution were not the overture to revolution.

There is moreover a section of the *bourgeoisie* that, quite indifferent to the interests of its class as a whole, pursues its own particular interests, which may even be inimical to those of its class.

These are financial magnates, big creditors of the state, bankers, and rentiers, whose wealth increases proportionately to the poverty of the people, and finally men whose business depends on the old political structure, e.g., *Dumont* and his literary lumpen-proletariat. These are also ambitious professors, lawyers and similar persons, who can only hope to obtain respectable posts in a state where betrayal of the people's interests to the government is a lucrative business.

These are certain manufacturers who do well out of their transactions with the government; contractors whose considerable profits depend on the general exploitation of the people; philistines who would lose their importance if political life were conducted on a larger scale; local councillors who under cover of the old institutions arrange their private shady affairs at the expense of the public; oil-merchants who at the price of their betrayal of the revolution have become Excellencies and Knights of the Eagle; bankrupt cloth-merchants and speculators in railway-shares who have become royal bank directors,[160] etc., etc.

"It is they who are the advocates of the imposed constitution." If the bourgeoisie has a *sympathetic heart for these poor brothers* and if it wants to be worthy of the respect of Montesquieu LVI, then it should elect
delegates in keeping with the imposed constitution.

Written by Marx

Neue Rheinische Zeitung Nos.
201 and 202,
January 21 and 22, 1849

THE TRIAL OF THE RHENISH
DISTRICT COMMITTEE OF DEMOCRATS[161]

[Karl Marx's Speech Delivered on February 8, 1849]

Gentlemen of the jury, if this action had been brought *before* December 5, I could have understood the charge made by the public prosecutor. Now, *after* the 5th of December, I do not understand how he dares to invoke against us laws which the Crown itself has trampled in the dirt.

On what does the public prosecutor base his criticism of the National Assembly and the resolution not to pay taxes? On the laws of April 6 and 8, 1848. And what did the government do on December 5, when it arbitrarily imposed a constitution and a new electoral law on the country? It tore up the laws of April 6 and 8, 1848. These laws are no longer valid for the supporters of the government, so why should they still be valid for the opponents of the government? On December 5 the government took its stand on a *revolutionary* basis, namely, on a *counter-revolutionary* basis. It is now confronted only by revolutionaries or accomplices. Even the mass of citizens who act on the basis of the existing law, who uphold the existing law in face of infringements of that law, have been turned into rebels by this government. *Before* December 5 opinion concerning the removal of the National Assembly, its dispersal and the introduction of a state of siege in Berlin could have been divided. *After* December 5 it is a well-established fact that these measures were intended to usher in the counter-revolution and that therefore every means could be used against a group that itself no longer recognised the conditions under which it *governed* and consequently could no longer be recognised as a government by the country. Gentlemen, the Crown could have preserved at least the semblance of legality, but it has not deigned to do so. It could have dispersed the National Assembly and then let the cabinet come forward and tell the country: "We have dared to carry out a coup d'état—circumstances have forced us to do it. We have disregarded the convention of the law, but there are moments of crisis when the very existence of the state is at stake. At such moments there is only *one* inviolable law—the existence of the state. There was no valid constitution when we dispersed the Assembly. Therefore no constitution could be infringed. But there existed two organic laws—those of April 6 and 8, 1848. Actually there is only *one* organic law, the *electoral law*. We ask the country to carry through elections in accordance with *this* law. We, the *responsible government*, will then appear before the Assembly that has emerged from these primary elections. This Assembly, we trust, will recognise that the coup d'état was an *act of deliverance* necessitated by circumstances. It will subsequently sanction the coup d'état. It will declare that we infringed a legal form in order to save the country. Let it pass judgment on us."

If the cabinet had done this, it would have had a *semblance* of right to arraign us. The Crown would have kept a semblance of legality, but it could not or *would* not do it.

The March revolution, as seen by the Crown, was a harsh fact. One harsh fact can be erased only by another harsh fact. By rejecting new elections on the basis of the law of April 1848, the cabinet *renounced its own responsibilities, thereby repudiating also the bar towards which it was responsible*. At the very outset it turned the appeal of the National Assembly to the people into a mere pretence, a fiction, a deception. By inventing a first Chamber based on the property qualification as an integral part of the Legislative Assembly, the cabinet tore up the organic laws, departed from the legal basis, falsified the elections and prevented the people from passing any judgment on the "act of deliverance" of the Crown.

And so, gentlemen, the fact cannot be denied, and no future historian will deny it—the Crown has made a revolution, it has overthrown the existing legal system, it cannot appeal to the laws it has itself so scandalously annulled. After successfully carrying out a revolution one can hang one's opponents, but one cannot convict them. Defeated enemies can be put out of the way, but they cannot be arraigned as criminals. After a revolution or counter-revolution has been consummated the invalidated laws cannot be used against the *defenders* of these laws. This would be a cowardly pretence of legality which you, gentlemen, will not sanctify by your verdict.

I have already told you, gentlemen, that the government has falsified the sentence which the people passed on the "act of deliverance of the Crown". The people nevertheless has already decided *against* the Crown and *for* the National Assembly. The elections to the second Chamber are the only lawful elections because they alone were based on the law of April 8, 1848. Practically all the deputies who were for the refusal to pay taxes were re-elected to the second Chamber, many of them even two or three times. Schneider II, my codefendant, is himself deputy for Cologne. Thus, the question of the National Assembly's right to vote for the refusal to pay taxes has virtually been decided already by the people.

But quite irrespective of this most authoritative judgment, you will agree with me, gentlemen, that in the present case no crime in the ordinary sense of the word has been committed, in this case no infringement of the law falling within your jurisdiction has occurred at all. Under ordinary conditions the existing laws are enforced by the public authorities; whoever infringes these laws or prevents the public authorities from enforcing them is a criminal. In the present case one public authority has infringed the law, another public authority, it makes no difference which, has upheld it. The struggle between these two political powers lies neither within the sphere of civil law, nor within the sphere of criminal law. The question of who was in the right, the Crown or the National Assembly, is a matter for history. All the juries, all the courts of Prussia cannot decide it. Only one power can supply the answer—history. I do not understand, therefore, how, on the basis of the Code pénal, we could be placed in the dock.

That this was a struggle between two powers, and only power can decide between two powers—that, gentlemen, has been declared by both the revolutionary and the counter-revolutionary press. This was proclaimed even by the organ of the government a short time before the struggle was decided. The *Neue Preussische Zeitung,* the organ of the present government, clearly realised this. A few days before the crisis it said approximately the following: It is no longer a question of right but of power, and the old monarchy by the grace of God will show that it still has this power. The *Neue Preussische Zeitung* correctly understood the situation. Power against power. Victory would decide for one or the other. The counter-revolution carried the day but we have seen only the first act of the drama. The struggle in England lasted over twenty years. Charles I came out on top several times and ended up on the scaffold. Who, gentlemen, can guarantee to you that the present cabinet and the officials who acted and continue to act as its tools will not be convicted of high treason by this Chamber or its successors?

Gentlemen, the public prosecutor has tried to base his accusation on the laws of April 6 and 8. I have been compelled here to demonstrate to you that it is these laws which acquit us. But I make no secret of the fact that I have never recognised these laws and never will. They never had any validity for the deputies elected by the people, still less could they prescribe the course of the March revolution.

How did the laws of April 6 and 8 come into being? By agreement between the government and the *United Provincial Diet.* It was an attempt to maintain continuity with the old legal system and to play down the revolution which had done away with that system. Men like Camphausen thought it important to preserve a semblance of legal continuity. And how did they preserve this semblance? By a series of obvious and absurd contradictions. Let us for a moment adopt the old legal point of view. Was not the very existence of Minister Camphausen, a *responsible minister,* a minister who had not climbed the bureaucratic ladder, unlawful? The position of Camphausen, the *responsible Prime Minister,* was unlawful. This officer, who does not exist *in law*, convenes the United Provincial Diet to have it pass laws it was not *legally* competent to pass. This inconsistent and self-contradictory playing with formalities was called legal advance, or maintenance of the legal basis!

But let us leave aside the form, gentlemen. What was the United Provincial Diet? It represented old decaying social relations. It was against these relations that the revolution was directed. And the representatives of the vanquished society are asked to endorse organic laws designed to recognise, guide and organise the revolution against this old society. What an absurd contradiction! The Diet was overthrown together with the old monarchy.

On this occasion we are confronted by the so-called *legal basis*. It is the more necessary for me to deal with this point since we are justly regarded as opponents of the legal basis, and since the laws of April 6 and 8 owe their existence to the formal recognition of the legal basis.

The Diet represented primarily big landed property. Big landed property was indeed the foundation of medieval, *feudal society. Modern bourgeois society, our* own society, is however based on industry and commerce. Landed property itself has lost all its former conditions of existence, it has become dependent on commerce and industry. Agriculture, therefore, is carried on nowadays on industrial lines, and the old feudal lords have now become producers of cattle, wool, corn, beetroots, spirits, etc., i.e., people who trade in industrial products just as any other merchant. However much they may cling to their old prejudices, they are in fact being turned into bourgeois, who manufacture as much as possible and as cheaply as possible, who buy where they can get goods at the lowest price and sell where they can obtain the highest price. The mode of living, production and income of these gentlemen therefore gives the lie to their traditional pompous notions. Landed property, as the predominant social factor, presupposes a *medieval mode of production and commerce.* The United Provincial Diet represented this medieval mode of production and commerce which had long since ceased to exist, and whose protagonists, though they clung to the old privi-

leges, likewise enjoyed and exploited the advantages of the
new society. The new bourgeois society, grounded on an
entirely different foundation, on a changed mode of production, was bound to seize also political power, which had
to be wrenched from the hands of those who represented
the interests of a declining society, a political power, whose
whole structure had been built up on the soil of entirely
different material conditions of society. *Hence the revolution.*
The revolution was consequently directed as much against
the *absolute monarchy*, the supreme political expression of
the old society, as against the *representatives of the estates*,
who stood for a social system that had been long ago destroyed
by modern industry or, at most, for the presumptuous ruins
of the dissolved *estates* which bourgeois society was overtak-
ing and pushing into the background more and more every
day. How then was the idea conceived to allow the United
Provincial Diet, the representative of the old society, to
dictate laws to the new society which asserted its rights
through the revolution?

Allegedly in order to maintain the *legal basis.* But what
do you understand by maintaining the legal basis? To maintain laws belonging to a bygone social era and framed by
representatives of vanished or vanishing social interests, who
consequently give the force of law only to these interests,
which run counter to the public needs. Society is not founded
upon the law; this is a legal fiction. On the contrary, the
law must be founded upon society, it must express the common interests and needs of society—as distinct from the
caprice of the individuals—which arise from the material
mode of production prevailing at the given time. This Code
Napoléon, which I am holding in my hand, has not created
modern bourgeois society. On the contrary, bourgeois society,
which emerged in the eighteenth century and developed
further in the nineteenth, merely finds its legal expression
in this Code. As soon as it ceases to fit the social conditions,
it becomes simply a bundle of paper. You cannot make the
old laws the foundation of the new social development, any
more than these old laws created the old social conditions.

They were engendered by the old conditions of society
and must perish with them. They are bound to change with

the changing conditions of life. To maintain the old laws in face of the new needs and demands of social development is essentially the same as hypocritically upholding the out-of-date particular interests of a minority in face of the up-to-date interests of the community. *This maintenance of the legal basis* aims at asserting minority interests as if they were the *predominant* interests, when they are *no longer dominant*; it aims at imposing on society laws which have been condemned by the conditions of life in this society, by the way the members of this society earn their living, by their commerce and their material production; it aims at retaining legislators who are concerned only with their particular interests; it seeks to misuse political power in order forcibly to place the interests of a minority above the interests of the majority. The maintenance of the legal basis is therefore in constant conflict with the existing needs, it hampers commerce and industry, it prepares the way for *social crises*, which erupt in *political revolutions*.

That is what adherence to the legal basis and the maintenance of the legal basis really mean. Relying on these phrases about the legal basis, which arise either from conscious deceit or unconscious self-deception, the United Provincial Diet was convoked, and this Diet was made to frame organic laws for the National Assembly the need for which was created by the revolution and which owed its existence to the revolution. And on the strength of these laws the National Assembly is to be judged!

The National Assembly represented modern bourgeois society as against feudal society, which is represented in the United Provincial Diet. It was elected by the people for the purpose of independently enacting a constitution to fit the conditions of life, which had come into conflict with the old political organisation and laws. It was thus from the very beginning a sovereign, constituent assembly. The fact that it nevertheless condescended to the views of the conciliators, was mere formal courtesy towards the Crown, mere ceremony. I need not here go into the question whether the Assembly—as far as the people are concerned—had the right to take a stand for conciliation. It considered that a collision with the Crown should be averted by a display of goodwill on both sides.

One thing is certain, however—that the laws of April 6 and 8, which were agreed with the United Provincial Diet, were formally invalid. The only material significance they have is that they state and lay down the conditions under which the National Assembly could really express the sovereign will of the people. The laws passed by the United Provincial Diet were merely a formula by which the Crown was saved the humiliation of having to proclaim: *I have been defeated!*

Now, gentlemen of the jury, I shall examine more closely the speech of the public prosecutor.

He says:

"The Crown ceded part of the power which had been wholly in its hands. Even in the ordinary course of things a deed of renunciation does not go beyond what is clearly stated in the words of renunciation. The law of April 8, 1848, neither grants the National Assembly the right to refuse to vote taxes, nor stipulates that Berlin must necessarily be the seat of the National Assembly."

Gentlemen, power lay *broken* in the hands of the Crown, and the Crown gave up power in order to save the fragments. You will remember that immediately after his accession to the throne, the King formally pledged his word of honour at Königsberg and Berlin not to concede constitutional government. You will remember that when opening the United Provincial Diet in 1847 the King solemnly swore that he would not allow a piece of paper to come between him and *his* people. After the March events of 1848, and even in the imposed constitution, the King proclaimed himself a *constitutional* monarch. He has put this paper, this piece of abstract, outlandish flummery, between himself and his people. Will the public prosecutor dare to assert that in conceding the agreement or the constitution, the King voluntarily contradicted in so manifest a way his own solemn declarations, that in the eyes of the whole of Europe he voluntarily committed so glaring an inconsistency! The King made the concessions which the revolution *compelled* him to make. Neither more nor less.

The popular analogy which the public prosecutor has

made unfortunately proves nothing. It is true, that if I renounce anything, I renounce only what I have *expressly* renounced. If I made you a gift, it would indeed be impudent if, on the basis of the deed of gift, you tried to compel me to undertake further obligations. But after the March events it was the people that made the gift and the Crown which received it. Obviously, the nature of the gift must be interpreted in accordance with the intentions of the giver and not those of the receiver, i.e., in accordance with the intentions of the people and not those of the Crown.

The absolute power of the Crown was shattered. The people had won the day. The two sides concluded a truce and the people was cheated. The public prosecutor himself has taken pains to demonstrate at some length that the people was deceived. To challenge the right of the National Assembly to refuse to vote taxes, the public prosecutor has explained to you in detail that if there was something of this kind in the law of April 6, 1848, it was certainly no longer to be found in the law of April 8, 1848. The interval of two days was thus used to deprive the representatives of the people of the rights which had been conceded to them two days earlier. Could the public prosecutor have more strikingly compromised the *honesty* of the Crown, could he have more irrefutably proved the *intention to deceive* the people?

The public prosecutor says further:

"The right to *adjourn and prorogue* the National Assembly is a prerogative of the executive power recognised in all constitutional countries."

As to the right of the *executive to transfer* the meeting place of the legislative chambers, I would like to ask the public prosecutor to cite even a single law or example in support of his claim. In England, for instance, under an old historical privilege, the King could convoke Parliament anywhere he pleased. There is no law stating that London is the legal seat of Parliament. As you know, gentlemen, in England the most important political liberties are generally sanctioned not by Statute Law but by Common Law; such, for instance, is the case with the freedom of the press. But should an English ministry take it into its head to transfer Parliament from London to Windsor or Richmond, it is sufficient to put the idea into words to realise how impossible it is.

True, in countries that have a constitutional government, the Crown has the right to *prorogue* Parliament. But it must not be forgotten that on the other hand all constitutions specify *for how long* the chambers can be prorogued and when they have to be summoned again.—Prussia has no constitution, one still has to be drafted; no legal time-limit for summoning a prorogued chamber exists, consequently no prorogation right of the Crown exists.—Otherwise the Crown could prorogue the Chamber for ten days, for ten years, or for ever. How could one be sure that the chambers would ever be summoned or allowed to meet for any length of time? The existence of the chambers juxtaposed with the Crown would be left to the discretion of the Crown, the legislative power—if one could speak of legislative power in this context—would have become a sham.

Gentlemen, this example shows where any attempt to compare the conflict between the Prussian Crown and the Prussian National Assembly with the conditions obtaining in constitutional countries leads to. It leads to the *maintenance of the absolute monarchy*. On the one hand, the rights of a constitutional executive power are conferred upon the Crown, on the other, there is no law, no tradition, no organic institutions able to impose on it the restrictions proper to a constitutional executive power. The representatives of the people are expected to play the role of a *constitutional* chamber in relation to an *absolute* monarchy!

Is there any need to explain that in the case under consideration it was not a matter of an *executive power* vis-à-vis a *legislative power*, that the constitutional division of powers cannot be applied to the *Prussian National Assembly* and the Prussian Crown? Let us disregard the revolution and consider only the official *theory of agreement*. Even according to this theory two sovereign powers confronted each other. That is beyond any doubt. One of these two powers was bound to break the other. Two sovereign powers cannot function simultaneously, side by side, *in one state*. This is an absurdity, like the squaring of the circle. Material force had to decide the issue between the two sovereign powers. But it is not our task here to go into the question of whether agreement was possible or impossible. It is sufficient that two powers entered into relations with each other in order to conclude an agreement. Camphausen himself admitted that agreement might not be achieved. From the rostrum he spoke to the advocates of agreement of the danger that faced the country if they did not come to terms. The danger was implied in the initial relationship between the conciliatory National Assembly and the Crown, and afterwards an attempt is made to hold the National Assembly responsible for this danger by denying this initial relationship and by turning the Assembly into a *constitutional chamber!* It is an attempt to overcome a difficulty by abstracting from it.

Gentlemen, I think I have shown you that the Crown had no right either to adjourn or to prorogue the Assembly of conciliators.

But the public prosecutor did not confine himself to examining whether the Crown had the *right* to adjourn the National Assembly; he has tried to prove that this adjournment was *expedient.* "Would it not have been expedient," he exclaims, "if the National Assembly had obeyed the Crown and moved to Brandenburg?" According to the public prosecutor, the expediency of such an act was due to the position of the Chamber itself. The Chamber was not free in Berlin, and so forth.

But is it not obvious what purpose the Crown pursued in ordering this removal? Had not the Crown itself divested all officially advanced reasons for the removal of any semblance of veracity? It was not a question of freedom of deliberation, but of whether the Assembly be dissolved and a constitution imposed, or whether a spurious Assembly be created by summoning more docile representatives. When, unexpectedly, a sufficient number of deputies arrived in Brandenburg to form a quorum, the pretence was abandoned and the National Assembly was dissolved.

Incidentally, it goes without saying that the Crown had no right to declare the National Assembly either free or unfree. No one but the National Assembly itself could decide whether it had the necessary freedom of deliberation or not.

It would be most convenient for the Crown if it could declare that the National Assembly was not free, that it was irresponsible and to ban it, whenever the Assembly passed resolutions the Crown disliked.

The public prosecutor has also spoken about the government's duty to protect the dignity of the National Assembly against the terrorism of the Berlin populace.

This argument sounds like a satire on the government. I will not speak here of its treatment of individuals, of men who, after all, were the elected representatives of the people. It sought to humiliate them in every possible way, they were prosecuted in a most infamous way and a sort of wild chase was organised against them. But let us leave aside individuals. How was the dignity of the National Assembly and of its *work* maintained? Its archives were given over to the military who used the documents comprised in the various departments, the royal messages, draft laws and preliminary studies, as spills to light pipes with, burned them in stoves, and trampled on them.

Not even the formalities of a legal warrant were observed; the archives were seized without even an inventory being drawn up.

It was part of a plan to destroy this work so dear to the people, in order to make it easier to vilify the National Assembly and to quash the planned reforms which were abhorrent to the government and aristocracy. Is it not simply ridiculous to assert after all this that the government transferred the National Assembly from Berlin to Brandenburg out of tender concern for its dignity?

Now I come to the statement of the public prosecutor regarding the *formal validity* of the resolution to refuse payment of taxes.

The public prosecutor says that in order to make the resolution on the tax refusal formally valid, the Assembly should have submitted it to the *Crown for sanctioning*.

But, gentlemen, the Crown itself did not face the Assembly, it was represented by the Brandenburg cabinet. Consequently, according to the absurd claim of the public prosecutor, the Assembly should have reached an agreement with the Brandenburg cabinet to proclaim that cabinet guilty of high treason and to prevent it from collecting taxes. What meaning can this demand have other than that the National Assembly should submit unconditionally to every request of the Brandenburg cabinet?

Another reason why the tax refusal resolution was formally invalid, says the public prosecutor, was that a motion can become law only after the *second reading*.

On the one hand, when dealing with the National Assembly they ignored *important* forms of procedure which ought to have been binding and, on the other, they expected the National Assembly to observe even the most unimportant *formalities*. As simple as that! A bill objectionable to the Crown is passed in the first reading, after which the second reading is prevented by force of arms, and the Bill remains invalid because there was no second reading. The public prosecutor does not take into consideration the exceptional state of affairs that obtained when, threatened with bayonets in their meeting hall, the deputies passed this resolution. The government commits one arbitrary act after another. It flagrantly violates the principal laws, the Habeas Corpus Act, and the Civil Guard Law.[162] It arbitrarily establishes an unlimited military despotism under the guise of martial law. It sends the deputies to the devil, and while on the one hand impudently infringing *all laws,* it, on the other hand, demands the most punctilious observation of even the *rules of procedure.*

Gentlemen, I do not know whether it is deliberate misrepresentation—I am far from assuming this on the part of the public prosecutor—or merely ignorance when he says: "The National Assembly did not want any *negotiations*" and it "did not seek any negotiations".

If the people blame the Berlin National Assembly for anything, it is for its desire for negotiations. If the deputies themselves regret anything, it is their desire for reconciliation. It was this desire for reconciliation which gradually alienated the Assembly from the people, caused it to lose all its positions, and finally, when it was not backed by the nation, exposed it to the attacks of the Crown. When at last it wanted to make a stand it found itself alone and powerless, precisely bceause it had not made that stand

and asserted itself at the right time. It first manifested this desire for reconciliation when it renounced the revolution and sanctioned the *theory of agreement,* when it degraded itself by turning from a revolutionary National Assembly into a dubious society of conciliators. It carried the weakness for negotiation to extremes when it accepted Pfuel's pseudo-recognition of Stein's army order as valid. The publication of this army order was itself a farce, since it could only be regarded as a comical echo of Wrangel's army order. Nevertheless, instead of going beyond it, the Assembly snatched at the attenuated interpretation of the Pfuel cabinet, which made the order meaningless. To avoid any serious conflict with the Crown, the Assembly accepted the feeble semblance of a demonstration against the old reactionary army as a real demonstration. It seriously pretended to regard what was not even a pseudo-solution of the conflict as the real solution of the conflict. So little did the Assembly want to fight, so keen was it on negotiations— and the public prosecutor describes it as pugnacious and quarrelsome.

Need I mention another symptom showing the conciliatory nature of this Chamber? You will remember the agreement between the National Assembly and Pfuel about the law suspending commutations.* If the Assembly was unable to destroy the enemy in the army, then it was above all necessary to win a friend in the peasantry. But it refrained from attempting even this. To negotiate, to avoid a conflict with the Crown, to avoid it at any cost—that was the Assembly's chief concern, which it placed above even its own self-preservation. And this Assembly is blamed for not wanting to negotiate, not attempting to negotiate!

It tried to negotiate even when the conflict had broken out. You know the pamphlet by *Unruh,*[163] a man of the Centre. You will have seen from it that every attempt was made to avoid a clash; that deputations were sent to the Crown and were turned away; that some deputies tried to argue with the ministers and were superciliously and arrogantly rebuffed; that the Assembly offered to make conces-

---

* See this volume, p. 199.—*Ed.*

sions and that these were derided. Even at the time when it could only be a matter of preparing for war, the Assembly still wanted to make peace. And the public prosecutor accuses this Assembly of not wanting to negotiate and not attempting to negotiate!

The Berlin National Assembly clearly nursed extravagant illusions and did not understand its own position and its conditions of existence, when *before* the conflict and even *during* the conflict it believed that an amicable arrangement and reconciliation with the Crown was still possible and worked towards it.

The Crown did not want and could not want reconciliation. Gentlemen of the jury, let us not deceive ourselves concerning the nature of the struggle which began in March and was later waged between the National Assembly and the Crown. It was not an ordinary conflict between a cabinet and a parliamentary opposition, it was not a conflict between men who were ministers and men who wanted to become ministers, it was not a struggle between two political parties in a legislative chamber. It is quite possible that members of the National Assembly belonging to the minority or the majority believed that this was so. The decisive factor, however, is not the opinion of the deputies, but the real historical position of the National Assembly as it emerged both from the European revolution and the March revolution it engendered. What took place here was not a political conflict between two parties within the framework of *one* society, but a *conflict between two societies,* a *social* conflict, which assumed a political form; *it was the struggle of the old feudal bureaucratic society with modern bourgeois society*, a struggle between the society of *free competition* and the *society of the guilds*, between the society of landownership and the industrial society, between a religious society and a scientific society. The *political* expression corresponding to the old society was the Crown by the grace of God, the bullying bureaucracy and the independent army. The *social* foundation corresponding to this old political power consisted of privileged aristocratic landownership with its enthralled or partially enthralled peasants, the small patriarchal or guild industries, the strictly separated estates, the sharp contradiction between town and country and, above all, the domination of the countryside over the town. The old political power—the Crown by the grace of God, the bullying bureaucracy, the independent army—realised that its essential material basis would disappear from under its feet, as soon as any change was made in the basis of the old society, privileged aristocratic landownership, the aristocracy itself, the domination of the countryside over the town, the dependent position of the rural population and the laws corresponding to these conditions of life, such as the parish regulations, the criminal law. The National Assembly made such an attempt. On the other hand that old society realised that political power would be wrenched from its hands, as soon as the Crown, the bureaucracy and the army lost their feudal privileges. The National Assembly wanted to abolish these privileges. It is not surprising, therefore, that the army, the bureaucracy and the nobility joined forces in urging the Crown to effect a coup de main, and it is not surprising that the Crown, knowing that its own interests were closely interlinked with those of the old feudal bureaucratic society, allowed itself to be impelled to a coup d'état. For the *Crown represented* feudal aristocratic society, just as the *National Assembly represented* modern bourgeois society. The conditions of existence in modern bourgeois society require that the bureaucracy and the army, which controlled commerce and industry, should become their tools, be *reduced* to mere organs of bourgeois intercourse. This society cannot tolerate that restrictions are placed on agriculture by feudal privileges and on industry by bureaucratic tutelage. This is contrary to free competition, the vital principle of this society. It cannot tolerate that foreign trade relations should be determined by considerations of the palace's international policies instead of by the interests of national production. It must subordinate fiscal policy to the needs of production, whereas the old state has to subordinate production to the needs of the Crown by the grace of God and the patching up of the monarchical walls, the social pillars of this Crown. Just as modern industry is indeed a leveller, so modern society must break down all legal and political barriers between town and country. Modern society still has *classes*, but no longer *estates*. Its development lies in the struggle between these classes, but the latter stand united against the estates and their monarchy by the grace of God.

The monarchy by the grace of God, the supreme political expression, the supreme political representative of the old feudal bureaucratic society, is consequently unable to make any *sincere* concessions to modern bourgeois society. Its own instinct of self-preservation, and the society which backs it and on which it leans will constantly impel it to retract the concessions it has made, to maintain its feudal character and to risk a counter-revolution. Counter-revolution is a constantly recurrent condition of existence for the Crown after every revolution.

On the other hand, modern society, too, cannot rest until it has shattered and abolished the political power, the traditional official power, by which the old society is forcibly preserved. For the rule of the Crown by the grace of God is the rule of antiquated social strata.

Hence no peace is possible between these two societies. Their material interests and needs bring them into mortal combat. One side must win, the other must lose. That is the only possible reconciliation between them. Neither can there be peace between the supreme political representatives of these two societies, between the Crown and the representatives of the people. Thus, the National Assembly had only the choice of either yielding to the old society or standing up to the Crown as an independent force.

Gentlemen, the public prosecutor has described the *refusal to pay taxes* as a measure "which shakes the *foundations of society*". The refusal to pay taxes has nothing to do with the foundations of society.

Generally speaking, why do taxes, the granting or the refusal of taxes, play such an important role in the history of constitutionalism? The reason is very simple. Just as serfs purchased privileges from the feudal lords with ready money, so did entire nations purchase privileges from feudal monarchs with ready money. Monarchs needed money for their wars with foreign nations and especially for their struggle against the feudal lords. The more trade and industry developed the greater grew their need for money. But the third estate, the middle classes, grew to the same extent and disposed of increasing financial resources; and in the same degree they purchased liberties from the monarchs by means of taxes. To make sure of these liberties they retained the right at definite intervals to renew the monetary obligations, i.e., the right to vote or to refuse to vote taxes. You can trace the details of this development especially well in English history.

In medieval society, therefore, taxes were the only bond between the emerging bourgeois society and the ruling feudal state, a bond which compelled the state to make concessions to bourgeois society, to meet its needs and adjust itself to its growth. In modern states this right to grant and refuse taxes has been turned by bourgeois society into a means of controlling the government, the body administering its common interests.

You will find therefore that *partial tax refusal* is an integral part of every constitutional mechanism. This type of tax refusal operates whenever a *budget* is rejected. The current budget is voted only for a definite period; moreover after being prorogued the chambers must be reconvened after a very short interval. It is thus impossible for the Crown to make itself independent. Rejection of a budget means a definite tax *refusal* if the cabinet does not win a majority in the new chamber or if the Crown does not nominate a cabinet in accordance with the wishes of the new chamber. The rejection of a budget is therefore the *parliamentary form of a refusal to pay taxes*. This form could not be employed in the conflict under consideration because a constitution did not yet exist, but had first to be produced.

But a refusal to pay taxes as it occurred here, a refusal which not only rejects a new budget but prohibits even the payment of current taxes, is by no means exceptional. It happened very frequently in the Middle Ages. Even the old German Imperial Diet and the old feudal Diets of Brandenburg passed resolutions refusing to pay taxes. Nor is there any lack of examples in modern constitutional states. The refusal to pay taxes led in Britain in 1832 to the downfall of Wellington's cabinet. And in Britain it was not Parliament which decided to refuse taxes, but the people which proclaimed and carried out this decision on its own authority. Britain, however, is the historic land of constitutionalism.

Far be it from me to deny that the English revolution, which brought Charles I to the scaffold, began with a refusal to pay taxes or that the North American revolution, which ended with the Declaration of Independence from Britain, started with a refusal to pay taxes. The refusal to pay taxes can be the harbinger of unpleasant events in Prussia too. It was not John Hampden, however, who brought Charles I to the scaffold, but only the latter's own obstinacy, his dependence on the feudal estates, and his presumptuous attempt to use force to suppress the urgent demands of the emerging society. The refusal to pay taxes is merely a sign of the dissidence that exists between the Crown and the people, merely evidence that the conflict between the government and the people has reached a menacing degree of tensity. It is not the cause of the discord or the conflict, it is merely an expression of this fact. At the worst, it leads to the overthrow of the existing government, the existing political system. The foundations of society are not affected by this. In the present case, moreover, the refusal to pay taxes was a means of society's self-defence against a government which threatened its foundations.

Finally, the public prosecutor accuses us of having gone further in the incriminating document than the National Assembly itself. He says, "For one thing, the National Assembly did not publish its resolution." Gentlemen, am I to give a serious reply to the accusation that the decision not to pay taxes was not even published in the *Statute Book*?

Furthermore, unlike us, the National Assembly did not incite to the use of *force* and in general did not take a revolutionary stand, but wanted to remain on the basis of the law.

The public prosecutor previously described the National Assembly as unlawful, now he considers it lawful—in each case to present us as criminals. But if the collection of taxes is declared unlawful, am I not obliged to resist by force the exercise by force of this unlawful action? Even from this standpoint, therefore, we were entitled to repel force by force. Incidentally, it is quite correct that the National Assembly wanted to act on a purely legal basis, by resorting to passive resistance. Two roads were open to it, the revolutionary road—it did not take it, those gentlemen did not want to risk their necks—or the refusal to pay taxes which did not go beyond passive resistance. It took the second road. But to give effect to its refusal to pay taxes the people would have had to take a revolutionary stand. The conduct of the National Assembly could by no means serve as a criterion for the people. The National Assembly, as such, has no rights; the people has merely entrusted it with the defence of its own rights. If the Assembly does not act in accordance with the mandate it has received, then this mandate lapses. The people then takes the stage itself and acts on its own authority. If, for example, a national assembly were to sell itself to a treacherous government, the people would have to kick them out, both the government and the assembly. If the Crown makes a counter-revolution, the people has the right to reply with a revolution. It does not require the sanction of a national assembly to do this. The fact that the Prussian government is attempting a treasonable assault has been stated by the National Assembly itself.

Gentlemen of the jury, to sum up briefly, the public prosecutor cannot charge us under the laws of April 6 and 8, 1848, when these laws have been torn up by the Crown. These laws by themselves are not decisive, as they were arbitrarily concocted by the United Provincial Diet. The resolution of the National Assembly regarding the refusal to pay taxes had the force of law both formally and materially. We went further than the National Assembly in our appeal. This was our right and our duty.

In conclusion, I repeat that we have seen only the first act of the drama. The struggle between the two societies, the medieval and the bourgeois society, will again be waged in political forms. As soon as the Assembly meets, the same conflicts will arise again. The *Neue Preussische Zeitung*, the organ of the government, already prophesies— the same people have voted again, that means the Assembly will have to be dispersed a second time.

Whatever new path the new National Assembly may choose, the inevitable result will be—either *complete victory of the counter-revolution* or a *new successful revolution*. It may be that the victory of the revolution is possible only after the counter-revolution is consummated.

Neue Rheinische Zeitung Nos.
231 and 232,
February 25 and 27, 1849

Published also in a separate
pamphlet entitled *Zwei politi-
sche Prozesse*, Köln, 1849,
Verlag der Expedition der
Neuen Rheinischen Zeitung

THE PROCLAMATION OF A REPUBLIC IN ROME[164]

The Italian Constituent Assembly is quite unlike the Frankfurt National Assembly. The Italians know that the unity of a country split into feudal principalities can only be established by abolishing dynastic rule. The Italians led the dance in 1848, and they are leading again in 1849. But what progress! Italy no longer has Pius IX nor France her Lamartine. The fantastic period of the European revolution, the period of enthusiasm, goodwill and florid orations, was fittingly concluded with fire-balls, massacres on a grand scale and deportations. Austrian Notes, Prussian Notes and Russian Notes were the most relevant replies to Lamartine's proclamations.

From their Pythian tripod of thoroughness and perseverance the Germans are in the habit of looking down with haughty disdain on the superficiality of the Italians. A comparison between the Italian 1848 and the German 1848 would provide the most striking answer. In drawing this comparison one would have to take into account that revolutionary Italy was kept in check by Germany and France, whereas revolutionary Germany was not restricted in her movements.

The *republic in Rome* is the beginning of the revolutionary drama of 1849.

Written about February 21, 1849

Neue Rheinische Zeitung No. 228,
February 22, 1849

[THE COUNTER-REVOLUTIONARY OFFENSIVE AND THE SUCCESSES OF THE REVOLUTION]

Cologne, May 9. The counter-revolution is advancing with swift strides, but the revolution advances still faster. While the counter-revolution has gained advantages in *Dresden,*[165] which make its victory probable, and has managed to introduce a *state of siege, censorship* and *martial law* by provoking a putsch in *Breslau* at the right moment, the revolution can point to quite different victories.

We do not speak of the quickly mounting *open rebellion of the reserve army* [*Landwehr*] in Rhenish Prussia involving the most "Prussian" districts, nor of the South German movement,[166] which is being betrayed everywhere by the governments, the bourgeoisie and the Frankfurt National Assembly; we speak only of those great events which, coming from outside, may give strong support and unity to the small, separate and helpless German movements—we speak of the Magyar and the French revolutions.

While the *Magyar revolution* is gaining one victory after another, and after the next decisive battle (which was to have taken place on May 5 or 6 at Pressburg) will move straight on Vienna and liberate the city, *France* suddenly enters a stage when the movement is developing again openly and in broad daylight. The underground development of the past months comes to a close; the defeat of the French army at Rome[167] has exposed and discredited the entire policy of the present government. The people reappears upon the scene—the people, the ultimate, supreme judge. Whether it happens at the elections or in the course of an open revolution, the French people will shortly give an impetus to the movement, which all Europe will feel.

The European dynasties will soon see that the chosen people of the revolution has not changed; the French revolution of 1849 will speak to them, not in Lamartinian phrases, but in the language of guns.

Written by Engels

Neue Rheinische Zeitung No. 294
(special supplement), May 10,
1849

[SUPPRESSION OF THE *NEUE RHEINISCHE ZEITUNG*]

Cologne, May 18. Some time ago Berlin demanded that the local authorities reintroduce a state of siege in Cologne. They intended to use martial law to suppress the *Neue Rheinische Zeitung*, but met with unexpected resistance. The municipal authorities of Cologne then turned to the judiciary here in order to achieve the same purpose by arbitrary arrests. But this failed on account of the legal scruples of the judiciary, just as it had failed twice before on account of the common sense of the Rhenish juries.[168] There was nothing for it but to resort to a *police ruse*, and this, for the time being, has achieved its purpose. *The "Neue Rheinische Zeitung" ceases publication for the present.* On May 16, its Editor-in-Chief *Karl Marx* received the following official note:

"The tendency of the *Neue Rheinische Zeitung* to provoke in its readers contempt for the present government, and incite them to violent revolutions and the setting up of a social republic has become stronger in its latest pieces" (!). "The right of hospitality" (!) "which he so disgracefully abused, is therefore to be withdrawn from its Editor-in-Chief, Dr. *Karl Marx*, and since he has not obtained permission to prolong his stay in these states he is ordered to leave them within 24 hours. If he should not comply with this demand, he is to be conveyed across the border. *Cologne*, May 11, 1849.

Royal Government
Moeller

"[Addressed to] Herr *Geiger*, Royal Police Director, here."

Why these absurd phrases, these official lies?

The trend and tone of the latest pieces of the *Neue Rheinische Zeitung* do not differ a whit from its first "trial piece". In that "first piece" we wrote among other things:

"Herr Hüser's idea (in Mainz) is but part of the larger plan of the Berlin reactionaries, who would like ... to deliver us defenceless ... into the hands of the army."[*]

Well, gentlemen, what do you say now?

As to our tendency, did not the government know it? Have we not declared before the jury that it was now "*the duty of the press to undermine the whole basis of the existing order*"[**]? Regarding the Hohenzollern princeling one can read the following in the issue of October 19, 1848:

"The King is consistent. He would always have been consistent, had not the March days unfortunately interposed that portentous piece of paper between His Majesty and the people. At present His Majesty apparently believes again, as he did prior to the March days, that Slavism has '*feet of iron*'; perhaps the people of Vienna is the magician who will turn the iron into clay."[***]

Is that clear, gentlemen?

And the "*social republic*"? Have we proclaimed it only in the "latest pieces" of the *Neue Rheinische Zeitung*?

Did we not speak plainly and clearly enough for those dullards who failed to see the "*red*" thread running through all our comments and reports on the European movement?

The November 7 issue of the *Neue Rheinische Zeitung* says, "Assuming that *arms* will enable the counter-revolution to establish itself in the whole of Europe, *money* would then kill it in the whole of Europe. European *bankruptcy, national bankruptcy* would be the fate nullifying the victory. Bayonets crumble like tinder when they come into contact with the salient 'economic' facts. But developments will not wait for the bills of exchange drawn by the European states on the new European society to expire.

"The crushing counter-blow of the June revolution will be struck in *Paris*. With the victory of the '*red*' republic in Paris, *armies* will be rushed from the *interior* of their coun-

---

[*] See *Neue Rheinische Zeitung* No. 1, June 1, 1848, "Hüser".—*Ed.*

[**] See *Neue Rheinische Zeitung* No. 221, February 14, 1849, "The First Trial of the *Neue Rheinische Zeitung*".—*Ed.*

[***] See *Neue Rheinische Zeitung* No. 120, October 19, 1848, "The King of Prussia's Reply to the Deputation of the National Assembly".—*Ed.*

tries to the frontiers and across them, and the *real strength* of the fighting parties will become evident. We shall then remember this June and this October and we too shall exclaim:

"*Vae victis!*

"The purposeless massacres perpetrated since the June and October events, the tedious offering of sacrifices since February and March, the very cannibalism of the counter-revolution will convince the nations that there is only one way in which the murderous death agonies of the old society and the bloody birth throes of the new society can be *shortened,* simplified and concentrated, and *that way* is *revolutionary terror.*"[*]

Is that clear, gentlemen?

From the very beginning we did not consider it necessary to conceal our views. During a polemic with the judiciary here, we told you:

"*The real opposition of the 'Neue Rheinische Zeitung' will begin only in the tricolour republic.*"[**]

And at that time we were speaking with the judiciary. We summed up the old year, 1848, in the following words (cf. the issue of December 31, 1848):

"The history of the Prussian middle class, and that of the German middle class in general between March and December shows that a purely *middle-class revolution* and the establishment of *bourgeois rule* in the form of a *constitutional monarchy* is impossible in Germany, and that the only alternatives are either a feudal absolutist counter-revolution or a *social republican revolution.*"[***]

Did we therefore have to advance our social republican tendency only in the "last pieces" of the *Neue Rheinische Zeitung*? Did you not read our articles about the *June revolution,* and *was not the essence of the June revolution the essence of our paper*?

Why then your hypocritical phrases, your attempt to find an impossible pretext?

---

[*] See this volume, pp. 148-49.—*Ed.*
[**] See *Neue Rheinische Zeitung* No. 129, October 29, 1848, "Public Prosecutor 'Hecker' and the *Neue Rheinische Zeitung*".—*Ed.*
[***] See this volume, p. 202.—*Ed.*

KARL MARX

We have no compassion and we ask no compassion from you. When our turn comes, we shall not make excuses for the terror. But the *royal terrorists*, the terrorists by the grace of God and the law, are in practice brutal, disdainful, and mean, in theory cowardly, secretive, and deceitful, and in both respects *disreputable*.

The Prussian official piece of paper goes even to the absurd length of speaking about the *"right of hospitality which was disgracefully abused"* by *Karl Marx,* the Editor-in-Chief of the *Neue Rheinische Zeitung.*

The right of hospitality which the insolent intruders, the anterior Russians (Borussians), forced upon *us, inhabitants of the Rhineland,* on our own land—this hospitality was indeed "disgracefully" abused by the *Neue Rheinische Zeitung.* We believe that we have thereby rendered a service to the Rhine Province. We have saved the revolutionary honour of our homeland. From now on the *Neue Preussische Zeitung* alone will enjoy the full right of citizenship in the Rhine Province.

In parting we should like to remind our readers of the words printed in the first issue we published in January:

"The table of contents for 1849 reads: *Revolutionary rising of the French working class, world war.*"*

And in the East, a revolutionary army made up of fighters of all nationalities already confronts the alliance of the old Europe represented by the Russian army, while from Paris comes the threat of a "red republic".

Written by Marx

Neue Rheinische Zeitung No. 301,
May 19, 1849

---

* See this volume, p. 205.—*Ed.*

[HUNGARY]

Cologne, May 18. At a moment when the actual entry of Russian troops turns the Magyar war into a *European* war, we are compelled to discontinue our reports on its further development. We can only once more present for our readers the course of this grand East European revolutionary war in a brief survey.

It will be remembered that in the autumn of 1847, even before the February revolution, the Diet at Pressburg, under the leadership of *Kossuth,* adopted a number of revolutionary decisions, such as those providing for the salability of landed property, the peasants' right to choose their own domicile, the commutation of feudal services, the emancipation of the Jews and equal taxation of all classes. On the very day the February revolution began in Paris (February 22) the Diet permitted Croats and Slavonians when dealing with their internal affairs to use their own language for official purposes and finally, by demanding a separate responsible ministry for Hungary, it made the first step towards a *separate Hungary.*

The February revolution broke out, and with it collapsed the resistance of the Viennese government to the demands of the Hungarians. On March 16, one day after the Viennese revolution, consent was given for the formation of an independent Hungarian government thereby reducing the association between Hungary and Austria to a mere personal union.

The now independent Magyar revolution made rapid progress. It abolished all political privileges, introduced universal suffrage, did away with all feudal dues, labour services and tithes—compensations being payable by the

State—brought about the union with Transylvania and succeeded in securing the appointment of Kossuth as Minister of Finance and the dismissal of the rebellious Ban Jellachich.

Meanwhile the Austrian government recovered from the blow. While the pseudo-responsible ministry at Vienna remained powerless, the camarilla at the Innsbruck Court grew steadily more powerful. It relied on the imperial army in Italy, on the national appetite of the Czechs, Croats and Serbs and on the stubborn narrow-mindedness of the Ruthenian peasants.

The Serbian insurrection, instigated with the help of money and emissaries from the Court, started in the Banat and Bácska on June 17. On the 20th Jellachich had an audience with the Emperor at Innsbruck and was reappointed Ban. Jellachich returned to Croatia, renounced allegiance to the Hungarian ministry and on August 25 declared war against it.

The treachery of the Hapsburg camarilla was plainly evident. The Hungarians tried once more to persuade the Emperor to return to constitutional methods. They sent a deputation of 200 members of the Imperial Diet to Vienna; the Emperor was evasive. Feeling ran high. The people demanded guarantees and brought about changes in the government. Traitors, who sat in the Pest ministry too, were removed, and on September 20 Kossuth was appointed Prime Minister. But only four days later the Palatine Archduke Stephan, the representative of the Emperor, escaped to Vienna and on the 26th the Emperor issued the well-known manifesto to the Hungarians in which he declared that the government was rebellious and dismissed it, appointing the Magyarophobe Jellachich governor of Hungary and encroaching on the most important revolutionary gains of Hungary.

The manifesto, not having been countersigned by an Hungarian minister, was declared null and void by Kossuth.

Meanwhile Jellachich, taking advantage of the disorganisation and treachery prevalent among the nominally Hungarian, but in reality old imperial, officers and general staff, advanced to Stuhlweissenburg. There he was defeated by the Hungarian army, despite its treacherous leaders, and driven back into Austrian territory to the very walls of Vienna. The Emperor and the old traitor Latour then decided to send reinforcements to Jellachich and to reconquer Hungary with the aid of German and Slav troops. But the revolution broke out in Vienna on October 6, and for the time being put an end to the royal and imperial schemes.

Kossuth immediately marched with a Magyar corps to the assistance of the Viennese people. At the Leitha·he was prevented from moving immediately on Vienna by the indecision of the Viennese Diet, the treachery of his own officers and the bad organisation of his army, which consisted for the most part of local militia. He was finally obliged to arrest more than a hundred officers, send them to Pest and have a number of them shot. Only after this did he dare to attack. But it was too late—Vienna had already fallen, and his undisciplined local militia was thrown back at Schwechat by the regular Austrian troops.

The truce between the imperial troops and the Magyars lasted six weeks. While both armies did their utmost to strengthen their forces, the Olmütz camarilla carried out a coup which it had been preparing for a long time. It forced the idiot Ferdinand—who had compromised himself by concessions to the revolution and was now useless—to abdicate, and placed on the throne Sophia's son, the boy Francis Joseph, whom it intended to use as its tool. On the basis of the Hungarian constitution the Pest Diet rejected this change of sovereigns.

Finally in the middle of December the war started. Hungary by then was practically surrounded by the imperial army. The offensive was launched from all sides.

From Austria three army corps, no less than 90,000 strong, under the supreme command of Field-Marshal Windischgrätz advanced southward from the Danube. Nugent with about 20,000 men marched from Styria along the left bank of the Drave. Dahlen with 10,000 men marched from Croatia along the right bank of the Drave to the Banat. Several frontier regiments, the garrison of Temesvár, the Serbian militia and the Serbian auxiliary corps of Knića-

nin, totalling 30,000 to 40,000 men commanded by Todoro-
vich and Rukavina, fought in the Banat itself. Puchner with
20,000-25,000 men was in Transylvania as was also Malkowski with 10,000-15,000 men, who had invaded it from Bukovina. Finally Schlick with a corps of 20,000-25,000 men
moved from Galicia towards the upper Theiss.

The imperial army thus numbered at least 200,000 regular, battle-hardened troops, not counting the Slav, Romance
and Saxon local militia and National Guards who took
part in the fighting in the south and in Transylvania.

Against this colossal fighting force Hungary could pit an
army of perhaps 80,000-90,000 trained soldiers, including
24,000 men who had formerly served in the imperial army,
and in addition 50,000 to 60,000 poorly organised Honveds
and local militia. This army was commanded largely by
traitors similar to the officers Kossuth had had arrested at
the Leitha.

But whereas Austria, a country kept down by force,
financially ruined and almost moneyless, could not yield
another recruit for the time being, the Magyars still had
great resources at their disposal. The Magyars' enthusiasm
for liberty, reinforced by their national pride, waxed stronger every day, providing Kossuth with eager fighters in
numbers unheard-of for such a small nation of 5 million.
The Hungarian printing press placed inexhaustible financial
resources in the form of banknotes at Kossuth's disposal and
every Magyar accepted these national assignats as if they
were hard silver coin. Rifle and gun production was in full
swing. All the army lacked was weapons, experience and
good leaders, and all this could be procured in a few
months. It was only necessary to win time, to entice the
imperial troops into the heart of the country where they
would be worn down by unceasing guerilla warfare and
weakened by having to leave behind strong garrisons and
other detachments.

Hence the plan of the Hungarians to withdraw slowly
into the interior, to train the recruits in continuous skirmishes and as a last resort to place between themselves and
their enemies the Theiss line with its impassable swamps,
which form a natural moat around the Magyar lands.

According to all calculations, the Hungarians should have been able to hold the area between Pressburg and Pest for two to three months even against the superior strength of the Austrians. But severe frosts suddenly set in covering all rivers and swamps with a thick layer of ice capable of bearing the weight even of heavy guns. This deprived the terrain of all features favouring defence, and made all fortifications built by the Magyar army useless and liable to be outflanked. And so it happened that before twenty days had passed the Hungarian army was thrown back from Ödenburg and Pressburg to Raab, from Raab to Mór, from Mór to Pest, and even had to leave Pest and withdraw beyond the Theiss at the very beginning of the campaign.

The other corps fared no better than the main army. In the south Nugent and Dahlen continued their advance towards Esseg, which was occupied by the Magyars, and the Serbs gradually approached the Maros line; in Transylvania Puchner joined Malkowski at Maros-Vásárhely; in the north Schlick descended from the Carpathians to the Theiss and made junction with Windischgrätz at Miskolcz.

The Austrians seemed to have practically finished with the Magyar revolution. They had two-thirds of Hungary and three-fourths of Transylvania in their rear, the Hungarians were attacked in front, on both flanks and in the rear. A further advance of a few miles would have enabled all the corps of the Emperor to make junction and draw the ring tighter until Hungary was crushed in it as in the coils of a boa constrictor.

The thing now—while the Theiss on the front still formed an insuperable barrier to the enemy—was to gain some breathing space.

This was done at two points: in Transylvania by Bem, and in Slovakia by Görgey. Both carried out operations which show that they are the most gifted commanders of our time.

On December 29, Bem arrived at Klausenburg, the only town in Transylvania still held by the Magyars. Here he quickly concentrated the reinforcements he had brought and the remnants of the defeated Magyar and Szekler troops,[169] and marched to Maros-Vásárhely, beat the Austrians and drove Malkowski first across the Carpathians into Bukovina and from there into Galicia, where he pushed on towards Stanislav. Then, swiftly turning back into Transylvania he pursued Puchner to within a few. miles of Hermannstadt. After several skirmishes and a few swift drives in various directions, the whole of Transylvania was in his hands apart from two towns, Hermannstadt and Kronstadt, and these too would have been taken if the Russians had not been called in. The 10,000-strong Russian auxiliary troops tipped the scales and forced Bem to fall back on Szeklerland. There he organised an uprising of the Szeklers, and with this achieved, he had the Szekler militia engage Puchner, who had reached Schässburg, while he bypassed Puchner's positions, moved straight on Hermannstadt and drove the Russians out, then defeated Puchner who had followed him, marched on Kronstadt and entered it without firing a shot.

Transylvania was thus won and the rear of the Magyar army cleared. The natural defence line formed by the Theiss now found its continuation in the Carpathian mountain range and the Transylvanian Alps, from the Zips to the borders of the Banat.

Görgey at the same time made a similar triumphal march in North-Western Hungary. He set out with a corps from Pest to Slovakia, for two months kept in check the corps of Generals Götz, Csorich and Simunich operating against him from three directions, and finally, when his position became untenable against their superior forces, fought his way through the Carpathians to Eperies and Kaschau. There he appeared in the rear of Schlick and forced him hurriedly to abandon his position and his whole operational base and retreat to Windischgrätz's main army, while he himself was already marching down the Hernád to the Theiss to join the main body of the Magyar army.

This army, which was now commanded by Dembiński, had likewise crossed the Theiss and had repulsed the enemy all along the line. It had reached Hatvan, six miles from Pest, when a stronger concentration of enemy forces compelled it to retreat again. After offering vigorous resistance at Kapolna, Maklar and Poroszló it recrossed the Theiss just at the moment when Görgey reached the Theiss at Tokaj. The meeting of the two corps was the signal for a new magnificent advance of the Hungarians. Newly trained recruits arriving from the interior strengthened the Hungarian army in the field. Polish and German Legions were formed, capable leaders had been trained or enlisted, and in place of the leaderless, unorganised mass of December, the imperial troops were suddenly faced by a concentrated, brave, and numerous army which was well organised and excellently led.

The Magyars crossed the Theiss in three columns. The right wing (Görgey) moved northwards, outflanked the Ramberg division, which had been following it, at Eperies and quickly drove it through Rimaszombat towards the main imperial army. The latter was defeated by Dembiński at Erlau, Gyöngyös, Gödöllö and Hatvan, and hastily retreated to Pest. Finally the left wing (Vetter) dislodged Jellachich from Kecskemét, Szolnok and Czegléd, defeated him at Jászberény and compelled him, too, to retreat to the walls of Pest. There the imperial forces stood along the Danube from Pest to Waitzen, surrounded in a wide semicircle by the Magyars.

To avoid exposing Pest to bombardment from Ofen, the Hungarians had recourse to their well-tried tactics of dislodging the Austrians from their positions by manoeuvres rather than by open frontal attacks. Görgey captured Waitzen and forced the Austrians to fall back beyond the Gran and Danube; he defeated Wohlgemuth between the Gran and Neutra, thereby relieving Komorn, which was besieged by imperial troops. Since its line of retreat was threatened, the imperial army had to decide on a hurried withdrawal. Welden, the new commander-in-chief, retreated in the direction of Raab and Pressburg, and Jellachich was obliged, in order to pacify his extremely refractory Croats, to hastily retreat with them down the Danube into Slavonia.

During their retreat, which rather resembled a stampede, Welden (and especially his rearguard commanded by Schlick) and Jellachich suffered further considerable reverses. While the latter's hard-pressed corps was slowly fighting its way through the Tolna and Baranya districts, Welden was able at Pressburg to concentrate the remnants of his army which were by no means capable of offering any serious resistance.

Simultaneously with these astonishing victories of the Magyars over the main Austrian army, Moritz Perczel pressed forward from Szegedin and Tolna towards Peterwardein, relieved it, occupied Bácska and moved into the Banat, in order to link up there with Bem who was advancing from Transylvania. Bem had already taken Arad and besieged Temesvár; Perczel stood at Werschetz close to the Turkish frontier; the Banat was thus conquered in a few days. The fortified Transylvanian mountain passes were at the same time held by the Szeklers, the passes in upper Hungary by the local militia, and Görgey with a considerable army stood at the Jablunka Pass on the Moravian-Galician frontier.

In short, in a few more days the victorious Magyar army, driving the remnants of the mighty Austrian Legions before it, would have entered Vienna in triumph and put an end to the Austrian monarchy for all time.

Hungary's separation from Austria had been decided in Debrecen on April 14; the alliance with Poland, openly proclaimed since the middle of January, was turned into reality by the 20,000-30,000 Poles who joined the Hungarian army. The alliance with the German Austrians, which had existed since the Viennese revolution of October 6 and the battle at Schwechat, was similarly preserved and sustained by the German Legions within the Hungarian army, as well as by the fact that the Magyars were faced with the strategic and political necessity of occupying Vienna and revolutionising Austria so as to secure recognition of their declaration of independence.

Thus, the Magyar war very soon lost the national character it had had in the beginning, and assumed a clearly European character, precisely as a result of what would seem to be a purely national act, as a result of the declaration of independence. Only when Hungary proclaimed her separation from Austria, and thereby the dissolution of the Austrian monarchy, did the alliance with the Poles for the liberation of both countries, and the alliance with the Germans for the revolutionisation of Eastern Germany acquire a definite character and a solid basis. If Hungary were independent, Poland restored, German Austria turned into the revolutionary focus of Germany, with Lombardy and Italy winning independence—these plans, if carried out, would wreck the entire East European political system: Austria would disappear, Prussia would disintegrate and Russia would be forced back to the borders of Asia.

The Holy Alliance, therefore, had to make every effort to stem the impending revolution in Eastern Europe—the Russian armies rolled towards the Transylvanian and Galician frontiers; Prussia occupied the Bohemian-Silesian frontier and allowed the Russians to pass through her territory towards Prerau, and within a few days the first Russian army corps stood on Moravian soil.

The Magyars, who clearly understood that in a few weeks they would have to deal with numerous fresh troops, did not advance on Vienna as quickly as one expected at the beginning. They could not take Vienna, as they could not take Pest, by a frontal attack without shelling the city, and this they were not prepared to do. Again, as at Pest, they were compelled to resort to outflanking manoeuvres, and this required time and the assurance that their own flanks and rear were secure. But it was here that the Russians menaced their rear, while if Vienna were seriously endangered strong detachments of Radetzky's army could be immediately expected from the other direction.

The Hungarians therefore acted very wisely when, instead of advancing swiftly on Vienna, they confined themselves to steadily forcing the imperial armies out of Hungary, enveloping them in a wide arc from the foothills of the Carpathians to the spurs of the Styrian Alps, dispatching a strong corps towards Jablunka, fortifying and covering the Galician mountain passes, attacking Ofen and rapidly proceeding with the recruitment of 250,000 men, especially from the reconquered western districts. In this way they secured their flanks and rear and assembled an army which need no more fear the Russian contingents than the once colossal imperial army. 200,000 soldiers of this glorious

Austrian army had invaded Hungary and barely 50,000 of
them had returned; the rest were either killed, wounded,
sick, taken prisoner or had changed sides.

True, the Russians threaten to send even more gigantic
armies. Some speak of 120,000 soldiers, others of 170,000.
According to the *Triester Freihafen*, the mobile army in
the field is expected considerably to surpass 500,000 men.
But the Russian love of exaggeration is well known: of the
figures they give only half are on the nominal rolls, and
of the numbers on the nominal roll again less than half are
really there. If, after deducting the number of troops required for the occupation of Poland, the effective Russian
aid amounts to from 60,000 to 70,000 men, the Austrians
can be glad. And the Magyars will be able to deal with
that number.

The Magyar war of 1849 has strong points of resem-
blance with the Polish war of 1830-31. But the great difference is that the factors which were against the Poles at
that time now act in favour of the Magyars. Lelewel, as
we know, unsuccessfully urged, first, that the mass of the
population be bound to the revolution by emancipating the
peasants and the Jews, and secondly, that all three partitioning powers be involved in the war and this war turned
into a *European* war, by raising an insurrection throughout
the old Polish territories. *The Magyars started at the point*
which the Poles only achieved when it was *too late*. The
Hungarians first of all carried through a social revolution
in their country, they abolished feudalism; their second
measure was to involve Poland and Germany in the war,
thus turning it into a European war. It started with the
entry of the first *Russian* corps into German territory, and
will take a decisive turn when the first *French* battalion
steps onto German territory.

By becoming a European war, the Hungarian war is
brought into reciprocal interaction with all other factors
of the European movement. Its course affects not only
Germany, but also France and England. The English bourgeoisie cannot be expected to let Austria become a Russian
province and it is certain that the French people will not
calmly contemplate the increasing attacks of the counter-

revolution on it. Whatever the outcome of the French elections, the army at any rate has declared for the revolution.
And the army today is the decisive force. If the army wants
war—and it does want it—then war it will be.

War will come. Paris is on the threshold of revolution,
whether as a result of the elections or of the army's fraternisation with the revolutionary party at the ballot-box.
While in Southern Germany the core of a revolutionary
army is being formed, which prevents Prussia from taking
an active part in the Hungarian campaign, France is on the
point of playing an active role in the struggle. A few weeks,
perhaps even a few days, will decide everything, and the
French, the Magyar-Polish, and the German revolutionary
armies will celebrate their fraternisation on the battle-field
before the walls of Berlin.

Written by Engels

Neue Rheinische Zeitung No. 301,
May 19, 1849

TO THE WORKERS OF COLOGNE

Finally we warn you against any putsch in Cologne. In the military situation obtaining in Cologne you would be irretrievably lost. You have seen in Elberfeld that the bourgeoisie sends the workers into the fire and betrays them afterwards in the most infamous way. A state of siege in Cologne would demoralise the entire Rhine Province, and a state of siege would be the inevitable consequence of any rising on your part at this moment. The Prussians will be frustrated by your calmness.

In bidding you farewell the editors of the *Neue Rheinische Zeitung* thank you for the sympathy you have shown them. Their last word everywhere and always will be: *emancipation of the working class!*

The Editorial Board of the *Neue Rheinische Zeitung*

Written on May 18, 1849

Neue Rheinische Zeitung No. 301,
May 19, 1849

Neue Rheinische Zeitung

Organ der Demokratie.

№ 301.   Köln, Samstag, den 19. Mai.   1849.

Abschiedswort der Neuen Rheinischen Zeitung.

F. FREILIGRATH.

An die Arbeiter Kölns.

Die Redakteure der Neuen Rheinischen Zeitung danken Euch beim Abschiede für die ihnen bewiesene Theilnahme. Ihr letztes Wort wird überall und immer sein: Emanzipation der arbeitenden Klasse!

Die Redaktion der Neuen Rhein. Zeitung.

Deutschland.

Proklamation an die Frauen.

Georg Weerth.

The last issue of the *Neue Rheinische Zeitung*

NOTES

1 *Neue Rheinische Zeitung. Organ der Demokratie* (New Rhenish Gazette. Organ of Democracy)—a daily paper published in Cologne from June 1, 1848, to May 19, 1849. As its name indicates, it was meant to continue the tradition of the *Rheinische Zeitung*, which Marx edited in 1842 and 1843. The paper was intended not only for the Rhine Province, whose centre Cologne was, but also for Germany as a whole. In April and May 1848, Marx and Engels did a great deal of preparatory work, such as raising the necessary funds for the publication of the paper by selling its shares, finding suitable correspondents and establishing contacts with democratic periodicals in other countries. p. 21

2 In September 1835 the French government promulgated laws which placed restrictions on juries and introduced severe measures against the press, i.e., larger sums had to be deposited by periodicals, and writers who attacked property rights and the existing political system were liable to imprisonment and heavy fines. p. 21

3 On May 19, Raveaux proposed that Prussian deputies elected to both the Berlin and the Frankfurt assemblies should have the right to be members of both parliaments. Auerswald, Prussian Minister of the Interior, expressed the same point of view in the decree of May 22, 1848, which is mentioned on p. 25 of this volume.

The *Berlin Assembly*, i.e., the Prussian National Assembly, was convened on May 22, 1848, "for the purpose of drafting a constitution by agreement with the Crown" (hence Marx and Engels frequently call it the Assembly of agreement or conciliation). The Assembly was elected under the electoral law of April 8, 1848, by universal suffrage and an indirect (two-stage) system of voting. Most of the deputies belonged to the bourgeoisie or the Prussian bureaucracy. p. 23

4 Using the clashes between soldiers and citizens of Mainz as a pretext, Hüser, the Prussian commandant of the city, imposed martial law. p. 23

5 An expression used by the Prussian Minister of the Interior von Rochow. p. 24

[6] The *Preparliament*, which met in Frankfurt am Main from March 31 to April 4, 1848, consisted of representatives of the German states who were either members of existing diets or had been elected by some association or public meeting. Most of the delegates were constitutional monarchists. The Preparliament passed a resolution for the summoning of an all-German National Assembly in Frankfurt and produced a draft of the "fundamental rights and demands of the German people". Although this document proclaimed certain bourgeois liberties it did not attack the basis of the semi-feudal absolutist system prevalent in Germany at the time.   p. 24

[7] The seventeen "trusted men" represented the German governments and were summoned by the Federal Diet, the central body of the German Confederation. They met in Frankfurt am Main from March 30 to May 8, 1848, and drafted a constitution for a German empire based on constitutional monarchical principles.   p. 24

[8] The Left wing of the Frankfurt National Assembly comprised two factions: the Left, one of whose most influential leaders was Robert Blum, and the extreme Left known as the Radical-Democratic Party. Among the deputies belonging to this party were Arnold Ruge, Franz Zitz and Friedrich Wilhelm Schlöffel.   p. 30

[9] The *Federal Diet*, which was set up in 1815 by a decision of the Congress of Vienna as the central agency of the German Confederation, consisted of representatives of the German states and had its seat at Frankfurt am Main. It had no real power. After the March revolution of 1848 reactionary forces tried to revive the Diet and use it to prevent the democratic unification of Germany.   p. 31

[10] Heine, *Deutschland. Ein Wintermärchen,* Kaput XVI.   p. 32

[11] According to this theory, which was advanced by Camphausen and Hansemann, the Prussian National Assembly was to prepare a constitution by agreement with the Crown (see Note 3).   p. 35

[12] This refers to the *second United Provincial Diet* (Vereinigter Landtag) which was convoked on April 2, 1848, and consisted of representatives of the eight Provincial Diets (based on the estate principle) then existing in Prussia. The second United Provincial Diet passed a law on the election of a Prussian National Assembly and sanctioned a loan which the first United Provincial Diet had refused to grant the government in 1847. The Provincial Diet was dissolved on April 10, 1848.   p. 36

[13] A Polish uprising took place in the Grand Duchy of Poznan after the March revolution of 1848. The aim of the movement, in which large numbers of peasants and craftsmen participated, was liberation from the oppressive Prussian rule. At the end of March the Prussian government promised to set up a commission for the purpose of carrying through reorganisations in the Grand Duchy (creation of a Polish army, appointment of Poles to administrative

and other posts and recognition of Polish as an official language in Poznan). As soon as the Poles laid down their arms, however, these promises were broken and the Prussian army mercilessly massacred the now defenceless insurgents. p. 38

[14] *Wyshehrad* (Vyšehrad)—a southern district of Prague with an old citadel of the same name on the right bank of the Vltava.

Hradschin (Hradčany)—the north-western district of Prague with an old castle which dominates the rest of the city. p. 38

[15] *The Slavic Congress* met in Prague on June 2, 1848. A struggle between two trends in the national movement of the Slavs living in subjugation in the Hapsburg empire became evident. The Right, moderately liberal wing, which consisted of the majority of the deputies including Palacký and Šafařik, the leaders of the Congress, sought to solve the national problem by preserving and strengthening the Hapsburg monarchy. The Left, democratic wing, to which Sabina, Frič, Libelt and others belonged, was strongly opposed to this course and wanted to act in alliance with the revolutionary and democratic movement in Germany and Hungary. Delegates of the Left took an active part in the Prague uprising and were subjected to cruel reprisals. On June 16, the Right-wing delegates who remained in Prague adjourned the Congress indefinitely. p. 38

[16] Engels refers to the spontaneous rising of textile workers in Prague towards the end of June 1844. The revolt, in the course of which mills were destroyed and machines smashed, was brutally crushed by Austrian troops. p. 41

[17] *Berliner Zeitungs-Halle*— daily paper, started in Berlin in 1846; in 1848 and 1849 it was an organ of the petty-bourgeois democrats.
p. 42

[18] The full title of this Committee, which was set up in Vienna in May 1848, was "Committee of Citizens, the National Guard and Students for Maintaining Safety and Order and Defending the Rights of the People". p. 42

[19] The political group formed around the daily paper *Le National* (published in Paris from 1830 to 1851) consisted of moderate bourgeois republicans headed by Armand Marrast; it was supported by the industrial bourgeoisie and a section of the liberal intellectuals. p. 45

[20] The political group that supported the French daily *La Réforme* (published in Paris from 1843 to 1850) consisted of petty-bourgeois democrats and republicans headed by Ledru-Rollin; petty-bourgeois socialists led by Louis Blanc were also associated with it. p. 45

[21] *Executive Committee*—the government of the French Republic set up by the Constituent Assembly on May 10, 1848, to replace the Provisional Government which had resigned. It existed until the establishment of Cavaignac's dictatorship on June 24, 1848. p. 45

²² The *Dynastic Opposition*—a parliamentary group headed by Odilon Barrot during the July monarchy (1830-48). It expressed the views of the industrial and commercial liberal bourgeoisie and advocated limited electoral reform, which it regarded as a means of preserving the Orleans dynasty and averting a revolutionary outbreak.   p. 46

²³ The *legitimists* were supporters of the "legitimate" Bourbon dynasty, which ruled in France from 1589 to 1793 and from 1814 to 1830. They upheld the interests of the hereditary big landowners.   p. 46

²⁴ Following the revolutionary actions of the Paris workers on *May 15, 1848*, a law was passed banning gatherings in the streets; steps were taken to abolish the national workshops and a number of democratic clubs were closed.   p. 48

²⁵ The *mobile guard* was set up by a decree of the Provisional Government on February 25, 1848, to fight against the revolutionary masses. These armed units consisted, mainly, of lumpen-proletarians and were used to crush the June uprising in Paris.   p. 49

²⁶ A reference to the uprising of 1785 which deposed William of Orange. But two years later, with the help of Prussian troops, he again became Governor of the Netherlands.   p. 60

²⁷ Under an agreement between Britain, France and Russia the Bavarian prince Otto, who was still a minor, was made king of Greece in 1832. He arrived in Greece accompanied by Bavarian troops and ruled as Otto I until 1862.   p. 60

²⁸ Engels is alluding to the reactionary policy of the Holy Alliance in which Austria, Prussia and Russia played a leading role. At a congress of the Holy Alliance, which began in Troppau in October 1820 and ended in Laibach in May 1821, the principle of intervention in the internal affairs of other states was officially proclaimed, and the decision taken to send Austrian troops into Italy in order to crush the revolutionary and national liberation movements there. French intervention in Spain with similar aims was decided upon at the Congress of Verona in 1822.   p. 60

²⁹ In the 1820s and 1830s Austria and Prussia supported the clerical and feudal party headed by Dom Miguel, which opposed any measures designed to restrict absolutism in Portugal.   p. 60

³⁰ Austria and Prussia supported Don Carlos, who in 1833 started a civil war in Spain in order to win the throne with the help of the clerical and feudal party.   p. 60

³¹ In February 1846 preparations were being made for an uprising whose aim was the liberation of Poland. Polish revolutionary democrats (Dembowski and others) took the initiative in organising it. But as a result of treachery on the part of the nobility and the arrest of the leaders by the Prussian police a general uprising was prevented and only local outbreaks occurred. That at Cracow was the only successful one; on February 22 the insurgents there set up a national government which issued a manifesto abolishing feudal

obligations. The Cracow uprising was crushed in the beginning of March 1846 by Austrian, Prussian and Russian troops. The three powers signed an agreement the following November incorporating Cracow in the Austrian empire.   p. 61

[32] The manifesto was issued on April 6, 1848.   p. 62

[33] *L'Alba*—an Italian democratic newspaper published from 1847 to 1849.   p. 62

[34] On June 28, 1848, the *Frankfurt National Assembly* decided to set up a provisional central authority consisting of the Vice Regent (the Austrian Archduke Johann) and an imperial ministry. Since the central authority had neither a budget nor an army of its own it possessed no real power; it supported the counter-revolutionary policy of the German princes.   p. 63

[35] The last four words are from Heine's poem *Anno 1829*.   p. 66

[36] For the background of the Prusso-Danish war see Engels's article "The Danish-Prussian Armistice", this volume, pp. 114-19.   p. 67

[37] *Fädrelandet*—a Danish newspaper published in Copenhagen from 1834 to 1839 as a weekly, then as a daily. In 1848 it was a semi-official organ of the Danish government.   p. 68

[38] On secret orders from the Prussian King, Major Wildenbruch on April 8, 1848, handed the Danish government a Note intimating that Prussia was waging the war in Schleswig-Holstein not for the purpose of dissevering these lands from Denmark, but exclusively to fight the "radical and republican elements in Germany". The Prussian government declined to give official recognition to such a compromising document.   p. 68

[39] The *Sound tax* was a toll which from 1425 to 1857 Denmark collected from all foreign vessels passing through the Sound.
                                                                    p. 69

[40] Heine, *Deutschland. Ein Wintermärchen*, Kaput VIII.   p. 71

[41] *Kölnische Zeitung*—a German daily which started publication in Cologne in 1802; during 1848-49 it supported the cowardly and treacherous policy of the Prussian liberal bourgeoisie and continuously attacked the *Neue Rheinische Zeitung*.   p. 77

[42] Under the Poor Law of 1834 the only relief available to the poor was to become an inmate in one of the workhouses, known as Poor Law Bastilles.   p. 77

[43] The *Chartist movement* began in the thirties and lasted till the fifties of the nineteenth century.   p. 78

[44] *La Réforme*—see Note 20.   p. 79

[45] *Le Populaire de 1841*—propaganda organ of peaceful utopian communism published in Paris from 1841 to 1852; until 1849 it was edited by Etienne Cabet.   p. 79

[46] *L'Union. Bulletin des ouvriers rédigé et publié par eux-mêmes*—a monthly published by a group of workers influenced by the ideas of Saint-Simon; it appeared in Paris from December 1843 to September 1846. p. 79

[47] *La Ruche populaire*—a monthly dedicated to utopian socialist views, published in Paris from December 1839 to December 1849. p. 79

[48] *La Fraternité de 1845. Organe du communisme*—a workers' monthly journal supporting Babouvism, published in Paris from January 1845 to February 1848. p. 79

[49] *The Northern Star*—an English weekly, central organ of the Chartists, founded in 1837 by Feargus O'Connor. It was first published in Leeds and from November 1844 in London. Engels contributed articles to the paper from September 1845 to March 1848. It ceased publication in 1852. p. 79

[50] The fight for legislative restriction of the working day began in Britain towards the end of the eighteenth century, and from the 1830s large sections of the working class were involved in it. As the landed aristocracy counted on using this campaign in its struggle against the industrial bourgeoisie, it supported the Ten Hours' Bill in Parliament. The Bill, limiting the hours of women and young workers, was passed by Parliament on June 8, 1847. p. 80

[51] A reference to the King's repeated promises to introduce a constitution in Prussia based on the estate principle. p. 83

[52] The treaties signed by Russia, Prussia and Austria in Vienna on May 3, 1815, and the final act of the Congress of Vienna signed on June 9, 1815, pledged that representative bodies and national political institutions would be set up in all Polish lands. An assembly representing the social estates and endowed only with advisory functions was convoked in Poznan. p. 88

[53] Black and white were the Prussian colours. p. 89

[54] See Note 31. p. 89

[55] A character in the comedy *Don Ranudo de Colibrados* by Ludwig Holberg, the Danish writer, depicted as a stupid, arrogant, impoverished nobleman. p. 90

[56] Words from the Polish national anthem. p. 90

[57] The Poznan Committee and the Prussian representative General Willisen concluded the *Convention of Jaroslawiec* on April 11, 1848. Under this agreement the Polish insurgents were to lay down their arms and disband. In return the Poles were promised the "national reorganisation" of Poznan, i.e., the formation of a Polish army, appointment of Poles to administrative and other posts and recognition of Polish as an official language. But the Convention was treacherously broken by the Prussian administration, and the national liberation movement in Poznan was brutally suppressed by the Prussian troops. p. 92

[58] On the orders of the Prussian General Pfuel the participants of the Poznan uprising who had been taken prisoner had their heads shaved and their hands and ears branded with lunar caustic (in German called *Höllenstein*, i.e., stone of hell), hence Pfuel's nickname. p. 94

[59] The *chambers of reunion* (*chambres de réunion*) were set up by Louis XIV in 1679-80 in order to justify and provide legal and historical reasons for France's claims to certain lands of neighbouring states. These lands were subsequently occupied by French troops. p. 94

[60] An ironic allusion to the war against Denmark waged in 1848 (for particulars of this war see Engels, "The Danish-Prussian Armistice", this volume, pp. 114-19). p. 95

[61] See Note 28. p. 97

[62] The *Polish constitution of 1791* reflected the aspirations of the progressive sections of the nobility and urban bourgeoisie. It abolished the *liberum veto* (the principle that resolutions of the parliament can be passed only unanimously) and the elective monarchy, provided for a government responsible to the parliament and granted the urban bourgeoisie various political and economic rights. The constitution was directed against feudal anarchy, it strengthened the central authority and restricted the rights of the feudal aristocracy. It recognised the legal force of commutation agreements between landowners and peasants, thus alleviating the position of peasant serfs to some extent. p. 98

[63] The term "Blacks" is an allusion to the Jesuit priests; "Black-Yellows" to the Austrians, since the colours of the Austrian flag were black and yellow. p. 102

[64] *Carbonari*—a secret political society organised in Italy in the early nineteenth century to fight for national independence. p. 103

[65] See Note 17. p. 105

[66] Meetings and demonstrations were held in Berlin on August 21, 1848, to protest against an assault, engineered by reactionary forces, on members of the Democratic Club in Charlottenburg. The demonstrators demanded that the Auerswald-Hansemann cabinet should resign and those involved in the incidents in Charlottenburg be punished; they also threw stones at a building in which Auerswald and other ministers met. The government retaliated with further repressive measures. p. 105

[67] From Ernst Moritz Arndt's poem *Der Freudenklang*. p. 106

[68] The armistice between Sardinia and Austria was concluded on August 9, 1848, after the capture of Milan by the Austrian army. It was originally meant to last six weeks but was prolonged. p. 108

[69] Heine, *Deutschland. Ein Wintermärchen,* Kaput XIX. p. 114

[70] *Morgenbladet*—a Norwegian newspaper founded in Christiania in 1819.   p. 115

[71] The *Neue Rheinische Zeitung* published the second, third and fourth articles of this series under the heading "The Crisis".   p. 120

[72] Royal decrees issued by the King of France on July 26, 1830, abolished freedom of the press, dissolved parliament and changed the electoral law, thereby reducing the electorate by three-quarters. These measures precipitated the French July revolution of 1830.
   On February 24, 1848, King Louis Philippe of France was overthrown.   p. 122

[73] In his message of September 10, 1848, Frederick William IV agreed with the view of the ministers that the resolution passed by the Prussian National Assembly on September 7, 1848, was an infringement of the "principles of constitutional monarchy" and approved the ministers' decision to resign as a protest against this action of the Assembly.   p. 123

[74] On August 9, 1848, the Prussian National Assembly accepted a proposal submitted by deputy Stein requesting the Minister of War to issue an army order to the effect that officers were expected to demonstrate their support of a constitutional system and that those who held different political views were bound in honour to quit the army. Schreckenstein, the Minister of War, did not issue such an order; Stein therefore tabled a similar motion once more, and this was passed by the National Assembly on September 7. Thereupon the Auerswald-Hansemann cabinet resigned. Under the Pfuel cabinet which followed, the decree, though in a considerably weakened form, was at last issued on September 26, 1848, but it remained on paper.   p. 125

[75] See Note 41.   p. 128

[76] After the ministers' resignation the King, in his message of September 10, 1848, asked them to continue to carry out their duties pending the appointment of their successors (see Note 73).   p. 128

[77] *Vossische Zeitung*—the name generally used for a Berlin daily newspaper which, since 1785, appeared under the title *Königlich privilegirte Berlinische Zeitung von Staats- und gelehrten Sachen.* Its owner was Christian Friedrich Voss. In the 1840s it adopted a moderate liberal stand.   p. 128

[78] *Berlinische Nachrichten von Staats- und gelehrten Sachen*—a daily, generally known as *Spenersche Zeitung* after the name of its owner; published in Berlin from 1740 to 1874; in 1848-49 it adopted a constitutional monarchist stand.   p. 128

[79] See Note 17.   p. 128

[80] The words Cromwell used when dissolving the Rump Parliament on April 20, 1653.   **p. 131**

[81] In the *Einleitung zu "Kahldorf über den Adel, in Briefen an den Grafen M. von Moltke"*, which Heine wrote in March 1831, he says with reference to the French revolution of 1830, "The Gallic cock has now crowed a second time, and in Germany, too, day is breaking."   p. 135

[82] On October 7, 1848, the Austrian Emperor fled from Vienna to Olmütz. Most of the Czech deputies of the Austrian Imperial Diet who belonged to the Czech National Liberal Party also left Vienna and went to Prague.   p. 138

[83] Heine, *Der Tannhäuser*, Kaput 3.   p. 138

[84] *Slovanská Lípa*—a Czech national society founded towards the end of April 1848. The leadership of the society in Prague was in the hands of bourgeois liberals (Šafařík, Gauč), who joined the counter-revolution after the Prague uprising, whereas the provincial branches were mostly led by members of the radical Czech bourgeoisie.   p. 144

[85] *Imperial Schinderhannes*—an allusion to Windischgrätz. Schinderhannes (Jack the Skinner), a name given to Johann Bückler, a robber chief living in Rhenish Hesse in the late eighteenth and early nineteenth centuries.   p. 144

[86] *Koblenz* during the French revolution was the centre of the counter-revolutionary émigrés.   p. 144

[87] The Pfuel ministry was dismissed by the King on November 1, 1848, and an openly counter-revolutionary ministry headed by Brandenburg and Manteuffel was formed. On November 9 a royal decree was issued transferring the Prussian National Assembly from Berlin to Brandenburg, a small provincial town. This was the beginning of the coup d'état which ended with the dissolution of the Assembly on December 5, 1848.   p. 150

[88] The reference is to an article published under the heading "The Brandenburg Ministry" in the *Neue Preussische Zeitung* on November 5, 1848.
Neue Preussische Zeitung—a daily published in Berlin from June 1848; it was the organ of the counter-revolutionary camarilla and the Prussian landed aristocracy. The paper was popularly known as *Kreuz-Zeitung* because it had an Iron Cross printed in its heading.   p. 150

[89] Seven of the economically backward Catholic cantons of Switzerland set up a Separate Federation in 1845 to resist the introduction of progressive bourgeois measures and to defend the privileges of the Church and the Jesuits. The Swiss Diet passed a resolution in July 1847 dissolving the Separate Federation, which thereupon took military action against the other cantons at the beginning of November. The army of the separatists was defeated by the troops of the federal government on November 23, 1847.   p. 152

10*

[90] The deputies of the Swiss Diet—the legislative Assembly of Switzerland up to 1848—had to act in accordance with the instructions they received from their cantonal governments; this greatly impeded the introduction of progressive measures.   p. 152

[91] During the bourgeois revolution (1820-23) in Spain, the Liberal Party split into a Right wing, the *Moderados,* and a Left wing, the *Exaltados.*   p. 153

[92] *Revue de Genève et Journal Suisse*—organ of the Radical Party, published under this title in Geneva from 1842 until 1861.   p. 155

[93] The Swiss Diet adopted a new constitution in 1847, which gave the central government more power, abolished the privileges of the monasteries and banned the Jesuit Order. The bourgeoisie gained this victory over the feudal and clerical reaction with the support of the popular masses.   p. 155

[94] The riot, which took place on October 24, 1848, was organised by the Catholic clergy and aimed at overthrowing the democratic government of this canton, which was established after the defeat of the separatists. The rising was quickly suppressed.   p. 156

[95] With reference to the Brandenburg cabinet the King said: "Either Brandenburg in the Assembly or the Assembly in Brandenburg." In its issue of November 9, 1848, the *Neue Preussische Zeitung* changed this to: "Brandenburg in the Assembly and the Assembly in Brandenburg."   p. 157

[96] This refers to the Hohenzollerns who became hereditary margraves of Brandenburg in 1417.   p. 157

[97] The Emperor Charles V, shortly before his death, is said to have ordered his own funeral service to be performed and he took part in these obsequies.   p. 157

[98] The criminal code of Charles V (*Constitutio criminalis carolina*), enacted by the Imperial Diet in Regensburg in 1532, was notorious for its excessively cruel penalties.   p. 157

[99] During the uprising of August 10, 1792, which overthrew the French monarchy, Louis XVI (Louis Capet) vainly sought protection in the National Assembly. The *Neue Rheinische Zeitung* published a series of articles under the heading "The Debates of the National Convention on Louis Capet, Ex-King of France" on June 19, 21, 22 and 26, and September 9, 1848.   p. 157

[100] The majority of Slav deputies in the Austrian Imperial Diet of 1848, who were associated with the bourgeoisie or the landowners, sought to set up a Slav federal state within the Hapsburg monarchy.   p. 158

[101] When on November 9, 1848, the Prussian National Assembly was informed of the royal decree suspending its session and transferring it from Berlin to Brandenburg, most Right-wing deputies obediently left the building.

[102] Schiller, *Die Jungfrau von Orleans*, Act III, Scene 6.   p. 161

[103] Shakespeare, *Troilus and Cressida*, Act III, Scene 3.   p. 161

[104] *Le Moniteur Universel*—a French daily published in Paris from 1789 to 1901. It was the official government organ from 1799 to 1814 and from 1816 to 1868. During the French revolution the paper published the parliamentary reports as well as the laws and decrees of the revolutionary government.   p. 162

[105] In its issue of November 3, 1848, the *Kölnische Zeitung* carried an article about an imaginary African tribe, the Hyghlans, an intermediate form between man and ape. On November 5 the *Neue Rheinische Zeitung* ridiculed the report, adding: "this discovery is at any rate of the greatest importance for the party of the howlers" (see Note 156) "for whom the Hyghlans will provide a fitting reinforcement".   p. 162

[106] According to the French Constitution adopted on November 4, 1848, the presidential elections had to take place in December 1848. The President as the head of the executive was given wide powers by the Constitution, which reflected the growing counter-revolutionary trend among the ruling sections of the bourgeoisie, who had been frightened by the June uprising of the workers of Paris. As a result of the December elections Louis Bonaparte became President of the Republic.   p. 162

[107] Despite the royal decree of November 8, 1848, transferring the sessions of the Prussian National Assembly from Berlin to Brandenburg, the majority of delegates decided to continue their deliberations in Berlin. They were thereupon expelled from the building where their sessions had been held hitherto; from November 11 to 13 the delegates met in the Berlin shooting-gallery.

The historical session of the French National Assembly in the tennis-court at Versailles took place on June 20, 1789.   p. 162

[108] See Note 41.   p. 162

[109] On November 14 and 15 the *Neue Rheinische Zeitung* published an article by Georg Weerth under the heading "The Refusal to Pay Taxes During the Struggle for the Reform Bill in England in 1832".   p. 163

[110] The *Democratic District Committee of the Rhine Province*, in which Marx played a leading role, directed the activities of the democratic organisations in the Rhine Province and Westphalia.

The Committee issued its appeal calling on the population to refuse to pay taxes at the beginning of the counter-revolutionary coup d'état, even before the Prussian National Assembly had passed a resolution to this effect. There was a wide response to the appeal in the Rhine Province. In its second issue of November 19, 1848, the *Neue Rheinische Zeitung* reported tax refusals in towns and rural communities, e.g., in Wittlich, Bernkastel, Bonn, Cologne and Neheim, and concluded by saying: "Only the revolutionary vigour of the provinces can safeguard Berlin, only the revolutionary vigour of the countryside can safeguard the large provincial towns, and especially the provincial capitals. *Refusal to pay taxes* (whether *direct* or *indirect* taxes) gives the *countryside* an opportunity to render an important service to the revolution."   p. 164

[111] The law safeguarding personal liberty passed by the Prussian National Assembly on August 28, 1848, was called *Habeas Corpus Act* by analogy with the English Act of 1679.   p. 165

[112] *Preussischer Staats-Anzeiger*—official organ of the Prussian government published in Berlin from May 1848 to July 1851. It was published as a semi-official organ of the Prussian government under the title *Allgemeine Preussische Staats-Zeitung* from 1819 to April 1848.   p. 167

[113] See Note 77.   p. 167

[114] See Note 88.   p. 167

[115] On *October 31, 1848*, a demonstration was held in Berlin as a protest against the cruelty with which the Austrian counter-revolution crushed the Vienna uprising. The demonstration ended when the unarmed engineering workers were attacked by the 8th Battalion of the Civil Guard. This incident provided the Prussian reaction with an excuse for replacing the Pfuel cabinet by the openly counter-revolutionary Brandenburg cabinet.   p. 167

[116] The *Kölnische Rathaus* (Cologne town hall), where the Prussian National Assembly met on November 14, 1848, was situated in the centre of Berlin. In the middle of the nineteenth century this centre was still called Kölln or Altkölln (Old Cologne).   p. 167

[117] This appeal led to the prosecution of Marx, Schapper and Schneider II (see this volume, pp. 227-47).   p. 168

[118] On *April 10, 1848*, a vast Chartist demonstration was to take place in London in connection with the presentation of the third Chartist Petition. The Chartist gathering was dwarfed by the large number of troops and special constables assembled by the government, and the planned march to Parliament was called off.

On *May 15, 1848*, the bourgeois National Guard frustrated the attempt of the revolutionary Paris workers to set up a Provisional Government.

On *June 25, 1848*, the rising of the workers of Paris was crushed.

On *August 6, 1848*, Milan was occupied by Austrian troops who defeated the national liberation movement in Northern Italy.

On *November 1, 1848*, the troops of the Austrian Field-Marshal Windischgrätz took Vienna.   p. 171

[119] The Sardinian-Lombardian army was defeated by the Austrian army under Radetzky at Custozza on July 25, 1848.   p. 174

[120] The royal order dissolving the Prussian National Assembly was issued on December 5, 1848. In the ministry's explanations accom-

panying the order the Assembly is accused of having disregarded the royal decree of November 8, ordering it to move from Berlin to Brandenburg, a measure allegedly designed "to protect the deputies' freedom of deliberation from the anarchistic movements in the capital and their terroristic influences".   p. 176

[121] The imposed constitution came into force on December 5, 1848, simultaneously with the dissolution of the Prussian National Assembly. This constitution provided for a two-Chamber Parliament elected by indirect suffrage. The number of citizens entitled to vote for the first Chamber was also restricted by a high property qualification. The wide powers which the constitution gave the Crown facilitated the further advance of the counter-revolution.
                                                                          p. 177

[122] *Die Jobsiade. Ein komisches Heldengedicht* (The Jobsiad. A Farcical Epos) is the title of a satirical poem by Karl Arnold Kortum.
                                                                          p. 177

[123] The Prince of Prussia was one of the most hated leaders of the reactionary camarilla. During the March revolution he escaped to England but returned to Berlin on June 4, 1848. On June 6, Camphausen sought to present the flight of the Prince as a journey undertaken for educational purposes.   p. 178

[124] The expression "superabundant patriotism" was used by Heine in the poem *Bei des Nachtwächters Ankunft in Paris*.   p. 178

[125] General Wrangel, who was associated with the reactionary Court clique, was, on September 15, 1848, appointed Commander-in-Chief of the Brandenburg military district, which at that time consisted of two parts, the Kurmark and the Neumark.   p. 178

[126] This ironical epithet was given to Camphausen by Marx and Engels. It is an allusion to *Allgemeine Geschichte vom Anfang der historischen Kenntniss bis auf unsere Zeiten,* by Karl von Rotteck, a well-known work at the time. Its subtitle ran: For Thinking Friends of History.   p. 178

[127] An allusion to the similarity existing between the measures proposed by Hansemann, the Prussian Minister of Finance, (i.e., a compulsory loan as a means of stimulating the circulation of money), and the views of Pinto, the Dutch stockjobber, who regarded the stock exchange as a factor speeding up the circulation of money.   p. 179

[128] The reference is to the revolt in the Netherlands from 1566 to 1609.
                                                                          p. 182

[129] An allusion to Camphausen, who formerly traded in oil and corn, and to Hansemann, who started as a wool merchant.   p. 185

[130] *Puer robustus sed malitiosus* (a robust but malicious fellow)—a modified quotation from the preface to *De cive* by Thomas Hobbes.
                                                                          p. 187

131 A decree on the establishment of a national representative body was issued on May 22, 1815. In it the King promised the setting up of provisional Diets, the convocation of an all-Prussian representative body, and a constitution. But only Provincial Diets with limited consultative functions were set up by a law issued on June 5, 1823.
p. 188

132 Under the *National Debt Law of January 17, 1820*, state loans could only be issued with the consent of the Provincial Diet.   p. 188

133 The *edict of February 3, 1847*, provided for the convocation of a United Provincial Diet (Vereinigter Landtag).   p. 188

134 The *Electoral Law of April 8, 1848*—see Note 3.   p. 188

135 A quotation from Hansemann's speech in the first United Provincial Diet on June 8, 1847.   p. 190

136 Marx is referring to Hildebrandt's novel *Kuno von Schreckenstein oder die weissagende Traumgestalt.*   p. 191

137 See Note 53.   p. 192

138 *Code pénal*—the penal code adopted in France in 1810; it was introduced in the parts of Western and South-Western Germany which Napoleon I conquered. It remained in force in the Rhine Province even after its incorporation into Prussia in 1815.   p. 195

139 Besides the ordinary police, a body of armed civilians was set up in the summer of 1848 for use against popular meetings and demonstrations and for espionage services. These plain-clothes policemen were called constables by analogy with the special constables in Britain, who had played an important part in frustrating the Chartist demonstration of April 10, 1848.   p. 195

140 The bourgeois-aristocratic constitution of Belgium adopted in 1831 after the victory of the bourgeois revolution of 1830 established a high property qualification, thus depriving a considerable part of the population of the suffrage.   p. 196

141 *Seehandlung* (short for *Preussische Seehandlungsgesellschaft*—Prussian Maritime Trading Company) was founded as a merchant bank in 1772 and enjoyed a number of important state privileges. It granted large loans to the government and in fact acted as its banker. In 1820 it became the bank of the Prussian state.   p. 197

142 A bill revoking exemption from graduated tax payments for aristocrats, officers, teachers and the clergy was submitted by Hansemann to the Prussian National Assembly on July 12, 1848. A bill revoking exemption from the land-tax was tabled by Hansemann on July 21, 1848.   p. 197

143 *Fra Diavolo*—a sobriquet of Michele Pezza, the Italian bandit (1771-1806).   p. 198

144 A reference to the General Assembly for the Protection of the Material Interests of All Classes of the Prussian People which met

in Berlin on August 18, 1848. The Assembly, which consisted mainly of big landowners, was convoked by the Association for the Protection of Property and the Advancement of the Well-being of All Classes of People. The name of the Association was changed by the General Assembly to: Association for the Protection of the Interests of Landowners. p. 200

[145] On July 31, 1848, troops attacked the Civil Guard in Schweidnitz, a Silesian garrison town, killing 14 people. p. 200

[146] See Note 74. p. 200

[147] On September 17, 1848, General Wrangel issued an army order in which he stressed that it was his task to maintain "public order", threatened those "who were trying to entice the people to commit unlawful acts" and called upon the soldiers to rally around their officers and their King. p. 200

[148] A statement to this effect was made by Frederick William IV on April 11, 1847, when he opened the first United Provincial Diet. p. 201

[149] Article 14 of the constitution which Louis XVIII enacted in 1814 read: "The King is the head of the State ... he issues the decrees and orders necessary for the enforcement of the law and the security of the State." p. 201

[150] From Schiller's *An die Freude*. The English translation is taken from *Poems by Schiller*, "Hymn to Joy", by Bowring, Chicago. p. 203

[151] After his election in 1846, Pope Pius IX initiated a number of liberal reforms to prevent the spread of the popular movement. p. 203

[152] *La Montagne* (The Mountain)—in 1848-51 the name was given to a group of petty-bourgeois democrats and republicans headed by Ledru-Rollin. Their newspaper was *La Réforme*. p. 203

[153] *The Prussian Association for a Constitutional Monarchy* was founded in June 1848 by a section of the Prussian landowners and of the bourgeoisie. The Association and its branches supported the counter-revolutionary policy pursued by the government. The activities of this Association earned it in the democratic press the nickname of "Society of Informers". p. 211

[154] *Citizens' Associations (Bürgervereine)* consisting mainly of liberal bourgeois arose in Prussia after the March revolution. Their aim was to maintain "law and order" within the framework of a constitutional monarchy, and to combat "anarchy", i.e., the revolutionary-democratic movement. p. 212

[155] The last article of the constitution imposed on December 5, 1848, provided for a rewording of the constitution by the two Chambers before its final promulgation. p. 212

[156] In 1848-49 the advocates of a bourgeois constitutional system in Germany called the republican democrats "agitators" and these in turn called their opponents "howlers". p. 216

[157] *Code civil*—the civil code adopted in France in 1804; it was introduced in the parts of Western and South-Western Germany conquered by France. It remained in force in the Rhine Province even after its incorporation into Prussia in 1815. p. 220

[158] In Britain in 1649 Charles I was beheaded, and in 1688 James II was deposed; in France the Bourbons were deposed in 1792 and again in 1830; in Belgium the revolution of 1830 ended the rule of William of Orange. p. 222

[159] By establishing low import duties on Dutch sugar, the trade agreement which Prussia (on behalf of the German Customs Union) concluded with Holland did considerable harm to the Prussian sugar industry and to the trade of many German towns. p. 223

[160] An allusion to Camphausen and Hansemann. p. 226

[161] The trial was held at the Cologne Jury Court on February 8, 1849. Marx, Schapper and Schneider II were accused of instigation to revolt on the basis of the Appeal issued by the Rhenish District Committee of Democrats on November 18, 1848 (see this volume, p. 168). The jury returned a verdict of not guilty. p. 227

[162] Although, under the *Civil Guard Law* passed by the Prussian National Assembly on October 13, 1848, the Civil Guard was completely dependent on the government, the counter-revolutionary forces were still afraid of it. The Berlin Civil Guard was disarmed on November 11, 1848, after Wrangel's troops marched into Berlin. p. 239

[163] Unruh, *Skizzen aus Preussens neuester Geschichte*, Magdeburg, 1849. p. 240

[164] A Constituent Assembly, elected in Rome on January 21, 1849, on the basis of universal suffrage—which was won as the result of the uprising of November 16, 1848—abolished the Pope's temporal power and proclaimed a republic. The Roman republic existed until July 3, 1849, when foreign intervention put an end to it. p. 248

[165] An uprising which began in Dresden on May 3, 1849, was almost completely put down by May 8. This rising marked the beginning of the struggle in Germany for the defence of the imperial constitution adopted by the Frankfurt National Assembly on March 28, 1849. p. 249

[166] In defence of the imperial constitution which was adopted by the Frankfurt National Assembly but rejected by many German states (including Prussia, Saxony, Bavaria and Hannover) risings took place in the Bavarian Palatinate, the Rhine Province and Baden early in May 1849, the people regarded this constitution as the only surviving gain of the revolution. The uprisings, however,

mostly led by petty-bourgeois democrats, were of a sporadic, spontaneous nature, and were ruthlessly crushed by the middle of July 1849.   p. 249

[167] In April 1849, the French government sent an expeditionary force into Italy to crush the Roman republic and restore the temporal power of the Pope, but the French troops were repulsed from Rome on April 30, 1849.   p. 249

[168] A reference to the trials of the editors of the *Neue Rheinische Zeitung* and of members of the Rhenish District Committee of Democrats (held in Cologne on February 7 and 8, 1849). In both cases the jury brought in a verdict of not guilty.   p. 251

[169] *Szeklers*—Hungarians living in the Transylvanian Alps.   p. 260

NAME INDEX

A

Archimedes (c. 287-212 B.C.)—Greek mathematician and physicist.—74

Arnim-Suckow, Heinrich Alexander, Freiherr von (1798-1861)—Prussian statesman, moderate liberal; Minister of Foreign Affairs (March 21-June 19, 1848).—36

d'Aspre, Constantin, Freiherr (1789-1850)—Austrian general.—103

Attila (d. 453)—King of the Huns (433-53).—104

Auersperg, Karl, Graf von (1783-1859)—Austrian general, commander-in-chief of the Viennese garrison in 1848.—146

Auerswald, Alfred von (1797-1870)—Prussian Minister of the Interior (March to June 1848).—25

Auerswald, Rudolf von (1795-1866)—Prussian statesman, Prime Minister and Foreign Minister (June to September 1848).—68, 70, 123, 190, 195

B

Ballin, Felix (born c. 1802)—Belgian merchant, radical democrat, member of the Democratic Association in Brussels; sentenced to death in 1848, then the sentence was commuted to 30 years imprisonment; released in 1854.—111, 112

Barrot, Camille Hyacinthe Odilon (1791-1873)—French bourgeois politician, leader of the liberal dynastic opposition during the July monarchy; from December 1848 to October 1849 he headed a ministry, which relied on the support of a counter-revolutionary monarchist coalition.—132, 204

Bassermann, Friedrich Daniel (1811-1855)—German politician, moderate liberal, member of the Baden Landtag, represented the grand duchy in the Federal Diet in 1848 and 1849, member of the Frankfurt National Assembly (Right Centre).—23

Bavay, Charles Victor (1801-1875)—Belgian officer of justice, Attorney General at the Brussels court of appeal from 1844.—111

Beaumarchais, Pierre Augustin Caron de (1732-1799)—French playwright.—220

Becker, Félix—French poet and revolutionary, took part in the Polish uprising of 1830-31, one of the organisers of the Belgian Legion formed in Paris in February and March 1848.—112

Beckerath, Hermann von (1801-1870)—German banker, a lead-

the Lyons rising of 1834; Paris police prefect from February to May 1848, deputy of the Constituent National Assembly; emigrated to England after the defeat of the June uprising.—79

Cavaignac, Louis Eugène (1802-1857)—French general and politician, bourgeois republican.—44, 46, 55, 57, 58, 108, 132, 137, 139, 173, 174, 175, 204

Charles I (1600-1649)—King of Great Britain (1625-49); executed.—158, 230, 245

Charles V (1500-1558)—King of Spain (1516-56), Holy Roman Emperor (1519-56).—157

Charles X (1757-1836)—King of France (1824-30).—158

Charles Albert (1798-1849)—King of Sardinia and Piedmont (1831-49).—102, 103, 108

Charles William Ferdinand (1735-1806)—Duke of Brunswick (1770-1806).—60

Cincinnatus, Lucius Quinctius (5th century B.C.)—Roman politician, patrician, model of ancient Roman virtue and simplicity.—65, 66

Cobden, Richard (1804-1865)—Manchester manufacturer, Liberal statesman, advocated Free Trade, one of the founders of the Anti-Corn Law League.—80

Cockerill, John (1790-1840)—British industrialist.—85

Colomb, Friedrich August von (1775-1854)—Prussian general, commander of a Prussian army corps in Poznan, 1843-48.—39

Compes, Josef Gerhard (1810-1887)—German lawyer, member of the Frankfurt National Assembly, 1848 to 1849 (Left Centre).—212

Cromwell, Oliver (1599-1658)—English statesman, leader of the bourgeoisie and the section of the nobility allied with it during the English revolution of the seventeenth century; Lord Protector from 1653 to 1658.—131, 158

Csorich (Čorič), Antun, barun de Monte Creto (1795-1864)—Austrian general of Croatian descent, helped to put down the October rising in Vienna in 1848 and the Hungarian revolution of 1848-49.—260

D

Dahlen, Hermann, Baron von Orlaburg (1828-1887)—Austrian officer, fought against the Hungarian revolution in 1848 and 1849.—257, 259

Damesme, Édouard Adolphe Marie (1807-1848)—French general.—54

Delescluze, Louis Charles (1809-1871)—French petty-bourgeois revolutionary, member of the Paris Commune, killed during barricade fighting in 1871.—110

Delolme, Jean Louis (1740-1806)—Swiss statesman and jurist.—124

Dembiński, Henryk (1791-1864)—Polish general, took part in the national liberation movement and the rising of 1830-31.—260, 261

Doggenfeld, Anton Vetter, Edler von (1803-1882)—Hungarian general, Kossuth's comrade-in-arms and Chief of the General Staff, 1848-49. After the defeat of the revolution he emigrated from Hungary.—261

Dronke, Ernst (1822-1891)—German writer, at first "true so-

INDEX OF AUTHORITIES

Allgemeines Landrecht für die Preußischen Staaten. Neue Ausg., 2 Th. in 4 Bdn., Berlin, 1817.—87-88, 124-25, 194-95

Arndt, Ernst Moritz, "Der Freudenklang". In: *Ernst Moritz Arndts ausgewählte Werke,* hrsg. und mit Einl. und Anm. vers. von Heinrich Meisner und Robert Geerds, Bd. 1-16, Leipzig, n.d., Bd. 3.—106

Beaumarchais, [Pierre-Augustin Caron] de, "La folle journée, ou le mariage de Figaro". In: *Œuvres complètes,* T. 5, n. p., 1785.—220

[Benkert, Franz Georg,] *Joseph Bonavita Blank's ... kurze Lebens-Beschreibung,* Würzburg, 1819.—82

Bible
—Exodus 3, 5.—71
—Job 1, 21.—202
—Matthew 13, 12; 8, 22.—106, 217

Blanc, Louis, *Histoire de dix ans. 1830-1840,* T. 1-5, Paris, 1841-1844.—79
—*Histoire de la révolution française,* T. 1-2, Paris, 1847.—79

[Brodowski, Kraszewski, Potworowski,] *Zur Beurtheilung der polnischen Frage im Großherzogthum Posen im Jahre 1848,* Berlin [1848].—83, 92

"Charte constitutionelle", June 4, 1814. In: *Le Moniteur universel* No. 156, June 5, 1814.—201

Code civil—see *Code Napoléon.*

Code Napoléon, Paris and Leipzig, 1808.—71, 220, 232

Code pénal, ou code des délits et des peines, Cologne, 1810.—111, 195, 229

Compte rendu des séances de l'Assemblée nationale, T. 1-10, Paris, 1849-1850. T. 2 and 4.—47, 48, 53, 132

["Constitutio criminalis carolina".] In: *Die Carolina und ihre Vorgängerinnen.* Text, Erläuterung, Geschichte. In Verbindung mit anderen Gelehrten hg. und bearb. von J. Kohler. I. "Die peinliche Gerichtsordnung Kaiser Karls V. Constitutio criminalis carolina". Kritisch hrsg. von J. Kohler und Willy Scheel, Halle, 1900.—157

"Declaration wegen Einziehung und künftiger Verwaltung der geistlichen Güter, ingleichen der Starosteien und anderer königl. Güter in Südpreußen und der von der ehemaligen Republik Polen neuerlich acquirirten Provinzen", Berlin, July 28, 1796. In: *Materialien zur Geschichte polnischer Lan-*

"Gesetz zum Schutz der persön-
lichen Freiheit. Vom 24. September 1848". In: *Gesetz-
Sammlung für die Königlichen
Preußischen Staaten* No. 42,
1848.—165, 239

"Gesetzbuch über Strafen". Aus
dem Franz. nach der officiel-
len Ausg. übers. von Wilhelm
Blanchard, zweyte verb. Aufl.,
Cöln, 1812.—111

Goethe, Johann Wolfgang von,
"Prometheus". In: *Goethe's
Werke*, Bd. 1-20, Stuttgart und
Tübingen, 1815-1819. Bd. 2.—
110

"Il Governo provvisorio alla Na-
zione Germanica", Milano,
April 6, 1848. In: *Raccolta
dei decreti, avvisi, proclami,
bulletini ec. ec. emanti dal
Governo provvisorio, dai di-
versi comitati e da altri dal
giorno 18 Marzo in avanti,*
Mailand, n.d.—62

"Grundrechte des deutschen Volkes". In: *Stenographischer Bericht über die Verhandlungen
der deutschen constituirenden
Nationalversammlung   zu
Frankfurt am Main*, Bd. 1-9,
Frankfurt a. M. und Leipzig,
1848-1849. Bd. 1-2.—135

Heine, Heinrich, "Anno 1829".
In: *Heinrich Heine's sämmt-
liche Werke*, Bd. 1 bis 18,
Hamburg, 1868. Bd. 16.—66
—"Bei des Nachtwächters Ankunft zu Paris", Bd. 17.—177
—"Deutschland. Ein Wintermärchen", Bd. 17.—32, 71, 114,
132
—"Einleitung zu 'Kahldorf über
den Adel, in Briefen an den
Grafen M. von Moltke' ", Bd.
14.—135
—"Der Tannhäuser", Bd. 16.—
138

—"Zur Beruhigung", Bd. 17.—
63

Hildebrandt, C., *Kuno von
Schreckenstein, oder die weis-
sagende Traumgestalt*. 2. Aufl.,
Bd. 1-3, Quedlinburg und
Leipzig, 1840.—191

Hobbes, Thomas, *Elementa phi-
losophica. De cive.* Editio nova
accuratior, Basileae, 1782.—
187

"Königliche Ordre an das Staats-
Ministerium, betreffend die
nationale Reorganisation des
Großherzogthums Posen", April 26, 1848, In: *Reden, Pro-
klamationen, Botschaften, Er-
lasse und Ordres Sr. Majestät
des Königs Friedrich Wil-
helm IV.* vom ... 6. März
1848 bis ... 31. Mai 1851, Berlin, 1851.—92-93

"Königliches Rescript", October 3, 1848. In: *Wiener Zeitung*
No. 275, October 5, 1848.—
256

Kortum, Karl Arnold, *Die Jobsiade.* Ein komisches Heldengedicht. Hrsg. von F. Bober-
tag, Berlin und Stuttgart
[1883].—177

["Manifest der Linken in der
Frankfurter Nationalversammlung".] In: *Neue Rheinische
Zeitung* No. 7, June 7, 1848.
—30-34

Molière [, Jean-Baptiste], "Le
bourgeois gentilhomme". In:
Œuvres complètes, T. 7, Paris, 1825.—186

"Motivirtes Manifest der radi-
kal-demokratischen Partei in
der konstituirenden Nationalversammlung zu Frankfurt
am Main". In: *Neue Rheinische Zeitung* No. 6, June 6,
1848.—30-34

"Patent die ständischen Einrich-

Volks. Vom 22ten Mai 1815". In: *Gesetz-Sammlung für die Königlichen Preußischen Staaten* No. 9, 1815.—188

"Verordnung über einige Grundlagen der künftigen Preußischen Verfassung. Vom 6. April 1848". In: *Gesetz-Sammlung für die Königlichen Preußischen Staaten* No. 11, 1848.—177, 227, 228, 230-32, 234, 235, 246-47

"Verordnung wegen der künftigen Behandlung des gesammten Staatsschulden-Wesens. Vom 17ten Januar 1820". In: *Gesetz-Sammlung für die Königlichen Preußischen Staaten* No. 2, 1820.—188

"Vorläufiger Entwurf einer Verordnung zur Ergänzung der Allgemeinen Gewerbe-Ordnung vom 17. Jan. 1845". In: *Kölnische Zeitung*, Erste Beilage zu Nr. 24 vom 28. Januar, 1849.—224-25

"Waffenstillstandsvertrag zwischen Preußen und Dänemark", Malmö, August 26, 1848. In: *Stenographischer Bericht über die Verhandlungen der deutschen constituirenden Nationalversammlung zu Frankfurt am Main*, Bd. 1-9, Frankfurt a. M. und Leipzig 1848 bis 1849. Bd. 3.—114-19, 131

"Wahlgesetz für die zur Vereinbarung der Preußischen Staats-Verfassung zu berufende Versammlung. Vom 8. April 1848". In: *Gesetz-Sammlung für die Königlichen Preußischen Staaten* No. 12, 1848.—121, 177, 188, 227-35, 246-47

Weichsel, F. F., "Deutschlands Einheit und der Entwurf des Deutschen Reichsgrundgesetzes", von den 17 Männern des öffentlichen Vertrauens überreicht am 26. April 1848, Magdeburg, 1848.—25

Wildenbruch [, Louis], "Note an die dänische Regierung", April 8, 1848. In: *Stenographische Berichte über die Verhandlungen der zur Vereinbarung der preußischen Staats-Verfassung berufenen Versammlung*, Beilage zum *Preußischen Staats-Anzeiger*, Bd. 1, Berlin, 1848.—68, 118

Wrangel [, Friedrich Heinrich Ernst, Graf von], "Armee-Befehl", Potsdam, September 17, 1848. In: *Neue Rheinische Zeitung* No. 109, September 22, 1848.—200, 220, 240

Periodicals

L'Alba. Giornale politico-letterario, Firenze, 1848.—62

Berliner Zeitungs-Halle, evening paper, Berlin
—No. 143, June 23, 1848.—42
—No. 194, August 24, 1848.—105-07

—No. 213, September 15, 1848.—128, 129

Berlinische Nachrichten von Staats- und gelehrten Sachen, Berlin, 1848.—128

Fädrelandet No. 179, July 13, 1848.—65

Le Populaire de 1841. Journal de reorganisation, Paris.—79

Preußischer Staats-Anzeiger, Berlin.—167
—No. 1, January 1, 1849.—219

Protokolle der Deutschen Bundesversammlung vom Jahre 1848, Frankfurt am Main, n.d.—90-91

La Réforme, Paris.—45, 79, 140
—No. 301, October 30, 1848.—140-43

Revue de Genève et Journal Suisse, Genève, 1848/49.—155

La Ruche populaire. Première Tribune et Revue Mensuelle. Rédigée et publiée par des ouvriers, Paris.—79

Le Spectateur républicain, Paris, 1848.—108

"*Stenographische Berichte* über die Verhandlungen der zur Vereinbarung der preußischen Staats-Verfassung berufenen Versammlung", Beilage zum *Preußischen Staats-Anzeiger*, Bd. 1-3, Berlin, 1848.—35-37, 69, 71-76, 118, 126, 127

"*Stenographischer Bericht* über die Verhandlungen der deutschen constituirenden Nationalversammlung zu Frankfurt am Main".—22-26, 63, 67, 82, 114-19, 131-33, 169-70

Triester Freihafen, Triest, 1849.—264

L'Union. Bulletin des ouvriers rédigé et publié par eux-mêmes, Paris, 1843-1846.—79

Vossische Zeitung—see *Königlich privilegirte Berlinische Zeitung von Staats- und gelehrten Sachen.*

Wiener Zeitung, 1848.—256

GLOSSARY OF GEOGRAPHICAL NAMES

Adelnau — Odolanów
Apenrade — Äpenraa
Breslau — Wrocław
Bromberg — Bydgoszcz
Eperies — Prešov
Esseg/Eszék — Osijek
Glogau — Głogow
Gran — Esztergom
Hermannstadt — Sibiu/Nagy
Kaschau — Košice
Klausenburg — Cluj/Kolozsvár
Komorn — Komaróm
Kronstadt — Braşow/Brassó
Küstrin — Kostrzyn
Maros — Vásárhely — Tîrgu — Mureş
Neutra — Nitra/Nyitra
Ödenburg — Sopron
Peterwardein — Petrovaradin
Prerau — Přerov
Pressburg — Bratislava/Pozsony
Raab — Györ
Rimaszombat — Rimavská Sobota
Schässburg — Sighisoara/Segesvár
Stuhlweissenburg — Székesfehérvár
Szegedin — Szeged
Temesvár — Timişoara
Thorn — Toruń
Waitzen — Vác
Werschetz — Vršac/Versec
Wreschen — Września